KRÚDY'S CHRONICLES

KRÚDY'S CHRONICLES

Turn-of-the-Century Hungary in Gyula Krúdy's Journalism

Selected, edited, and translated
by John Bátki

With an introductory essay
by John Lukacs

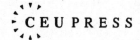 CEU PRESS

Central European University Press

English edition published in 2000 by
Central European University Press

Nádor u. 15
H-1051 Budapest
Hungary

400 West 59th Street
New York, NY 10019
USA

Distributed in the United Kingdom and Western Europe by
Plymbridge Distributors Ltd., Estover Road, Plymouth, PL6 7PZ,
United Kingdom

ISBN 963-9116-78-5 Cloth
ISBN 963-9116-79-3 Paper

Library of Congress Cataloging in Publication Data
A CIP catalog record for this book is available upon request

Printed in Hungary by Akadémiai Nyomda

CONTENTS

John Lukacs

The Chronicler and the Historian

It is a truth NOT universally acknowledged that the novelist and the historian deal with much of the same matter. Or, to put it differently: that every novelist is a historian by nature, while he is a novelist by choice. The novel—unlike the epic, or the drama, or the lyric—is not an original literary form. Notwithstanding its occasional forerunners, the novel appeared in the eighteenth century in England and Europe—at the same time as the professional and "scientific" study of history began (and 250 years later it may have run its course, while the writing of history goes on). During their parallel but separate evolution the nineteenth-century appearance of the historical novel was but another, now perhaps also closing, chapter. But what some of us recognize now is that their nature is not separate but overlapping. For the instrument of the novelist and of the historian is the same: everyday language; a prose for the purposes of a narrative. Their subjects, too, are the same: the description of people and of places with whom (unlike in the mythical or heroic verse epic) we can identify. That "fiction" and "nonfiction" are not entirely the airtight and separate categories we have learned to know. In this erosion of a once definite boundary there are all kinds of dangers for the future of history, since the historian, unlike the novelist, must not and cannot invent people (and events), no matter how plausible. At the same time he ought to recognize that there is rich material for him in many a novel; that the novelist's eye may see things that may elude the sight of the historian (and not only the pedantic members of his tribe). Maupassant once wrote that the aim of the realistic novelist "is not to tell a story; to amuse us or to appeal to our feelings, but to compel us to reflect, and to understand the darker and deeper meaning of events"—and of people, men and women. Both his eye and his hand must be deft: ergo Flaubert's classic desideratum, the *mot juste*. Which is where a master of language such as Gyula Krúdy enters.

Few people, if any, think of Krúdy as a historian. Many do not think of him as a novelist either: rather as a unique, perhaps unsurpassable, master of prose. No use to argue the latter back and forth—in part because Krúdy cannot be categorized. But, alas, almost all professional historians writing about the Hungary and Budapest of Krúdy's lifetime have, by and large, ignored his contributions to the history of that period, to their loss. I said something about this in 1983 when, for the first time after my emigration from Hungary, I was invited to give a talk at the Historical Institute in Buda, where I chose "History-writing and Novel-writing" as my topic ["Történetírás és regényírás: a múlt étvágya és íze." Published in *Történelmi Szemle* XXVIII, 2, 1985]—three years before my essay on Krúdy appeared in *The New Yorker*. I said that my historian colleagues ought to give some consideration to some of the writings of Hungarian novelists such as, say, Krúdy or Kosztolányi. Yet that was not the place or the occasion to expatiate upon the nature and the essence of Krúdy's *historianship*. Now, at John Bátki's invitation, the time has come to say some things about *that*.

To begin with: Gyula Krúdy was deeply conservative and a traditionalist. He had a great, and abiding, respect (more: a love) for old standards, old customs, older people. (His favorite season, as he himself often wrote, was autumn—and after that, winter.) He had—there was a duality in his personal life, as there is in the lives and minds of most people—a nostalgic, almost hopeless, and surely a melancholy longing for an older Hungarian way of life that was no longer his: of bright mornings in small country houses, with the odor of freshly ironed linen (let me add that *his* personal linen was always immaculately clean, even during long alcohol-ridden nights), of fresh butter shining atop a layer of green leaves; of old cupboards, old papers, old paintings, their scents and their contents. And let me go a step further: *le style c'était cet homme*. He adored the Hungarian Biedermeier, even though there was nothing very Biedermeier in his personal life. His style was not old-fashioned—except in the near-fantastic treasure of his knowledge and employment of ancient Hungarian words (especially of much of the Hungarian fauna and flora) and sometimes of older Hungarian verbs and their conjugations. Was he, then, a *modern* Hungarian writer? Yes and no—or, more precisely, more no than yes. His style was surely not traditional. It was inimitable and startlingly novel; but it was not really modern either. That is why, in the essay about Krúdy mentioned above, I dared to say that he was greater than Proust: because he was more than a chronicler of society and more than an analyst of human nature; because, unlike Proust, his writing was saturated with history as much as, if not more than, with sociography. Among the other values of his jewel-laden writing Krúdy was the Homer of a now forever sunken Hungarian past; and, unlike Homer, even when his scenes were mystical, they were not mythical but real.

He wrote about people and places that really existed. In the earlier phase of his writing he wrote, at times, about very old, medieval people and places; his imaginative power made them alive and real. But this is not what the present collection is about. When, after about 1910 or 1911, he began to write more and more about Budapest, he became a chronicler of the people and places that he knew. Like every first-class writer he wrote about men and women and things that he knew and understood: and both the quantity of his knowledge and the qualities of his understanding were immense—but in his case his intuitive understanding was not simply the result of accumulated knowledge: as Pascal had said about mankind at large, he understood even more than what he knew. His portraits of Hungarian political personages (mostly of the 1880 to 1920 period, and also of Francis Joseph) are not only superbly written—they deserve to be studied and pondered by historians. (It is at least interesting that he seldom wrote much about other writers and that there is practically no literary criticism by him.) Because of the obviously limited, or nonexistent, interest of non-Hungarian readers in these people, Bátki has had to limit the number included in this volume. But what belongs here, too, is his essayistic description of places, mostly in Budapest, and of their atmosphere, at a certain historical time: another treasure-trove for historians of a particular city and period. The scents and the colors are all there in his details: their evocations arise instantly in the reader's eyes, ears, and, yes, also in his nostrils. This is how Krúdy was more than a "chronicler" (though he would have been satisfied with such a designation); he had all the makings—the knowledge and the talent—of an analytical historian.

As he became older his interest in history, reaching further and further back into Hungary's past, grew. During the last decade of his life more and more of his articles dealt with historical personages. We know too, from his mention of them in his writings, that he read, avidly and with admiration, writers such as Carlyle and Thackeray—the former's book about the French Revolution and the latter's small masterpiece on the four Georges—in Hungarian, of course, since Krúdy knew no English, nor indeed any foreign language. (His favorite author was Dickens.) The mention of Carlyle and Thackeray should suggest, too, Krúdy's inherent understanding of the inevitable connections between literature and history, since neither of these two were professional historians. But it is not only that historians read (or ought to have read) them with profit. They, like Krúdy, were attracted by the deeper meaning of historical people and places and events: as the French critic Émile Faguet once wrote about Tocqueville, they peered under the surface, to understand the often hidden character of movements.

Krúdy was compelled to write; and while on one level he felt like writing more and more about history, on the practical level of his life he had to turn out more and more articles, often day after day, for different Budapest newspapers, fleeing from his innumerable debts. That was the reason why he became largely ignored and was forgotten by most people during the last decade of his life: he wrote too much; he was no longer interesting; he was passé. Such a depreciation we no longer share. Ever since 1940 his reputation has risen, again and again. Whether the "historian" Krúdy will be appreciated as is Krúdy the "novelist" remains questionable. It may be enough for us to state that he does not accurately fit into either of these categories, whether overlapping or not. He was *sui generis* a great writer, until the end.

The particular qualities of Krúdy's historianship are threefold. There are his descriptive powers; his insight; and his historical sense. Or, in other words: the genius of his eye; of his heart; and of his mind. His descriptive powers are the same whether he writes novels or essays or chronicles; and, as with all great writers, his *mots justes* are not only there in his adjectives and adverbs but also in his verbs and nouns. His insights are those of a startlingly profound wisdom about human nature (which, of course, is an indispensable requirement for any historian worth his profession)—and they are insights even about men and women whom he did not intimately know, but no matter. To this let me add two other qualities. One is his generous, often magnanimous, kindness. This secretive and introvert man, who could sit for long hours in company and remain silent and who had plenty of bitterness in his life, wrote about men and women with understanding and forgiveness, with occasional irony but without sarcasm. Without sharply focusing on their shortcomings and faults, his portraits sing softly, with his unsurpassable melancholy music, full of harmonies, impressionistic, as in a chromatic and chord-laden key. And their world, and his world, are sinking, if not altogether sunk: a world where the high and highest classes still counted: the end of the aristocratic age (*az úri világ*) in Hungarian history, and indeed in European history. His respect and reverence for the aristocracy is devoid of snobbism or of snobbery: again and again he *understands*. Finally—in order but not in importance—there is Krúdy's astonishing comprehension of the largest and deepest movements of history. One stunning example of this may be found in his article about Russia, written but a few days after the March Revolution of 1917. "The European revolutions (when such were still imaginable, and even if politely middle class) ploughed deeper beneath the topsoil of the histories of nations than the present skirmish in Russia..." After this tsar a new kind of tsar would be coming; and the eternally passive Russian masses would go on to live and suffer, as is their wont. He thus foretold Stalin, way beyond Kerensky or Lenin, years before anyone would hear the former's name. (Would he have understood Hitler? We cannot tell—Krúdy died in May 1933, at the very time when that extraordinary man had come to power.) In this sense Krúdy exemplified yet another astonishing quality, apparent only here and there in the words of the greatest poets of mankind: the genius of a prophet. But, like the greatest historians of mankind, he was essentially a Prophet of a Past...

Tiszaeszlár, Fifty Years Later

1. A Mysterious Killing by the River Tisza

Fifty years ago, around Eastertime, newspaper editors sounded the knell that was to be louder than all the bells ringing in old Budapest steeples.

They were sounding the death knell for Eszter Solymosi, a fourteen-year-old girl from Tiszaeszlár. Although the girl had not yet been found—dead or alive—rumors were going around that she had been killed by the Jews, who had used the blood of the Christian girl for their Passover rites. The story had it that they had cut her throat and collected her blood, in, of all places, their temple, where they had enticed the girl who was on her way back from the village store carrying house-paint for the woman in whose service she was employed.

Then, as hearsay had it, the girl's body was put on a cart and then floated by raft down the River Tisza.

Even fifty years ago it must have taken a lively imagination to make up a story like that.

Yes, the country was rife with phantasmagorias back then, just as in our own days.

The first report of the alleged Tiszaeszlár killing surfaced in the Nyíregyháza weekly *Nyírvidék*, after which the Budapest papers picked up the scent, signaling the start of the nationwide, and eventually Europe-wide, campaign accusing or defending the raggedy *shochetim* of Tiszaeszlár.

At the time, fifty years ago, no other affair could have torn open more brutally the recently healed wounds of Hungarian society, which still deemed the events of 1848/49 to be the only worthwhile topic of discussion—although a sizable party was emerging in support of letting bygones be bygones and beginning a new historical era as of 1867, the year of the Compromise with Austria.

But the sympathies of the nation were still largely with the Independence Party; most people denounced Liberal ideas as untenable. But in the area of societal contacts the adherents of the two opposing parties managed to put up with each other. The real rupture in the fabric of society was created by the Tiszaeszlár case, which profoundly stirred even the most sober individu-

1

als. Weeks and months were to pass before contemporary onlookers found the proper framework for judging this sudden development. At first not even the most clear-headed people knew how to proceed.

The smartly executed, old-fashioned gendarme-style investigation; the explicit testimony given by Móric Scharf, the son of the congregation's *shammes*; the corpse floating in the Tisza (which was not, however, identified by Mrs. János Solymosi as her daughter) all seemed to confirm the guilt of the Tiszaeszlár Jews. Moreover, certain domestic and foreign historians chimed in with claims that they could cite other cases similar to the Tiszaeszlár blood libel from the history of the Jews.

During the investigation, which lasted more than a year and a half, there were months when the cause of the incarcerated Jews appeared hopeless; not even the most liberal individuals dared raise their voices in defense of these Jews lest they themselves be accused of acting as accomplices. All testimony given during interrogation seemed to implicate the Jews, whose fate was considered to be worth less than a plugged coin. It seemed that, like drowning men, they would only drag down with them anyone who offered a helping hand. The most courageous hearts trembled in the general panic. The most astute minds dared not deny that a crime had been committed. There were frequent reports, "planted" in the newspapers, of individual Jews converting specifically on account of the Tiszaeszlár events.

Even the popularity of the near demigod Lajos Kossuth, then living a hermit-like existence in exile in Turin, was threatened, when, in his frequent messages to Hungary, he chose to side with the Jews. Domestic politicians, personages of far lesser stature, deemed it best to remain silent in the hope that some biblical miracle would clear up an affair rooted in superstition.

Fifty years ago the cause of the Jews in Hungary appeared to be at an all-time low. It was in that most liberal era—when the aged Kálmán Tisza had apparently brought about the conditions necessary for directing the future of Hungary toward new ideals and modern development, and when the "Age of Francis Joseph" with its grand agenda and nationwide prosperity was about to establish a solid footing for Hungarians in the Dual Monarchy—that the "Francis Joseph concept" received a tremendous blow, the ship of state began to founder, and the horizon turned cloudy. On Good Friday, the winds of religious hatred cast swaying shadows of the trees that conjured up images of hanged men swinging from the branches.

Now, fifty years later, few people remember these turbid, phantasmagoric and ghost-ridden mood-swings of Hungarian society. At times the thermometer reached the highest pitch of fever bearable by the human organism and the psyche of the social construct. Time after time the aged Tisza must have felt the earth shake under him, jarring the old desks at the ministerial offices which until then had been peacefully amassing piles of documents in the expectation that the awarding of decorations for public service was to be their only business in times to come. And now the government in this hospitable land was forced into the position of punishing people who, "one instinctively felt", were innocent... Let us face it: even fifty years ago only a tiny minority of the public actually believed the horror story that Móric Scharf, the adolescent son of the *shammes*, recited like a lesson learned by heart when questioned about what had happened at the Tiszaeszlár synagogue.

What follows is the story of how a handful of judicious individuals, who retained their clarity of mind even in this Shakespearean night, managed to stem the rumbling earthquake that was approaching and thereby forestalled truly major damage to the best part of the nation.

2. Those Dashing Independence Party Deputies

In those days an outstanding physique was still an indispensable requirement for election to the Chamber of Deputies on an Independence Party ticket. Even if the candidates of those times were unable to compete with Lajos Kossuth, who was considered to be the most handsome man ever born to a Hungarian mother, nevertheless one still had to "cut a fine figure" in order to appeal to the voters of pro-Independence districts.

Géza Polónyi was a most virile-looking, broad-shouldered man with a somewhat Gypsy-like, pockmarked face, and most of his female clients were slightly in love with him. His law office did in fact handle many cases involving women, and his name was mentioned in connection with a wide variety of ladies.

Károly R. Eötvös was also a man of burly stature; at that time he had not yet become the paunchy and bald figure familiar to a later generation. He still possessed all of his curly locks, wore traditional Hungarian-style, close-fitting garments, and emanated the kind of poetic air seen in portraits of the young Kisfaludy.

Gyula Verhovay was one of the most dashing figures of his day. About him, alas, we possess hardly any feminine recollections, for after his battles in the political arena he retired to his village to devote his days to one woman only, whom he addressed as "Nanny", and both he and Nanny have now been dead for quite some time. But till the end of his life he remained proud of the sword-scar on his forehead, acquired in a duel with Géza Polónyi at the time of the Tiszaeszlár trial. Independence Party deputies were forced to fight duels among themselves, since they could not find suitable opponents among the government-party representatives.

Győző Istóczy was also a handsome man; formerly a judge he became embittered after one of his decisions was overturned by a higher court, and decided to join the radical wing of the Independence Party.

The parliamentary representative of the Tiszaeszlár district, Géza Ónody, was likewise proverbially good-looking, "like an officer of the Guard"; he was the first to make an incendiary speech about the "murdered" girl after hearing about the shocking case from his local constituents. Probably Géza Ónody was a gentleman in a rather chaotic state of mind, further inflamed by local public opinion to demand the investigation of this extraordinary case.

More or less every parliamentary representative, who enjoyed his privileged position as a result of the confidence of the electorate, had something to do with the Tiszaeszlár trial. The "Saintly Old Man", Lajos Mocsáry, the leader of the Independence Party, was unable to refrain from occasional statements—nor were the witty Lulu Meszlényi and Ignác Helfy, Kossuth's proxy. Likewise, Pál Hoitsy, a man with a European vision, as well as Gyula Lits, the "military expert" of the Independence Party, had to have their say. In whom could the nation have confidence when an outrageous case like this one needed to be prosecuted, if not in the opposition deputies, who were practically obliged to keep bringing up the affair lest it gradually fade away during the lengthy investigations. For, lo and behold, as soon as a single anti-Jewish demonstration broke out in Pozsony, Kálmán Tisza ordered non-Hungarian troops to quell it! Thus one could not expect any action from the government party to appease the inflamed public mood. Old Vidliczkay, the famous "midnight orator", the first to filibuster in Hungary, was importuned by his Nyíregyháza constituents to speak about something other than the wretched Csángó people (whose repatriation from Bukovina was a current topic of discussion) in the Chamber of Deputies presided over by Tamás Péchy, who was also quite dashing, flanked by his secretaries István Rakovszky, Albert Berzeviczy and Ferenc Fenyvessy, gallants every one of them.

It was obvious that Kálmán Tisza was stalling and prolonging the investigation (for almost fifteen months), while he sat in his office in Buda Castle, smoking the cigars named after him, or took long walks back home at his Geszt estates, sucking on his long-stemmed pipe.

Whom could the populace trust, the opposition asked, if not the deputies— "offshoots of the very soul of the people", oftentimes elected in defiance of the gendarmerie or the revenue officers—when something like this Tiszaeszlár case came along to disrupt the equanimity of even the most tranquil folks?

So the Independence deputies, who stood for "the people's own heart and soul", did not have it easy when they visited their districts for Easter or Pentecost. They were inundated with hundreds of questions.

And most of the voters wanted to hear some reassuring information about the Tiszaeszlár case.

3. Count Dessewffy's Fateful Intervention

The investigation into the affairs of the Máramaros raftsmen who had clandestinely floated the corpse away had become so drawn out as to indeed neutralize the work of the local gendarmerie (that had seemed conclusive, after the interrogation of Móric Scharf and the other witnesses)—whereupon the "inaction of the somnolent county officials and the halfhearted efforts of the national government were interfered with by a hand from abroad". (That was how they worded it in those days. It is best to insist on the exact terms used back then if we want an accurate image of the times.)

This "foreign hand" was none other than the Parisian daily Le Figaro, a publication which was highly respected even in Hungary, although its readership here was relatively smaller than in other foreign countries.

A May issue of Le Figaro carried a letter from its Viennese correspondent, according to whom the interrogation of the accused in the Tiszaeszlár trial, and especially the questioning of the easily influenced, simple-minded raftsmen, was much enhanced by the "nail-studded Swedish whip". (We may wonder how this term entered the story in the Paris newspaper; it is most unlikely that the raftsmen, Jankel Szmilovics and Dániel Herskó, both principal defendants, made statements about being tortured to the Viennese correspondent of Le *Figaro*.)

One reader of Le *Figaro* from Szabolcs county responded to this story—this was none other than Count Dessewffy, known throughout the land as the "Count of Királytelek".

The largest landowner in the county, he was famous for living in aristocratic isolation and reading only foreign newspapers.

Who would ever have believed that A. de Dessewffy would speak up in a case discussed in the daily papers, a man who saved his public pronouncements for the annual Upper Tisza Flood Control Association meetings where he would submit proposals for taming the unruly river, usually accompanied by cash contributions.

The "Count of Királytelek" had the reputation of being something of an eccentric on account of his flood control projects, which were inspired by river engineering reviews from abroad. At one of the flood control meetings he once went as far as to compare our meandering Tisza to the Mississippi River.

Of all people it was the reclusive Count Dessewffy, devoted only to science and his "peculiar hobbyhorse", who chose to respond in public to the article in Le *Figaro* about the "nail-studded Swedish whip" (which might have been a reference to the *karikás*, a traditional long whip)—by reflecting on the repercussions of this entire Tiszaeszlár affair.

A. de Dessewffy's statement was published in the form of a letter to the editor of Le *Figaro*, and it dealt a crushing blow to those who still entertained some glimmer of hope for the innocence of the Tiszaeszlár Jews.

A record number of copies of Le *Figaro* sold in Hungary on that day in May when the letter from Count Aurél Dessewffy, Szabolcs county landowner, was published.

It is true that anti-Semitism in Hungary has assumed threatening proportions and, I will admit, has even instigated riots, but the guarantee of public safety is in Mr. Tisza's hands, and it is to be hoped that there will be no recurrences of the Pozsony riots.

It is also true that the reaction caused by the exclusive, selfish, and often hostile behavior of our Jewish compatriots is now being acknowledged beyond doubt even in those circles that are mindful of the history of the past fifteen years.

In any case it is essential that a rapprochement take place, and sooner or later this will happen; but in the meantime the cup is filled to the brim, and one must handle it very cautiously lest it spill.

Our Israelites will follow the example of their French and English coreligionists, and their fine qualities and many talents will, without doubt, secure for them the goodwill and recognition they deserve.

A. de Dessewffy

This letter from the "Count of Királytelek" was thus launched, via the Paris daily Le *Figaro*, on its journey into public opinion.

Its first effect was the arraignment of the incarcerated Jews and the appointment of the court date for their trial.

"Well, the eccentric count's letter has brought on the calamity," said those clever folks who would have preferred to see the matter hushed up while still at the investigation stage, before the story of that Easter in Tiszaeszlár exploded into a full-scale, Europe-wide scandal.

4. Lajos Kossuth's Messages Defend the Innocents

In those days the Hermit of Turin expressed his views on issues of public interest in letters addressed to the deputy lieutenants of the counties.

These messages from Kossuth were mostly responses to the eightieth birthday greetings flooding him from Hungary and other parts of the world.

And the words of the eighty-year-old Kossuth were respected as Gospel truth.

The marvelous thing was that each of his letters was different; not once did he repeat the same sentence or phrasing.

"No matter how long a human life is, it is no more than a fleeting moment", he writes for example to the Deputy Lieutenant of Fehér county. For those who like trivia, he also adds that he has lived 29,270 days thus far.

"But eighty years are a very great length of time for that 'fleeting moment' called human life. The board upon which the hand of time has scored one's age eighty times has no room left for 'hope'."

Kossuth also sent individual replies to the local governments, the municipal council of Budapest among them, that had greeted him on his birthday. "Foreigners who visit Budapest speak of the city in terms of the highest praise... I, too, delight in my beautiful memories of Budapest... Since I last saw the city (alas, for that 'last') I have felt not only great pride on account of her remarkable development, but I also bow my head in homage..."

However, in the letter addressed to the Deputy Lieutenant of Zemplén county (his birthplace) he speaks about more topical matters. His voice is more familiar in the letter sent to the county of his birth, the usually high-flown tone is more intimate here, beyond the courtesies of "a poor exile addressing his home folks". He warns his native county against a malicious and evil exploitation of the "Jewish question", for surely the charges brought are so vicious that the innocence of the accused is bound to be established sooner or later...

But Kossuth's letter was not able to obstruct the march of events. The Nyíregyháza court proceeded to charge with murder Salamon Schwarcz, the *shochet* from Tiszaeszlár; Ábrahám Buxbaum, a schoolteacher from Ibrány; Lipót Braun, the *shochet* from Udvar; and Hermann Volner, a day laborer. Another eleven men, including József Scharf (the father of Móric Scharf, the star witness for the prosecution) were charged with aiding abetting, as accessories to the murder. Thus a total of fifteen individuals were charged by the court—for committing the murder "by means of the slaughtering knife", and for helping to conceal the crime and transport the corpse by means of cart and raft. Fifteen prisoners now sat in the Nyíregyháza jail, awaiting their fate.

5. Károly Eötvös Conducts of the Defense

The prisoners, like any other incarcerated persons, could do little else beside grow beards—but the outside world was profoundly shaken by the indictment delivered by the court.

In all of Hungary perhaps no more than a few hundred people really believed in the authenticity of the "Tiszaeszlár Hoax" (that is, in the actual fact of ritual murder)—the same people who also gave credence to the forged "Talmud" recently published by Rohling. Now this "Tiszaeszlár Hoax", as a result of the decision by the Royal Court, began to assume the proportions of a menacing shadow on the horizon, some dark, unknown, ghostly form capable of wreaking havoc in a civil society that had been fairly calm until then. Could the shochetim, obeying some ritual law, actually have bled the Christian girl to death? ... Could the testimony of the backward Móric Scharf prove true in its claim that the members of an entire Jewish community had conspired to kill an innocent servant girl and to get rid of the corpse by floating it down the river? If yes, the consequences would have been incalculable.

The jailed victims therefore had to find competent defense attorneys capable of ensuring that justice would be upheld in the midst of the hysteria surrounding the trial.

Until this time only Heumann, a bright and burly Nyíregyháza lawyer, had been active on behalf of the accused Jews. He had appeared in court during the interrogation of the witnesses to represent the impoverished prisoners who could not be expected to pay an honorarium for his troubles. On the other hand he had received more than his share of abuse for "hindering", by his intervention, a murder case that seemed to have been proved as "plain as day". While the defense was under his management matters did not progress very auspiciously; with each passing month the authorities came up with fresh evidence pointing to the guilt of the Jews (perhaps the most shattering was the testimony of the raftsmen who claimed that emissaries from the Tisza-eszlár Jews had commissioned them to float the corpse away, and that they had seen the body transported to the raft by cart). During all this time only the prosecuting magistrate seemed to produce any witnesses.

A young Budapest lawyer, Miksa Székely, the son of a Nyíregyháza tobacconist, assisted Heumann with the case.

But it was obvious that the two of them were incapable of defending the fifteen accused, even though Heumann proved to be a fearless, rock-solid, brilliant bulwark against a torrent of blows. (His surviving papers and correspondence, which the writer of these lines has had the opportunity to consult, are proof that he was not intimidated by such harassment as the frequent broken windows at his house and the death threats he received while defending the detained Jews. He remained a stalwart believer in the triumph of justice, even though it was seemingly receding into the distance during the repeated rounds of investigations.)

Finally, after almost a year and a half of incarceration, just before the setting of the date for the final trial—as they said in those days "under the shadow of the gallows"—it at last occurred to the coreligionists of the innocent sufferers to secure the services of an effective defense attorney for the Tiszaeszlár trial.

There was in those days a Jewish association known by a variety of names. The Budapest representative of this association began to look for a defense lawyer with a national reputation, to make sure that justice was done in the case of the men who were victims of the Blood Libel. Where could such a courageous defender, who also enjoyed universal esteem, be found? Only among the members of the Independence Party, those heroes we referred to earlier. Among them were to be found men who dared to speak out not only in times of national peril and tribulation but also against a flagrant act of injustice. Among them were famous lawyers such as Géza Polónyi and Károly Eötvös—although there were also others such as Verhovay, Istóczy and Ónody who professed world-views that diverged from those held by the majority of Independence Party deputies. (Géza Polónyi had launched a newspaper called Nemzeti Ujság to counter Verhovay's Függetlenség, while Károly Eötvös, along with Adolf Agai, was a contributor to Egyetértés, the daily run by Lajos Csávolszky, the brilliant "newspaper king", who offered a splendid mix of Independence Party politics and Liberal ideals. It is reassuring for a student of the history of those times to see that the journalists of fifty years ago knew their métier even in a world that had seemingly gone haywire. Every line published in the contemporary press had a purposefulness to it.)

The name of Károly Eötvös came foremost in assembling the list of defenders in the Tiszaeszlár case. This Independence Party deputy seemed to be cooler, more collected, steadier, and even more distinguished than the brilliant Géza Polónyi, who occasionally proved to be somewhat nearsighted in individual combat against a great variety of opponents. Besides, at that time he was occupied in a case involving a mail robbery in Graz. [...]

In those days Károly Eötvös went about wearing the clothes typical of a respectable country gentleman of the 1880s: boots and tight-fitting Hungarian breeches, the knee-length braided jacket named after Ferenc Deák, and a fringed tie knotted around an open collar. In this outfit he would attend the Chamber of Deputies or the impassioned meetings of the Independence Party, intimate, familial gatherings always rife with intramural squabbles fueled by personal animosities ("While the dog barks, the caravan moves on"). Károly Eötvös, who in his old age was to be revered as a demigod for his equanimity, back in the 1880s was often capable of pounding the table, as a matter of historical record. In debates he always had ready at hand one or two ancient examples—some old jurist or national hero—ready for citation.

Upon being recruited—by the above-mentioned Jewish association that was protecting the rights of the impoverished brethren—to organize and lead the defense of the Tiszaeszlár accused, Károly Eötvös suddenly transformed into a doctor. "With graying hair" (as he liked to say) he took up the study of forensic medicine, investigating the varieties of cadavers by studying autopsy records. Unhurried and deliberate, as befitted a gentleman of the old-time world of county-court judges, he advanced in his studies. Little by little, in the course of his afternoon siestas, he read through many an autopsy record from court archives, including some that were two hundred years old. He consulted the notoriously curmudgeonly Professor Kovács, a terrifying figure in medical students' anecdotes, and, under the pretext of debates with him, learned much that was relevant. Likewise, after immersing himself in court records of autopsies, he paid a visit to Professor Scheuthaler (who later, as an expert witness in the Nyíregyháza trial, informed the court that he had personally conducted over forty thousand post-mortems).

In the meantime Károly Eötvös had not exchanged a single word with his defendants, the Jews incarcerated in the Nyíregyháza jail. He did write three letters to Heumann, his defense associate, to inquire about the progress of the case. These letters, written in his minuscule hand, are larded with seemingly insignificant queries. He did not seem to be interested in the so-called murder aspect of the case at all. He spent his time studying cadavers in order to prove to the Royal Court at Nyíregyháza that the corpse retrieved from the river (which, needless to say, exhibited no sign of murder) was identical to the missing Eszter Solymosi and that the "cause of death" was drowning. The extraordinary figure of the famous defense attorney was often seen in the anatomy laboratories of old clinics where young medical students were dissecting cadavers. There he stood, with his high forehead and full beard and wearing his braided and frogged suit, among the medical students listening to anatomy lectures, paying especial attention when the cadaver of a drowned person lay on the dissecting table. And he would examine the cadavers of aged nuns as well as of young *filles de joie*, to gain insight into the mysteries of post-mortem changes to the corpse. It could be that he did not so much as glance at a single legal paragraph during the months in which he prepared his defense, but he consulted all the textbooks available on forensic medicine... As contemporary wits put it, his extraordi-

11

nary mind acquired such a store of expert knowledge that he would have been able to prove the corpse of a hundred-year-old grandmother to be that of Eszter Solymosi.

Fortunately there was no need for this. The Nyíregyháza court refused to accept the credibility of the prosecution's star witness, the half-witted Móric Scharf, whose testimony was revoked, and, as the truth emerged in the course of the final trial, the accused were acquitted of the charges brought against them.

(27 March, 1932)

Frigyes Podmaniczky's Beard

In certain respects I may consider myself a fortunate man: I have witnessed just about every nineteenth-century fashion in beards. Although I myself, even in my earliest youth, have never sported more of a beard than what is visible in certain portraits of Byron or Pushkin, still, even this minimal fuzz suffices to enroll me in that great assembly of men who have employed their beards to influence politics, public opinion, and fashion; to imply dignity, nobility, superiority—and even to further affairs of the heart, letting a superstitious beloved snip off a few strands before leaving on a journey...

I recall still seeing the beards worn by collaborators in honor of Haynau well after the London brewery workers (incited by Hungarian émigrés) had given a sound thrashing to the former commander in chief of the Austrian imperial forces occupying Hungary after 1849. Dyed-in-the-wool imperial bureaucrats expressed their hopes for the return of Haynau and their refusal to acknowledge the passing of their day by letting their beards grow long and shaggy on each side. This was the type of beard you saw on old men who muttered curses at the world as they sat on benches along the Buda esplanades.

I have seen the vogue of the Kossuth-style beard, difficult to groom and therefore somewhat symbolic. The man with a Kossuth beard obviously had no ambition to appear at a court ball. Official neglect, and occasionally persecution, was the lot of this beard which was sometimes seen on priests, such as the Hungarian Piarists at the Podolin college near the Polish border, where higher authorities rarely came to visit. And even if they did, the monks could claim that their tight-fitting ecclesiastical collars made daily shaving an impossibility.

And who can forget the beards of the Tiszaeszlár Jews, who kept Hungary in a state of turmoil for years a generation and a half ago? The youth of those days often pulled and tore, and even set fire to, the *shochetim*'s reddish-brown or salt-and-pepper beards. Yes, even though medieval persecution, scorn, mockery, and defeat were the lot of such a beard, it still had its fanatical adherents. Wearers would conceal these telltale beards under their kaftans in the daytime, but in the hours of the night they would stubbornly flourish them like the characters in old romantic operas.

And let us not forget Garibaldi's beard, individual hairs of which were once sold glued to papers carrying seals of authenticity, while shreds of linen bearing drops of Garibaldi's blood were marked with the date on which the Italian freedom fighter had shed his blood. In its day the Garibaldi beard was almost as popular in Hungary as the Kossuth beard. Women dreamt of warriors with Garibaldi beards seeking shelter in their gardens, and the brave barber who dared to display a shop sign featuring a gentleman with a Garibaldi beard was once the talk of the town in Pest.

And how about the so-called Petőfi beard, which in the nineteenth century usually signaled a definite penchant toward patriotic poetry. However, this fashion failed to develop to its full extent, for in the past century no authentic portrait of Petőfi existed. In fact all those "close friends", "fellow *honvéds*", and "eyewitnesses" who delivered pronouncements about Petőfi and the 1848/49 War of Independence in the *Honvéd* magazine (edited by Kuszkó) that was published for decades in Kolozsvár, gave such confusing accounts of the poet's appearance that even Petőfi's friend Mór Jókai could no longer tell the truth from the lies. Thus the "Petőfi beard" was never fully authenticated—and neither was the style of beard worn by the ancient Magyars, that Miklós Szemere affected (and that was dubbed, by that gentleman's admirers and lickspittles, the "Huba beard"). Likewise, neither the Henry IV nor the Bonaparte beard ever caught on in Hungary; these could be seen in their original forms in their native land.

After this brief survey we may address that period of the beautiful nineteenth century when any gentleman in this land who wanted to amount to anything had to grow, groom, and wear, amidst universal esteem, a so-called Francis Joseph beard. Orders and decorations found their place as a matter of course in the vicinity of such a beard.

In his youth Francis Joseph had reddish-blond hair and his face was somewhat smaller than those of most Habsburgs, whose double chins command respect from the vantage of centuries. Historical portraits show that those Leopolds and Ferdinands possessed faces of grander dimensions than most ordinary mortals. Francis Joseph, on the other hand, had a face of average size, decidedly undersized for a Habsburg who was expected to convey all the

14

majesty of a mighty empire. I will let a future scholar track down the identity of the talented court barber who invented the so-called Imperial beard. (I grew up among Hungarian men who preferred the fine, solemn Lajos Batthyány-style beard, so I could never become truly enthusiastic about the Imperial beard.)

One thing is certain: the young man with reddish-blond hair who, in the early 1850s, rode in a four-horse carriage through the lowlands of eastern Hungary to get acquainted with this realm that had recently been subdued with the aid of Russian armies, wore, according to contemporary eye-witnesses, thinnish, barely visible side whiskers and a small mustache; while the mature man of 1867, wearing the coronation robes of St. Stephen in front of the primate of Esztergom, who was about to crown him Apostolic King of Hungary, wore, according to contemporary accounts, full but not overly long brown muttonchops. This newfangled style of beard became the object of public admiration at the next carnival ball of the Industrial Association at which Gyula Andrássy gave the Budapest dames a whirl on the dance floor, while the excluded *misera plebs* had a chance to study this beard on the cheeks of the lackeys and coachmen waiting outside the Redoute building. For a while the fashion remained restricted to court circles, the imperial family and their servitors; but eventually the whiff of court atmosphere became sweeter and sweeter, wafting on the winds from the Viennese Hofburg and the royal palace at Buda, to circulate throughout all of Hungary. Queen Elizabeth had much to do with the growing popularity of the Imperial House in Budapest, especially after she spent a summer at the Villa Kochmeister near Városmajor for the health of her infant children. She was frequently seen walking from Buda Castle Hill, along the Vérmező, toward the villa, allowing local matrons to take in every detail of her couture.

Naturally at first it was the womenfolk who began to copy Elizabeth's frou-frous, her narrow waistline and long straight skirts. Those ladies especially who were built like the queen—tall and slender—were eager to follow the new fashion...

Well, if women were willing to forget the events before the coronation, then who could blame all the henpecked husbands who now began to eye their bare or hirsute faces in the shaving mirror, wondering how that new-style beard would look on their physiognomies? The first to adopt the new fashion were those men who had Kossuth beards in 1848 and Haynau beards in 1849, and who had then tried in succession the beard-style of each successive department chief until, after the coronation, they settled on the Francis Joseph beard. Thus old army officers angling for a commission in the newly forming *honvéd* units soon grew Imperial beards; likewise, bureaucrats aiming to stay in office a few more years until retirement sought the protection offered by such beards. After the Imperially bearded attained official positions there was a general movement in the barbershops of the capital, as well as in the provinces, toward the transformation of beards. But the fingers of these Figaros were not fast enough to win positions in the new regime for every aspirant. Many a face was deemed untrustworthy because it retained traces of vanished Kossuth, Batthyány, and Garibaldi beards. Thus plenty of the finest Francis Joseph beards were stranded without an official post.

Times changed but the beard remained.

But these early beards (harking back to the time of the coronation), whether successful or not, gradually wandered off to the graveyards, and now only a few lugubrious family photographs remain as evidence of the early experiments by the paterfamilias. In the wake of this pioneering generation came the real onslaught of the Imperial beard, which governed and directed Hungary from the 1870s until defeat in the Great War. This beard received the decorations and medals at court; it created bank directors, founded insurance companies, pronounced loyal sentiments from the Lord Lieutenant's chair; and portrait painters soon learned that a successful portrait had to depict a gentleman with an Imperial beard.

Our hero, Frigyes Podmaniczky, is of this glorious era of the Imperial beard when the style enjoyed a practical monopoly in the land and the wildest Kossuth beards had turned white.

Even the Francis Joseph beards began to start graying, keeping pace with the sovereign, but it was far more practical and comfortable to grow old and bald together with the portrait known throughout the land from the coins minted at Körmöcbánya, than in the style of Kossuth, the Hermit of Turin, who no longer wore a beard in his old age while his trembling hand penned the messages that were heeded by fewer and fewer people at home! That Imperial beard, trained bilaterally, stood for permanence, security, and freedom from care, in human lives as well as on the face profiled on silver forint coins. Imperial beards were worn by letter carriers who strove to attain promotion after many years of faithful service. The same beard became the politician, who, for the sake of his career, thought nothing of the daily care it required. Frigyes Podmaniczky's corpulent old butler, who was mostly seen chatting with the likewise corpulent waiter of the White Swan in the doorway of the hotel while his master was having his lunch at the Pannónia across the street, could tell many a tale about all the work that went into making Podmaniczky's beard perhaps the finest in all of Hungary, after Francis Joseph's.

The fat old butler waited in front of the White Swan, even though Frigyes Podmaniczky did not like to be assisted, not even when crossing the bustling Kerepesi Road. He was a stubborn man who refused to grow old even when he could barely make his way about on foot. He was a hero who had stepped forth from one of his own Romantic novels, a man who wanted to remain a man to the end.

For crossing from one side of Kerepesi Road to the other was not an easy task to negotiate for someone with Frigyes Podmaniczky's mobility. As long as the old-time horse-drawn tram still passed this way the conductor always blew his horn and slowed down, having gotten accustomed to watching the tall old man in the checked suit and top hat slowly making his way across, taking tiny steps that were not without a certain dignity. Budapest cabdrivers who had been around would know him by name and would slow down their mad pace for the pink-jowled old gentleman with the stiff bearing and white beard who wore colorful shirts (patterned with riding whips and jockey caps!), slowly crossing from the White Swan to the Pannónia. That still left the villagers' carts that rattled into town with the *komondor* running in their wake, and provincial buggies carrying the wives of rural notables who still covered their heads with scarves but placed a hat on top...not to mention riders speeding by on velocipedes, popularly dubbed "mad knife-grinders"... Yet in spite of all the dangers of being knocked down and run over, even in the middle of the roadway the old baron never altered his slow and even pace, not even when village drovers appeared with herds of mooing cattle on Kerepesi Road.

The highly visible, enormous Francis Joseph beard sported by the baron halted all traffic, whether urban cabdrivers or village drovers.

Stepping up on the sidewalk presented no problem for the baron, who was well versed in climbing the stairs at the old Liberal Party clubhouse. [...]

Ah, that was a beautiful world! The finest Imperial beard in Budapest shone far and wide among all other beards. Respect and the obeisance due to a patrician surrounded this beard, even in the dining room at the Pannónia, where the guests who had arrived at dawn from the countryside would start to rattle the silverware against the water glass as early as a quarter past eleven, and would loudly nag the waiter about the tardiness of their lunch. Waiting for their meal, these provincials would carve their own toothpicks, using horn-handled hunting knives; they cared not a whit about man or beast when it came to their long-anticipated beef consommé ("Plenty of greens in it, waiter!") with the marrow bone and boiled beef on the side—but these guests would pause as they tied the napkin around their necks when the famous Imperial beard appeared behind the glass door of the entrance.

"Here comes Podmaniczky!" exclaimed even those who were in the midst of pondering whether to order tomato sauce or horseradish with their ribs. The arrival of Podmaniczky postponed the pleasures of the palate for a moment. (Legend has it that the notorious trencherman "Pátri" Szűcs, treated to lunch here by Miklós Szemere, a resident at the Pannónia, was so astounded by the lively checked pattern of Frigyes Podmaniczky's coat—a pattern woven at a Czech mill exclusively for the baron—that he forgot to place his order for scallions with his boiled beef, an unheard-of omission.)

The baron had his own small table in a corner of the dining room. It was small but suited one man comfortably, and he always ate his lunch alone. He spooned up his puréed vegetables, nibbled at the chicken breast, smacked his lips after the sweet noodles. The old waiter who served his food bustled about him with a self-importance that implied that the immediate fate of the country depended on these efforts. The pink and bald baron—whose healthily glowing pate greatly resembled that of Francis Joseph—ate his lunch, calmly impervious to the curious onlookers. He drank his seltzer and nodded off after lunch without fail.

Many a time I had looked at that dozing Imperial beard, which even then emanated such dignity that the provincial matrons and crimson-cheeked misses lunching at nearby tables would instinctively lower their voices a notch or two as they discussed their night at the Folk Theater, while their menfolk modulated the ardor of their argument over wool prices or the quality of agricultural products. The children were sent out to be entertained by the doorman in the vestibule. Everyone was a shade quieter after lunch in the dining hall while the president of the Liberal Party dozed in a corner. I was deeply absorbed in contemplating the former novelist, author of *The Lady with Blue*

Sunglasses, *The Lowlands Hunting Lodge*, and other novels, whose career in literature had brought him to this pinnacle.

I wondered if he ever thought about having been a novelist in his youth...while my eyes rested on the dignified old man surrounded by his nimbus of splendid political triumphs.

Indeed, he did.

But that is another story.

(28 August, 1924)

The Bridegroom of Andrássy Avenue

"If we were to consider matters district by district, we could say that the Inner City first began to be choked off by the Sixth District, also known as Teréz-város. It was somewhat like the parricide practiced by certain primitive tribes, where the young people get the old out of the way", said Baron Podmaniczky, who could be called the Founder of Budapest, even though his given name was Frigyes and not Romulus or Remus.

I had the honor of accompanying the baron on his walks a few times, from Erzsébet Square (where he was born) to the Inner City, where he spent the happy days of his youth, on to Andrássy Avenue, which had been built up by him. Frigyes Podmaniczky, in the course of these walks that were equally dear to him in both winter and summer, always gave proof that he remained a faithful lover of this city even when Budapest had long forgotten her old bridegroom who had become her betrothed on a summer Sunday in 1856 by the pond in the Municipal Park. It was then that the young Frigyes Podmanicz-ky, recently returned from his travels abroad, swore the oath to dedicate his life to the beautification of Budapest. The witnesses at the ceremony consisted of a Pest hansom cab (for the baron never set foot in a two-horse hackney), the military band playing on the island in the pond, and Podmanicz-ky's own heart of gold.

"After Andrássy Avenue was built up it was especially the members of the fair sex who lapsed in their loyalty to the Inner City, having discovered the perfect milieu for displaying themselves on this splendid new avenue which, although it was named after a mere Foreign Minister of the Monarchy, instantly surpassed Koronaherceg [Crown Prince] Street in popularity. Yes, on occasion women have been known to ignore differences in rank, especially where affairs of the heart are concerned", said the well-known baron in the course of our walk. He no longer inscribed his aphorisms in souvenir albums but dropped them in the course of conversation, which is a sure sign of wisdom.

"Yes, Gyula Andrássy was a handsome man indeed, but it still took some luck to be adored by women the way he was, in his day. Had he not been pockmarked, and therefore thinnish of beard and mustache, I would have understood my friend's great success with women. But I must conclude that the avenue named after him became an instant hit with the women of Budapest because its width provided ample opportunity to flaunt each new hat, each wide skirt, each parasol, each high heel paraded in full view on this spacious boulevard—instead of them being obscured on the winding, overcrowded alleys of the Inner City, especially during the noontime promenade. On the three-fathom-wide asphalt of the Andrássy Avenue sidewalk each fashion plate, each impeccable outfit could be shown off to best advantage.

"On Andrássy Avenue no one had her train stepped upon, no one's galloping steed was forced to come to a halt (since I had a separate roadway built for people on horseback, recalling how difficult it had been to gallop about in the Inner City during the days of my youth)—nor did provincial gentlemen from all parts of the country, here to show off their skill as drivers, have to curb their fleet equipages. Bánffy of Boncida could freely parade his horses that were branded with 'BB' and trained to bite. Yes, Andrássy Avenue was the freeway of aristocratic liberties where everyone found their own delights, amusements, and good cheer—and for this reason I refrained from erecting a temple here for any clerical religion, other than the arts. I transplanted the Opera here, bringing it over from the National Theater, and this is where La Traviata had its first great success, to mention only one grand opera. The gaiety of Andrássy Avenue bestowed, in one fell swoop, a metropolitan atmosphere to the Terézváros district which it traversed. Granted, good times could be had in Budapest formerly, even on the odd-numbered side of Király Street (which belongs to another district, Erzsébetváros), but you truly entered Budapest, the world-renowned, only after you crossed to the other side of the street and entered the Sixth District, where the very air seemed to be different. The asphalt, too, was smoother here and the buildings were whitewashed more frequently. The horse-drawn omnibus coming from Buda went down the length of Király Street in those days, but no one would ever board it before the St. Theresa's stop except for older citizens too intimidated to take the street car. Reaching St. Theresa's Church, where the omnibus entered the Sixth District, the conductor would take a look in his mirror, twirl his mustache, and toot his horn; from this point on he would give a free ride to a passenger on the seat next to him—usually some maid on her day off, heading for the Municipal Park. Here all the old ladies from Buda were helped off

22

the bus, their tickets being valid only to this stop; and the ark would fill up with energetic youths as young misses clambered up to the top-tier seats for the speeding ride down Andrássy Avenue, toward which the omnibus headed after turning onto Nagymező Street. On certain spring afternoons there were so many lovely girls seated in that bus that you needed to look no further if you wanted to find a wife in Budapest."

In the course of his walks Frigyes Podmaniczky would inspect, beside the Opera House, the other edifices on Andrássy Avenue that "he had had built", and, strolling past these palazzos, he listed their owners, whom he knew personally, having originally sold the lots to them.

"Naturally the landlords became aware of this 'Terézváros air'—and even though it was not sold by the bottle as Margit Island air used to be during the last century they did start to raise rents as soon as Andrássy Avenue began to be fashionable. The saplings along the avenue were growing taller, and even though we did not go as far as the folks in London who considered the chopping down of a three-year-old tree a capital crime, our Andrássy Avenue acquired a canopy of leafy boughs. And the women promenading under these trees on a Friday evening were just as pretty as those on a Saturday night, for the Jewish residents mingled here most fortuitously with the Christians—although I must say that back then, 'in my time', we did not allow religious differences to influence our appreciation of the fair sex. The ladies would display their finest outfits, their most charming smiles, and their most bewitching walk when they went for a stroll on Andrássy Avenue. In all of France there was not enough silk and perfume for the women of Budapest, so some of them had to make do with domestic products. Meanwhile the landlords were hiking rents at such a rate as to imperil the auspicious promise of Andrássy Avenue."

Evidently the baron privately blamed these landlords for not being satisfied with having the "loveliest" ladies of the capital promenading in front of their buildings, for the baron himself never became a landlord, not even when he was an old man and deserving of such status.

"No, I could never understand Harkányi, Táfler, or for that matter the Swiss Molnár, who asked higher rents in his Andrássy Avenue apartment house than for his other properties, even though he had acquired this lot at a bargain price, just as I did the Opera House lot. Back then we were happy to have anyone build here on Hermina Fields, which used to be a marshy, reedy wetland just like those frequented by Alföld hunters and outlaws—and where, today, the Italian diva sings Aida for the Budapest audience. They kept screwing the apartment rents higher and higher, as if the windows opening on Andrássy Avenue were made of diamonds. My friend Ilkey, who owned a building on the corner of Újvilág and Hatvani Streets where the Opera House was originally going to be built, was fully justified in complaining to me that developing Andrássy Avenue was tantamount to committing parricide against the Inner City. Citizens without a prospect of receiving a baronetcy or a patent of Hungarian nobility strove to achieve whatever rank they could—such as being a landlord on Andrássy Avenue. Why, a landlord on Andrássy Avenue would consider himself superior to one on Váci Street even if the latter's grandfather had already been a landlord in the capital.

"So the landlords on Szervita Place and Koronaherceg Street—barons, counts, and respectable patricians among them—began to look askance at me after Andrássy Avenue became the showplace of the world. At every step they would remind me of the crime I had committed against Korona Street, where I had lived as a junior clerk at court; against Párizsi Street, where I strolled each day; against Kristóf Square and Váci Street, where I had spent some of the happiest days of my youth in the days when I introduced countesses to the pleasures of taking walks in old Pest, and my friend Eliz Szapáry had persuaded even the most reserved countesses to show their faces at least once a day on Váci Street.

"All that remained was for some peeved Inner City resident on an upper storey of the Tüköry Palace to lie in wait for my daily passage, clutching a vase full of water, or ladies to order their maids to empty chamber pots on my head, or their janitors to drive me away with broom in hand. I did not need to wait until the white-bloused milliners of Korona Street started to stick their tongues out at me before I realized that, although I had done my beloved city a service by building up Andrássy Avenue, I had caused just as much damage to my long-time home, the Inner City, by creating a new fashionable district.

"Therefore I launched a pro-Inner City movement among my circle, for beneficial movements are always welcome. Our aim was the revival of the Inner City. I composed an appeal to the gentlemen of my acquaintance, the signatories of which would pledge to confine, to the extent that it was possible, their shopping, residence, entertainment, and even their daily walks, to the Inner City. My appeal was addressed to 'Friends of the Inner City', and I had my old friend Kálmán Tisza sign it first among the members of the Liberal Party. The appeal I prepared for the National Casino was signed at the top by Count István Károlyi. He already nursed a special grudge against Andrássy Avenue, for it was on account of its development that he had fought his fatal duel with Zichy-Ferraris, an affair he naturally regretted, for any gentleman is bound to feel pity for another who is mortally wounded by his bullet. My appeal was signed by all the Kegleviches, Wenckheims, and Szapárys; by Baron Üchtritz (who, in spite of being a landlord in the Józsefváros district, still resided on Magyar Street), Elemér Batthyány, Leona Csekonics; and by the gentlemen of Pest county led by Gyula Gullner, who liked to stay at the Országos Casino that was built in place of the former 'Arany Sas' hotel. My humble efforts on behalf of the Inner City produced close to a hundred signatures, but there was another group at the 'Vadászkürt', led by Vidacsek and others of the gilded youth, known as the 'terrorists' for they set out to teach a lesson to all who spent their money at Andrássy Avenue night spots instead of the Inner City.

"The residents of the Inner City were gratified by my appeal. The Váci Street promenade was crowded day after day by those who considered this their patriotic duty; the storekeepers on Koronaherceg Street prospered once again. Authentic high society was recaptured from the clutches of Andrássy Avenue: gentlemen and especially ladies of distinction limited their noontime walks to the familiarly winding narrow and cozy streets of the Inner City, where they knew exactly whom they would meet at the next street corner, from whom to expect winged compliments, and precisely what the gallants would be saying—for there are certain greetings and expressions that ring true only in the Inner City and sound false anywhere else. After all, on Andrássy Avenue, who would ever reply with fashionable nonchalance when asked how he was feeling: 'Fine, just like any other count!'"

Baron Frigyes Podmaniczky, having built up Andrássy Avenue and having crowned her with the Opera House and placed the Grand Ring Boulevard around her waist (for the Old Baron had a hand in that as well), after issuing his appeal took a manful stand by the side of the Inner City, for his was a soul of infinite loyalty. After the Millennial Exhibition of 1896 he no longer frequented Andrássy Avenue and the Opera House, refused to be celebrated, and continued to live like a hermit in the Inner City, preferring not to leave that district. Each day he took his constitutional on Váci Street, considering this to be his public duty even though he had retired from public life.

"After the top hat and the high boot heel they invented the bicycle with its big wheel for the elevation of men of short or medium stature. As for me, I had invented Andrássy Avenue, the Royal Castle Garden and the Danube promenade for the elevation of a formerly small and insignificant Budapest. I placed a beautiful setting around the ladies of Budapest by commissioning Károly Lotz to paint the Opera House frescoes, having the boxes upholstered in crimson velvet and lighting up the grandest chandeliers. I doubt there is a man who has done more for the ladies of Budapest (for whom I still possess the deepest esteem and sentiments). I know they will forgive me for never marrying—perhaps for the simple reason that I was never able to choose just one from among them", concluded the Old Baron at the end of our walk.

(9 November, 1930)

The St. Stephen's Day Traveler

"We're going to Budapest on Stephen's Day!" used to be a bright promise, toothsome as honey-cake, heard so often back in the old days. For in the Hungarian consciousness St. Stephen's Day had always occupied a place similar to Christmas, Easter, and Pentecost... It was a day full of expectations, even for those who had otherwise little to expect. A day celebrated by everyone as if it were their very own name day. A day, coming at the end of summer, that once more recalled the joys of that season, for as far back as one could remember there had never been an overcast Stephen's Day; on the contrary, it had always been a day of fair weather and golden sunshine.

"Back in those days they still roasted oxen on Vérmező!" Such are the reminiscences of the occasional historians who somehow manage to turn up every Stephen's Day to prove, by means of their recollections, that today's generation in fact does not have the least idea of what it really meant to live in Hungary.

Well, it is true enough that the butchers' apprentices used to parade a flower-bedecked ox with gilded horns all over the city, but I never actually saw them roast one, for it would have been highly unlikely that they could have felled, cut up, and dressed an ox in that field without a supply of water, even if they had been able to start a fire suitable for roasting it. Perhaps the coronation of Francis Joseph was the last time that the Pest guild of butchers had sacrificed an ox for the purpose of actually roasting it in the open and distributing the semi-raw meat among the poorer folk. But in any case on St. Stephen's Day one could find everywhere food stalls serving pork chops grilled in the open, the way it had been done at fairs for centuries. In taverns where the floors were covered with wood chips, various kinds of *pörkölt* (braised meats) and goulashes were served, along with the wine. These latter dishes came to be especial favorites among Hungarians when they began to be called "zone breakfasts" (as just about everything was called "zone" in Hungary after the Minister of Transport Gábor Baross introduced the term for railway travel). If memory serves me well, a zone breakfast used to cost twelve

27

kreuzers, and it consisted of a glass of beer, a few bits of braised meat, and a slice of bread. Four forints allowed you to travel to Budapest from the greatest distances, such as Brassó—for the idea behind the zones was that the rates did not increase beyond a certain point, the aim being to attract people from the most distant parts of Hungary to the capital city. Stephen's Day was most appropriate for this, for then, in addition to the zone fares, travelers enjoyed all sorts of other discounts. Yes, it was indeed a glorious state to be a traveler in Hungary round about St. Stephen's Day.

Verily, Gábor Baross had been a graduate of the old Hungarian county administration. Such an administration was capable of handling just about anything; nothing was impossible for it. The wisdom of the county *alispán*, the power vested in the chief magistrates, used skillfully, was able to accomplish the most diverse aims, so that the public administration of Hungary could be said to be a model of its kind. Gábor Baross, in bringing the railroads under government management, only did what he had learned back in his own county administration where all power resided practically in the hands of one man, the *alispán*. As soon as you crossed over into a county you were able to tell what kind of *alispán* it had. The state of the bridges, highways, and villages would either sing his praises or else damn him. Even the smallest roadside tavern stood as character witness for the *alispán*. And so Gábor Baross became, as it were, the *alispán* of the Hungarian railways.

The train conductor with his grand mustachio, who represented the Hungarian state on railway lines extending to the borders, went about his duties in government service as if the *alispán* of the railroads were traveling incognito on that very train. The track-watchman was always on time with his red flag, for one never knew when Gábor Baross would decide to inspect his watchmen. He would set out unexpectedly—like an *alispán* of the old school who had heard bad news about one of his village notaries or district magistrates— and the Püspökladány stationmaster would suddenly be visited by the spectacle of a tall, bearded, broad-shouldered gentleman elbowing his way into the office. As for those small branch lines that were the subject of so many anecdotes in the old days, they received more than their share of visits from the *alispán* of the railways after they came under government management. And those old-fashioned cages in which the doors were locked on the passengers as in some prison, those dangerously crowded third- and fourth-class

28

carriages that had once upon a time "zoned" the country bumpkins; those small towns where the stationmaster's chief worry was the proper banking of the local skittle grounds, all saw plenty of Baross, who, if need be, avoided the trains and arrived on a hand-driven rail car—which had to be lifted off the rails in a hurry when a passenger train appeared around the bend!

It was Gábor Baross who made the Hungarian state railways into what they are now, although he gave no more thought to the matter than a county *al-ispán* to the execution of his duties.

Gábor Baross had his opponents—for instance one of the daily papers practically owed its existence to its attacks on him—but then every man of genius has his enemies in his day. This sort of thing is especially prevalent in Hungary, where even Sándor Wekerle had enemies, although this stout gentleman, who was bandy-legged as a result of his great body weight, had promised everything to everyone, and the funicular to Buda Castle was always full of satisfied customers. Gábor Baross was stingy with his promises, but his actions spoke louder than any words in making travel throughout Hungary safe, friendly, welcoming, and inexpensive, even for those old-fashioned folks who were loath to travel because of rumors of guests dispatched by outlaws at some far-flung inn.

The zone-system is memorable in the recent history of Hungary for all those who would never have visited Budapest without this innovation. For travel to the capital had not been easy before Gábor Baross's zones; conditions still very much resembled the state of affairs when, at the site of the present central railway terminal, provincial carters cracked their whips to attract customers. Trains did not have regular connections. For example, the train for Kassa arrived in Miskolc at midnight but did not leave until morning. The waiting room at the Püspökladány station always overflowed with a milling crowd of people whose trains were still somewhere far off. I can't say that the station restaurant suffered as a result, for in those days among veteran travelers railway station restaurateurs possessed nationwide reputations such as various inns had for travelers by *post chaise* in the time of Dickens. The Püspökladány station was famous for its *pörkölt*, braised meat prepared with tomatoes and green peppers, ample solace for the traveler's tribulations. The wine at Füzesabony was recommended by experienced passengers just as often as the red wines available on the Graz line in Austria. If you passed through Kassa you had to sample the local ham—usually there was time enough to consume two portions before the towering locomotive of the Tátra express pulled in. At the Nyíregyháza station restaurant a regular Christmas pig-sticking feast was available the year round, thanks to the ministrations of the renowned pork butcher Balczár. Pozsony had croissants filled with poppy seeds and walnut; Érsekújvár resounded with the music of a Gypsy band... It was the irregularity of trains that allowed the railroad restaurateurs to do their absolute best; their cooks did not have to dread the engine-driver's third whistle signaling the inexorable departure of the train. It was an amicable age that allowed you ample time to ruminate after your meal and make friends with gentle travelers from distant parts; time to converse about affairs of national importance—the crops, the wine-harvest and other matters that were always of interest to Hungarians.

Well, Gábor Baross, the *alispán* of the railways, sounded the whistle for the passing of precisely these station restaurants by not even leaving enough time between trains for a man to down a glass of beer to wash away the dust of his journey; it was curtains for those endless luncheons, and many a chef became suicidal as a result of Gábor Baross's insistence on transporting Hungarians at top speed towards the capital. As the old saying goes "All roads lead to Rome"—and just so did the minister of iron-ways direct the entire nation's traffic towards Budapest. No more would a freight train be allowed to stand in melancholy meditation at some romantic little station where only the clicking telegraph apparatus was awake... The whole country began to hurry, and if Gábor Baross acquired enemies as a result of introducing this modern pace into the Hungary of old, I can understand their animosity. After all, not all folks were in such a hurry to spend their money in the capital.

But Stephen's Day was an exception when no one would curse the engine-driver for stoking up the locomotive, for it was desirable to arrive at the capital as early as possible. Not everyone had relatives with apartments in Budapest where the country cousins could show up amidst much rejoicing, as so often depicted on the pages of old humor magazines. The digs rented out to law students by the month were now occupied by hearty families from the provinces, and the student could go sleep at his favorite café. With the coming of St. Stephen's Day the innkeepers with their silk skullcaps, the doormen with their gold braid, and the ever-present waiters crowded the hotel entrances to receive hordes of guests who came to sojourn at the "Horse", the

"Swan", the "Eagle", the "Griff", and others, for such were the hotel names in fashion in those days.

"I want the same room as I had last year!" the country squire would exclaim, hopping down from his hansom cab. "The one where I can count from the window how many shoppers are entering the Kerepesi Bazaar."

Another, rather corpulent, guest gives orders: "I don't want to wake the staff in the middle of the night, so make sure there is a bootjack in my room, that's what I'm used to."

Whereas a third St. Stephen's Day guest would insist: "Under no circumstance will I take a room next to a married couple, for they quarrel all night and I can't get a moment of sleep."

Small wonder that old Boz the novelist spent much of his life at inns where stagecoaches liked to stop—for even today one can learn many amusing things in the lobby of a hostel. All sorts of whimsies, oddities, and secret desires hide in the travelers who come to Budapest from distant parts of the country. The eccentricities of a whole nation would be on display around St. Stephen's Day. There was the man who left home intending to make a thorough study of the changes in the capital since the days of his youth, only to stay all day long in the room at the inn where he was ensconced. He was afraid to strike out on his own in the city that seemed unrecognizable after all these years. The streets had acquired new names; it was no use searching for a familiar face, not even at the tavern where that reliable old waiter had always placed the same dishes in front of him on the occasion of former visits— for such old waiters have a way of remembering the preferences of a guest, even if he stays away for years... I do believe the St. Stephen's Day traveler rejoiced even if he caught a glimpse of one of those typical, large-mustached porters, as long as he was still at his customary old post.

The Budapest municipal council, the clever shopkeepers and entrepreneurs would rack their brains for weeks ahead about what unforgettable entertainment—beside the ox-roasting, horse races, flying flags and shop windows—to offer the St. Stephen's Day travelers streaming into the capital. Yet the visitor from the countryside was sometimes most pleased by recognizing an ancient waiter or a walrus-mustached old porter from the capital of the old days. One never knows what people will like.

I hear that after a hiatus of so many years, when war, revolutions, and other miseries have prevented the proper observation of the great celebrations of

Hungarian life, the St. Stephen's Day traveler is once more as eagerly awaited in Budapest as in the old prewar days. True enough, we must pick up the broken thread that ties today's Hungarians to the good old days, to the generations now turned to pale shades who contemplate the present with a silent, disapproving shake of the head. No matter how much life in Hungary has changed, the past and its amiable customs cannot be stripped away. There are times when all of us would like to encounter the days of our youth again, regardless of any unpleasant memories; there are days when we firmly believe in the return of our lost happiness if only we could once more partake of the roast ox on St. Stephen's Day, if only we could once more travel inexpensively in Gábor Baross's zone, and taste that "zone" *pörkölt* again, if we could regress a good way into the zones of that past, away from the uncertain present and still more uncertain future. Yes, there are days...

It is possible that on the upcoming St. Stephen's Day the traveler, the amiable guest, the long-absent country cousin is again preparing to visit Budapest, smiling, curious, and at full speed, just as before; it is possible that now we shall resume our former lives which had to be interrupted at some point to allow us to see clearly who and what we were back when we did not fully esteem ourselves. Let our country friends come again and be amazed that the horse-drawn trolleys no longer run on Kerepesi Road. Let them wander again with wife and children, and a rucksack left over from the old days, lost on the streets of Budapest and still looking for the airship in which the actress Ilka Pálmay ascended on a bygone St. Stephen's Day. And yes, let them go searching for long-gone old hostels. Enthusiastic, bursting with curiosity and a will to learn, they will visit all those sights offered to visitors of the capital: museums, galleries, hills and bastions, the Danube and the Parliament, statues and monuments, all of which were once recorded in fine picture albums. Let them all come and make the name day of our first king again as holy, devout, and heartwarming as it was back in the nineteenth century when gigantic energies strove to educate our country in greatness and mighty wills were knocking at the gates, yet the past, the great past of the nation, was never forsaken for the sake of the greedy present.

"We're going to Budapest on Stephen's Day!" will once again be the message resounding throughout Hungary.

(20 August, 1926)

Catholic Crusading Knights of Yore: Their Glory and Their Decline

"...In those days there were considerable difficulties for the true faith in the land. The Knight of St. Louis had to do battle for weeks and months in the arena as a champion of the Holy Roman Church. The Semitic race, which had only recently discarded its yellow garb, demanded more substantial rights in addition to the right of moneylending. The ashes of John Hus and Hieronymus Savonarola, scattered in the wind, were resurrected and the *hajdúk* of Gábor Bethlen pounded the table in the Lower Chamber, fighting for the freedom of the sons of Shem." Thus reads a passage in my novel *The Crimson Coach*, first published twelve years ago in 1913. Since then four editions have sold out but religious issues are still most topical in Hungary, beside such lesser problems as not everyone having enough to eat. We had fought some splendid battles for the various religions as we approached the so-called enlightened twentieth century. "Fin de siècle," said the Budapest sophisticates, referring to the unusual phenomena in the last years of the nineteenth century. There were fin de siècle hairstyles and also ladies' hats to mark the great calendrical turn in the world of women. Still, it was religious matters that caused the greatest commotion. The structure of society was creaking and heaving as a result of the new crusade led by Counts Nándor Zichy and Albert Apponyi. The Canons and Reverend Fathers Prohászka and Huttkay, having found the activities of the Catholic Circle on Molnár Street wanting, founded the Pázmány Association, in whose chambers on Gyöngytyúk Street the Catholic writers and journalists were hosted by Monsignor Tóthfalussy, the Erzsébetváros parish priest, at dinners prepared by his far-famed cook for the delectation of old, bunion-footed editors and ardent young poets. The writer of these lines had also joined those who sang the praises of this lady who cooked for the parsonage, although his literary ambitions rather attracted him to the Molnár Street Catholic Circle, where in the course of readings at literary soirées József Kaposi, editor of *Magyar Szemle*, introduced the young writers he deemed worthy to Hungary's most prominent politicians. I was one of those introduced at the time...

I don't know what has made me trot this out after the passage of so many years—perhaps it is the approaching Advent season that recalls the beautiful Catholic ladies of those days, the unforgettable bishops and aristocrats vying with Tancred of the Holy Land: Advent, when we set out once more, lamp in hand, in the dark, toward the fragrant auroral Mass, the *rorate*, just as we did once upon a time when the bells at dawn signaled the end of the literary soirée at the Catholic Circle and the swansdown-pure ladies and noble gentlemen proceeded from the high-minded session of the Circle straight to the Franciscan Church. Advent approaches with its devout blue dawns, like a fairy-tale, like some otherworldly herald in advance of the greatest holiday of the year to announce the birthday of the Christ-child, and nowadays the times are again such that it is not only the pious villagers and small-town folk who leave their footprints on the snowy paths leading to church, but devout footfalls are heard even in the sleepy metropolitan dawn, just as twenty-five or thirty years ago when in our religious crises we so gladly escaped from solitude, insomnia, doubts, and hesitations toward the gently tolling church bells.

...Ah, how bright the banquet hall of the Catholic Circle shone when the young writer stepped onto the podium for his first appearance in the flesh in front of the distinguished public... Not quite as dignified as the poets depicted in etchings from the good old days, for his face was flushed with excitement and his voice trembled more shamefully than during any exam he had ever taken. He wondered if his clothes were truly the latest fashion and was unsure that his shaggy hairstyle would please the sensitive young ladies who had recently graduated from the English Misses'... Success was unpredictable here, for an awkward bow, an indelicate sentence, a misplaced emphasis could spell disaster for the reader in front of the most fastidious audience in Hungarian society... Yes, the young writer had to pay many a visit to the miracle-working saints' chapels in the capital to make sure he would not fluff his lines and that he would score a resounding success at the Catholic Circle, from where it would be smooth sailing into the ardently coveted literary salons of the day.

...Real princesses sat in the front row!

Yes, princesses, who had landed on Molnár Street straight out of fairy-tales. Next to them sat wives of Knights of the Golden Fleece, spouses of actual privy councilors. I do believe that in those days Budapest ladies dreamt of some day sitting in the front row at the Catholic Circle. There was one princess with a most benevolent face, about the same age as Mary at the time of her heavenly Assumption; her motherly gaze hung on the trembling young poet. She nodded her fine head, the color of pale old gold, in his direction, and whispered some solemn admonition into her neighbor's ear, then listened as devoutly to the words spoken from the podium as if it was Holy Scripture. Her Serene Highness was the most attentive listener I would ever have at a reading. The banquet hall was full, but it was for her ears only that I read my "Tale of the Wizened Old Man". Years later, when my eyes and ears had become more open to the world, I found out that this benevolent old princess, who never missed a literary reading, did not know any Hungarian.

...The diocesan bishops and other high-ranking ecclesiastical figures were relegated to the second row, although their chairs were upholstered in purple. Once I saw there Cardinal Lőrinc Schlauch of Nagyvárad, listening with sympathetic nods to the callow vaporings of some young littérateur; thus this bishop of the wealthiest county, one of the finest minds of his age, proved himself a man of such good will as only the greatest minds can be. The slogan of the times was "Support Catholic writing", and the highest prelates found time to bestow their subdued but gratified applause on the young poets introduced at the Catholic Circle.

...Everywhere in those splendid halls were violet-scented ladies and lily-of-the-valley-complexioned young misses, whose devout visages and conservative hairstyles always seemed to emanate some heartfelt prayer. They came here in a most festive mood, having no doubt planned for days in advance to meet at the Catholic Circle on the appointed evening, possibly having inquired from their gentlemen acquaintances about the writers scheduled to read at the soirée. The information they received could not have been derogatory, for back then our lives were as pure as snow, white as meerschaum before it is soiled by soot and smoke. The standing room was taken up by handsome gentlemen with that noble bearing one could only glimpse in the old days at those Catholic Circle gatherings. Benevolent, modest, well-mannered faces, glances free of hatred, anger, and scorn, as if these coreligionists were at a family meeting ruled by soft-spoken, gentle manners that make contact so pleasurable. Army officers with gilded collars and young men eager to help; silver-haired ministerial advisers and university students radiating St. Imre's humility; refined provincial gentry who thought nothing of

35

traveling by train in wintertime to spend an evening at the Catholic Circle; also teachers of religion and chaplains resembling French *abbés*: these were the folks who stood, listening with attention, lining the walls. The scene exuded friendliness, optimism, and encouragement, as if everyone present had empathized with the significance of a young writer's public début at a national forum... Who would have believed that in a decade or two these splendid specimens would be gone forever from Hungarian society?

As you may imagine, there had to be certain antecedents to a young writer's admittance to this House of Lords. First of all one had to know Ritter Lajos Kaczvinszky and the Reverend József Kaposi.

These gentlemen could be found in a small, single-storey mansion-like house with a garden on Új Street, where the doors were thrown open on Mondays and Wednesdays in the evening hours to receive writers and their manuscripts. This was the location of the editorial offices of *Magyar Szemle*, a weekly that was arguably one of the finest Catholic periodicals ever published in Hungary.

Ritter Kaczvinszky had not a word of Hungarian, ergo he was a Hungarian publisher. He was a stout, kindhearted man who showed a martial manner toward writers, mostly to prevent them from walking away with the shirt off his back. He had a silver-haired sister on whose hands enormous kisses were bestowed by writers more conversant with worldly ways. Kaczvinszky sat distrustfully among his antique furniture—many of the items museum pieces—and listened with misgiving while the writer made his petition. Then he would breathe a sigh of relief when it became apparent that it was only a matter of money—always money. The amount he paid for a poem, story, or essay is nowadays inconceivable even for the most prosperous papers: five forints, always in brand-new bills that snapped and crackled as if he had printed them on the spot. (In those days finicky individuals who liked to have only fresh, new banknotes about their person were not such a rare species.) Many were the writers, driven by dire need, who rushed from some remote part of town to this friendly house with its stained-glass windows, and strutted off light of heart like cocks of the walk. Kaczvinszky was always at home, always had money, was always wary at first and then relieved when he learned that all the writers wanted was some money... The ardent Catholicism of this good Polish knight was the motive force for many a young writer's persisting in a literary career and not leaving the path of devotion for some easier and more secure trail.

Another corner of the rose garden at the mansion on Új Street led to the editor of *Magyar Szemle*, József Kaposi, doctor of philosophy, who could have ended up as a bishop had he not decided to give up his ecclesiastical career. But back in those days he was still a solemn young priest who received in his editorial office even the humblest little writer with the utmost reverence due to a member of the Academy. I have encountered all sorts of editors since then, but will never forget this kind, intelligent, and sympathetic young man. He could not have been more than twenty-six years old, but writers twice his age turned to him as to a father. Old Imre Gáspár, László Torkos, Arnold Vértesi—so many passé authors and forgotten names!—confided in him their literary plans, works in progress, hopes and discouragements. A young writer does not yet know resignation and compromise, the whole world is his. But old writers who live to see themselves half submerged into the past need all the encouragement they can get to keep them from sinking into fallow depression. This good priest was also a true mentor to younger writers, reading their works in their presence and offering corrections and advice, instruction and encouragement; he was one of those editors of the old school who nurtured entire generations of writers. Károly Vadnai and Miklós Nagy were such editors in their own day and age. The growing seedlings needed sheltering care. The young tree's growth had to be directed, the trunk propped up with a stake if boughs sprouted prematurely. József Kaposi could spend hours tinkering with a poem or story in which he found something to his liking. He inquired about his writers' family problems and was not loath to show up at a Józsefváros tavern if he discovered a tendency toward carousing, so harmful to the young... He raised funds among the prelates and the aristocracy to support the publication of works by young writers. Bibliophiles are well acquainted with the fine editions József Kaposi published. This was what went into the education of Catholic writers in those days.

Since not even the most Catholic *Magyar Szemle* could exist without a Jew, the editorial offices were managed by a gentleman named Schwartz.

The career of the Catholic writer went on to other paths from the Új Street mansion, but one could never forget the *Magyar Szemle*, just as one never forgets one's schools. Once you made the grade at *Magyar Szemle* you were ready to be presented to an audience including princesses and countesses at the Catholic Circle. You were entitled to enter the Zerge Street palace of Cardinal Lőrinc Schlauch and make an offering of your books, nor did you have to wait long in the anterooms of the St. Stephen Association if you showed up with literary projects...

That man named Schwartz had a mailing list of some two thousand names in his desk drawer, and these addresses were so valuable that they were never trusted to the printer: he personally wrote the mailing labels each week. Yes, these two thousand hard-core supporters of Catholic literature, the first to receive the young author's works, were the audience addressed by the poet's lines—these two thousand subscribers would decide whether Catholic literature needed that particular new writer. Provincial parish priests, gentlemen and ladies living in the country, who in those days still followed literary happenings with sufficient interest, could judge whether Dr. József Kaposi had made the right choice in his latest discovery. I must admit that there was little occasion for debate: publication in *Magyar Szemle* conferred crusading knighthood, the status of Catholic author.

...Naturally not every Catholic writer stayed within the confines of this isolated readership. The great Budapest newspapers, desirous of providing reading matter suitable for every stratum of the populace, were eager to offer space to these "crusading knights". Some of these champions were so seduced by their new public that they did not return to Uj Street, or to the most Catholic Józsefváros where their careers had been launched... Good József Kaposi awaited in vain the return of these birds who had flown the coop. At the Catholic Circle the princesses, countesses, prelates, and generals still frequented the literary soirées for a while, but talented young writers were harder to come by. "It would seem that the Protestants and Jews have won in both politics and literature", they concluded. Needless to say, by Protestants and Jews these unforgettably kind folks meant the upsurge of Liberals. Nándor Zichy and Albert Apponyi had lost the battle in politics, and since back then, too, the nation lived mostly for and by politics, the defeat had its effects in literature as well. At the Pázmány Association fewer and fewer people showed up to praise the cuisine of the Erzsébetváros parish cook and membership ranks thinned; by now everyone was crowding the rooms of the Otthon Circle, for the word was out that this was where writers were made—even though here not even a cup of coffee was offered, much less those patriarchal pig-sticking feasts. Jenő Rákosi kibitzed at the card tables and orated about his thirty million Hungarians.

...Was it worth leaving Molnár Street and Józsefváros behind, along with the devotional life? We knew it was time to quit these environs when, soon enough, we discovered that those unforgettable princesses themselves were starting to show up in theater boxes at performances of plays by "depraved" Jewish authors. Likewise the doorman at the Opera House could be heard calling for the countesses' equipages on nights when some opera on an Old Testament theme was performed with great-bearded Jews singing in title roles. Jewish publishers were making unheard-of headway; these German-speaking booksellers issued the majority of books purchased by the public. The daily *Magyar Állam*, the last bastion of Catholic ideals, ceased publication for lack of patronage; *Alkotmány* was still appearing, but with an ever-decreasing circulation. As a final blow for the crusading knights József Kaposi, the fabulous gardener in the nursery of Catholic literature who had created such a lovely flower garland of poets and writers around him, abandoned his editorial endeavors, gave up organizing readings for bishops and princesses, and furthermore even renounced his ecclesiastical career in favor of having his love consummated at a civil wedding ceremony. This was the ultimate and greatest blow suffered by the splendid cause of Catholic literature and its crusading knights. No longer was there a mentor to guide young writers in the direction of Catholic ideals; no longer was the esteemed editor there to nurture writers both new and old; the publishing house that delighted in beautiful editions of upstanding, moral works folded. Good Ritter Kaczvinszky from then on was so intimidated when he came across a living writer that he hid his wallet and it was never seen again.

At that time, when one after another the crusading knights were abandoning the Catholic strongholds (although after the passage of two decades they would return to these ever reliable halls), when liberal ideas were stoking up the country as if it were a giant locomotive, when even Catholic literature came to be labeled "sectarian", the term applied to Jewish writing, at a time when liberalism became so widespread that even newborn babes in the cradle were called liberals, only one old writer remained loyal to the Catholic faith, and that was Imre Gáspár. His name is little known today; once he had been a promising poet who was overcome by poverty and ill fortune. This old writer now confessed that back in the glory days of Hungarian Catholicism he had been a secret Protestant. Although born into the Lutheran faith he had accepted assignments from the most Catholic periodicals, wrote devotional poetry, religious polemics, essays on Catholicism. And now, when politicians and writers had come to abandon the good cause, this old, owl-like writer asserted that he wanted to set right his former error... He had been a Protestant until now, but now that Protestants and Jews were so fashionable he would once and for all become a Catholic. So he received holy baptism from the hands of Father Bangha at the Jesuits' Church in Józsefváros, choosing the lame gardener of the cloister as his godfather.

But for some time to come the fine days of crusading knights were over— momentous events had to happen before Hungarians would no longer boast of being "Liberals".

And once again we are attending early morning Mass.

(22 November, 1925)

Somosy, the Man Who Taught Budapest a Lesson in Nightlife

[...] The name in the title of today's pensum will resound for some time to come in Budapest; at times as blaring as the paper trumpets of the Terézváros fair, at other times as mellow as the solitary cello played by an aging man-about-town for whom nothing else matters from bygone days beside the fact that he was young once. Well, the sound of Somosy's name should call forth female figures seen nowadays only on the rim of a musical clock where they perform their charming but monotonous dance, old ladies about whom no one would believe that they had worn red-heeled shoes once upon a time when men were willing to die for their garters with the ardor of medieval knights off to the Holy Land. How modestly these old nannies now slink close to the walls of churches, they who had formerly kicked up their heels so high that they nicked the kettle drummer's nose! Oh, they now pass with eyes downcast toward decrepit, outlying streets—they whose eyes had once been ready to swallow up all of young Budapest. The trembling hands now clutching the mug that contains their pittance of coffee or soup had once scattered gold, pearls, and silks around town with a prodigality that kept the entire male population of the capital toiling to satisfy their whims... No, let's not look for those young ladies of bygone days who had danced on the stage under Somosy's supervision—anyway, they would surely deny that they had ever splashed water, like a fountain, on the bald head of the bandleader in the pit below.

Somosy will symbolize young Budapest as long as people are forced to escape the cheerless present by turning to the rosy mirror reflecting their happy days.

It was Somosy who taught Budapest to enjoy nightlife, lighthearted late-hour revelries, just as smalltime *filles de joie* in the hands of the right director become *grandes dames*, past-mistresses of the art of living.

...Even so, there are still some old men around, resembling ancient yellowed music-hall playbills, who insist that Somosy did not invent nightlife in Budapest but merely perfected it. "Somosy!" they wave, "all he did was entice the Blaue Katze's audience to switch to his own newly opened Orfeum." (The Prologue for opening night had been sent by Jenő Heltai from Paris.) The Prince of Wales was no longer coming to Budapest, to have the Viennese danseuse Jeanette Waldau place her red sabots in his lap; there were no pre-dawn hurrahs shaking up the downtown end of Király Street sending meek burghers to their windows in a tizzy, as if an earthquake had hit; no more did the windows of those ancient tenements fill with heads covered by nightcaps and mobcaps whenever a notorious carouser rambled past, painting the town red. The tough fiacre-drivers were replaced by even tougher ones who were hired by Somosy to bounce rowdy guests, together with their coachmen, from his newly opened music hall, until gradually order was restored. The Blaue Katze had grown old, its days were numbered. Jeanette Waldau, cursed by so many abandoned wives and fiancées, moved back to Vienna and opened a milliner's shop in an outlying district, giving poor factory girls a lesson in fashions—after the styles she set had conquered the other capital of the Dual Monarchy. A similar (or worse) fate awaited the rest of the enchant-resses of the Blaue Katze: "Boriska", Pepi Niemayer, Frau Honett, Mirzl Léner, all of whom had once made barber and aristocrat alike ready to walk on their hands in the streets of Budapest. "New girls have arrived in town", as the businessmen would say. The old girls, if they did not find other careers in time, ended up peeking through the scarlet curtains of the new music hall and startled gentlemen would avoid them on the street, as if they had seen a ghost returned to haunt... Once I witnessed a painful scene outside Somosy's Orfeum: the scarecrow figure of a down-at-the-heels former beauty, with a funny little foppish hat, threw herself in front of the pair of grays pulling a red-wheeled fiacre in which a "new girl" was seated next to the man who had once sworn eternal fidelity. An ordinary tale, but enough to set your hair on end as you walk on—as if invisible steps were following you from your own past.

True enough, Mr. Somosy wiped out old-fashioned Budapest nightlife by launching his enterprise.

His music hall has been described many times by better qualified observ-ers, but to get a real sense of the place the latter-day reader would have had to sit at one of the tables laid with damask and silver in that hall where the air was thick with tobacco smoke. The silver bucket with a bottle of bubbly and the equally frosty lily-of-the-valley complexion of the lady of the night would have been *de rigueur* by the tableside.

A true gentleman would show up wearing tails (this was the first and foremost lesson Somosy had to teach the capital)—a mere dinner jacket would not do for anyone aspiring to be a man-about-town. The silver bucket, the thick cigar, cigarettes from eastern lands and the dazzling girl at your table would only have been conspicuous by their absence. The flower vendor placed her bouquet on the table without asking and the girl at the table was obliged, as a matter of business policy, to pin the corsage on her bosom. The waiters would serve a variety of dishes without being ordered, like so many djinns in the dream of the wanderer—for they knew just about every guest's taste and spending power. No, in this music hall you never had to call for the waiter's attention by clinking your beer-glass with a four-kreuzer coin, nor did you have to worry about finding a suitable personage to replenish the dwindling supplies in your thinning wallet. Hartmann and Lefkovits were there, and God only knows what other moneylenders, seated with the friendliest of smiles at an inconspicuous table somewhere near the cloakroom. One heard many tales about these kindly folk who operated at rather usurious rates. (One of these nocturnal Rothschilds was named Schreiber, known all over town by his nickname "Schreibie".) Also on hand was the deaf jeweler who carried fortunes in his vest pocket and smiled even more slyly than his rings. And when the waiter obligingly took your card for delivery into the hands of one of the artistes on the stage, out in the kitchen, famous for its cuisine, the chef would set about preparing one of his specialties with a knowing smile.

And the dancing girl was already on her way, wrapped like some fleecy cloud, to make her theatrical entrance.

But let us pause here for a moment, to clear Mr. Somosy's memory... Not every actress appearing on the music-hall stage would come to our table after her number was over. In fact it would be more correct to say that the artiste who responded to the invitation was the exception to the rule. It was mostly actresses hailing from Budapest or Vienna who agreed to have supper in the conservatory with their "cousin" or "fiancé" after the performance.

For in Mr. Somosy's music hall, members of the troupe led the lives of saints.

On the Mozsár Street side there were two small rooms where the artists and artistes had their meals before or after performances. Mr. Somosy placed the greatest emphasis on smooth service and on the high quality and international tone of the fare in these chambers. (Soon it would be proverbial in

Hungary that Central Europe had two restaurants where one could eat well. One was the dining car attached to international trains, frequently resorted to by gourmets taking the five-o'clock "sportsman" express, for by the time the Gypsy band at the Érsekujvár station had struck up to greet the train the waiters were already setting the dining-car tables for dinner for a meal that was worth the trip to Vienna, where the poor traveler could also look forward to a taste of boiled beef at Frau Sacher's establishment. The other dining table in Hungary that made it worth your while to take knife and fork in hand and undo the bottom-most vest button was Mr. Somosy's dining hall on Mozsár Street, which boasted windows no larger than an ordinary apartment's and an entrance so modest that only those in the know could find it. Mr. Somosy had actually played the joke [also told about Francis Joseph and a Hungarian minister] of three times in a row replacing the plates and eating utensils of an absent-minded guest who, awaiting his soup or roast, compulsively wiped his plate and fork with the napkin. Mr. Somosy was proud of his kitchen and worried when the famous Excentrique did not eat with the requisite appetite; was disconsolate when at dinner the nomadic Escamoteur plunged into a reverie about some other town where he had once performed and barely touched his food; became seriously upset when the lady aerialist, in a fit of jealousy because of her partner, petulantly pushed her plate away... Well, he had no reason for anxiety once the Budapest epicures discovered the secret of Mozsár Street, the small eatery behind curtained windows where guests were served beef and beer we nowadays only read about in Dickens' novels.)

So I repeat: not every time did the enchantress of the stage rise to the proffered bait of dinner in a private room, not even if the baldest waiter or the doorman, Popovits himself, who wore hussar pantaloons, was initiated into the plan.

As for the visiting foreign artistes, they were strictly off limits at Mr. Somosy's music hall.

Yes, this man Somosy, whose name was linked to so many wild adventures in Hungary, adventures that men would not have dared confess to their wives even on their deathbeds; Somosy, whose very name brought shudders to inexperienced young women of the capital and the provinces until, accompanied by a proper chaperone, they attended one of his shows; this same Somosy, known to variety artistes the world over as the last stop in Europe east of Ronacher's in Vienna where it was worthwhile accepting an engagement: this Mr. Somosy maintained stricter supervision over his artistes than many a mother superior over her nuns.

The artistes were usually quartered on the premises, behind those first-floor windows that gave on Nagymező Street, and none dared disturb their rest. No, this was not the place where a Gypsy band could be sent to serenade under the actress's window, as was still the custom in many parts of Hungary. Not even the most ardent man-about-town could ever get close enough to the high-wire ballerina to throw himself at her feet... By this I don't mean to imply that these strange, mysterious migrants, who traveled in all directions of the wind on their predetermined itineraries that were as regular as those of birds of passage, never shed a single feather during their Budapest sojourns. Certain legends from the time of Mr. Somosy persist, linking one or another dashing Budapest Lothario with a migrating swallow of the south or an ermine of the north, but the old-time agents who booked these artistes swear that those lady performers who traveled with such clockwork punctuality on western European trains and lingered not a whit longer in London, Paris, Berlin, and Vienna than required by the contractual obligations of their engagements, indeed ignored the lieutenants of the guards in the audience at Somosy's establishment.

Perhaps my circle of acquaintances was not broad enough to garner a truly intimate scoop about Baroness Rhadek, for instance, who made her entrance by bursting onto the music-hall stage on horseback, and who, in the course of her Budapest sojourn, was not seen once in the conservatory of the Orfeum where the famous Gypsy band leader, Lajos Munczy, laid his full-bodied salt-and-pepper beard along his violin, coaxing the latest Parisian tunes out of his instrument. But according to the grapevine of the day, as conveyed by waiters in the know, the baroness, after performing her equestrian bravuras, would proceed straight to her room to indulge in a cold bath. Captain Cody the sharpshooter likewise did not mix with the public, but brooded over his glass of beer in the solitude of the Mozsár Street taproom. In general Mr. Somosy required the artists he employed to maintain, offstage, the same illusion as they exerted in the magic circle of the limelight. Mr. S. believed that a true artist must not mingle with civilians in real life, for that sort of thing destroyed illusion and was harmful for business. Even Carola Cecilia, for years the queen of the Orfeum when the *Frauenbataillon* ran for some three hundred performances, whenever she felt like having a good time (which happened not infrequently) would forego the Orfeum's conservatory and take her entourage across Andrássy Avenue to camp out at Beliczay's well-known coffeehouse, entrusting her jewel-case to one of her most loyal courtiers, Diogenes Blau the Budapest stockbroker, while she served champagne from her low-cut shoes to count and cabdriver alike. But as I said, Mr. Somosy took the utmost care to have his actresses preserve the glamour of their stage presence by remaining unreachable for the public at large. Who would believe nowadays that an actress was not allowed to receive visitors in her dressing room?

But who was this celebrated man whose name echoed in the Budapest night even louder than Friedmann's, who would introduce flashy American-style advertising for the entertainment palace at the Millennial celebrations a few years later?

I remember him as a man of about sixty, who was as dignified as Nepaleck, the Imperial Court Chamberlain. Back in those days beards were de rigueur for men. Any gentleman of consequence felt obliged to grow a beard reflecting his rank and character. According to the old maxim a beard was bankable, and gentlemen of the old school laved the hirsute growth under their chins with egg yolk to promote a bushy luxuriance, while a tea rinse softened the beard. In those well-mannered days a man would think twice before scratching his beard in public! Mr. Somosy sported a fine Imperial beard à la Francis Joseph—perhaps in order to consign his past to oblivion, for back in the revolutionary days of '48 he had danced the *verbunkos* at the Kerepes tollgate to attract recruits for the rebel army of General Klapka. The adventurous young man had been a famous dancer, having run away from his wealthy and prominent family's home in Győr in order to lead the life of an itinerant actor, dancer, and buffoon—a passion that was not so unusual in the nineteenth century.

So a barely graying Imperial beard marked the tall, slender figure of this man who, at sixty, always tended to imitate courtly manners with his ceremonious comportment. Who knows what orders and decorations he would have been in line for had he not been obliged to retire from directing his Orfeum... Was the founder of the first Hungarian music hall a spendthrift? I cannot say that he had the least resemblance to any of the old roués, "*alter Dráhrer*" as they were called then, those elderly lions who showed no inclination to age. He was simply the one gentleman in Pest who had at least as many dress suits as Francis Joseph's master of ceremonies. These dress suits were as splendid as the enchantment he cast over a Budapest that was still in its infancy, the magic that promoted its rapid growth into a metropolis where more and more men wore tails without being professionally required to do so. One could say that Somosy, with his Imperial beard, dictated the design of tails in Budapest, although the city had its share of noted tailors. For quite a while he remained sole arbiter of the type of flower one wore in one's lapel, and he cued the audience, as well as his waiters, as to when to applaud the stars of his Orfeum. Yes, Somosy was the "leading man" of fashion in Budapest.

He was the reigning prince of the high life...whereas all his life he followed a sober, healthy, and sane regimen, smoking cigars only when he had to popularize some new brand that had appeared in town to compete with the cigars of Havana and their German imitations. For instance, he brought into fashion the *Tisza* cigar—who knows, possibly at the behest of the Minister of Commerce.

He indulged in champagne only when beseeched to do so by representatives of the champagne makers. (The handsome Miklós Kapy, the eventual sales manager of the Pécs champagne firm responsible for making the Hungarian bubbly a respectable item at nightclub tables, was still a captain of the hussars in the days when Mr. Somosy began his campaign to get his public used to the idea of always having a bottle of the effervescent wine at the dinner table, along the lines of the Parisian model.) Also, he was the first to hold a large-scale masked ball at his music hall, and for decades these Orfeum masked balls became the pre-eminent event of the Budapest ball season... With Countess Andrássy, née Countess Kinsky, as his partner he would open the ball, the guest list of which would be carefully studied by other notable organizers of Budapest entertainments, such as Béla Aczél, Gedeon Rohonczy and Pali Szapáry...

So how was it possible for this celebrated personage of Budapest nightlife to end his days among miserably reduced circumstances in a windowless little hole-in-the-wall room across the street from his Orfeum? Ferenc Rajna, who had appeared so many times on the Orfeum stage while the *Frauenbataillon* craze was still on, has written somewhere, quoting Somosy, that the theater is a barely tolerable business when it is going poorly, but God help you when it is doing well... For then it breaks even the most capacious directorial exchequers. This is what must have happened in Mr. Somosy's case: his Orfeum became too popular. The audience was overflowing night after night, and these audiences demanded more and more. True, entrance cost one whole forint, but the renowned acts from abroad, world-famous entertainers, stars of the variety world had to be paid a prince's ransom in order to fill the Budapest Orfeum night after night. Somosy paid dearly for the tempo he dictated. At the age of sixty he was no longer capable of shining, of setting off sparkling fireworks each and every night. He tired of tails, corsages, Robinettis, Bambullas, Carola Cecilias, of Kmoch and Der Herr von Rück: of everyone in short, even of the raging demands of his public, and he broke down. He was destroyed by being the talk of the whole town, by everyone's desire to have a good time at his place. Nonetheless, it is part of this extraordinary man's story that Somosy's famed star of fortune shines once again—for his descendants. His great-granddaughter, a little girl of eight, was introduced on the stage of the Operetta Theater the other night, on the premises where her great-grandfather had given Budapest lessons in how to become a metropolis.

(17 May, 1925)

The Court Kept by Miklós Szemere

...The pistol shot rang out and the ace of hearts fell with a hole through its center from the bullet-stop board set up three rooms away.

"Well, we're ready for target shooting at Szentlőrinc, our hand's as steady as ever," remarked the red-nosed Gyula Erdélyi, picking up the perforated card. Mr. Szemere replaced the pistols of fine workmanship in their case and eyed his hands for some time. Would these hands hit the mark out at the Pest-szentlőrinc rifle range, where he would have to demonstrate to the assembled university students that their host still had a steady hand?

*

In those days Mr. Szemere was out of favor with Francis Joseph and was making princely sacrifices for the promotion of sport in Hungary to show the monarch that he was good at other things beside gambling. For not long before, Francis Joseph had taken the unusual step of intervening in the affairs of the Vienna Jockey Club after word had reached him that gentlemen from various parts of his realm were gambling for vast stakes at the club's card tables. Naturally the Hungarians were the ringleaders, with the Poles as poor seconds—although they, too, had a reputation at card games. Outstanding among the most profligate Hungarian gamblers was a gentleman hailing from Zemplén county, a retired imperial and royal ambassadorial attaché, one Miklós Szemere; representing the Polish side at the green baize table was a certain Count Potocki, younger brother to the governor of Galicia. Inevitably, these two great card players came to a showdown. The elder gentlemen of the Jockey Club, those who tried to avoid unnecessary excitement and preferred to have others sit on tenterhooks instead, looked forward with great interest to the meeting of the Polish and Hungarian noblemen, for the Derby meet was drawing to its close and boredom loomed on the horizon of life in the capital.

Count Agenor Goluchowski, the Monarchy's Foreign Minister at the time, although himself not a gambler, was a passionate kibitzer. (He had plenty of time on his hands; all was calm on the foreign affairs front.) Moreover, he was a distant relation of the Galician governor's brother, who was sojourning in Vienna more or less under his tutelage. So the Minister for Foreign Affairs was also present at the Jockey Club the night the two fearless card players finally met head on. Among the kibitzers there were other prominent gentlemen who occupied positions of high honor and dignity at court, a truly fit audience for the duel at cards.

The game ended at dawn. Mr. Szemere, the cold-blooded Hungarian, triumphed over the panicked Pole who ended up owing him several million crowns. Not even the oldest members of the Jockey Club could recall a card-table loss that had come close to this. The customary rule—payment within twenty-four hours—had to be suspended in view of this staggering sum, and Mr. Szemere announced that Potocki could pay whenever he felt like it. But not so Potocki the elder, Governor of Galicia! He took the first train to Vienna, mustered all the credit at his disposal to pay for his brother's gambling debt, and then filed a complaint to Francis Joseph against the Hungarian card player.

Francis Joseph was astounded to hear about the card game, being a most frugal man who knew the value of money. He immediately summoned the Viennese chief of police...

"Herr von Szemere has twenty-four hours to leave Vienna!"

This was the reason why Mr. Szemere was now forced to pass his time in Budapest. But just to show that he had no need for the Polish count's millions he dedicated a sizable chunk of his Szentlőrinc estates to the construction of the largest shooting range in Hungary. He would show Francis Joseph what kind of stuff he was made of.

*

Did Francis Joseph eventually conclude that his punishment of the Hungarian gentleman had been too harsh? Something must have happened, for after the passage of about a year the Viennese police lifted the ban, but in the meantime Mr. Szemere was exiled to Budapest. And so he organized great festivities at Pestszentlőrinc, for (as he imagined) this would annoy Francis Joseph.

In those days a handful of Boers, by virtue of their wonderful marksmanship, were holding off the mighty British in South Africa. Miklós Szemere admired the bravura of the Boers, as he did all acts of bravery. He diligently studied the news from England where he had several correspondents; as time went by the Boers were still unvanquished thanks to their superior abilities with the rifle.

"This is how we must be, if our small nation is to survive in the great world!" Mr. Szemere exclaimed, and from his chambers at the Hotel Pannónia issued an invitation to the William Tells of the country, conferring with the most outstanding marksmen to plan a strategy for training Hungarian youths to match the Boers in sharpshooting. "You never know when we may need it," said the gentleman who was so rich in ideas.

The grand old man of Hungarian marksmen, Colonel Gusztáv Elek of Pazony, was notorious for hitting silver forints tossed in the air, and there were other gentlemen known to be in the habit of putting out candles at the end of long hallways by firing their pistols at the flame; there were legendary hunters with a reputation for never wasting powder. These illustrious men were all gathered at the meeting convened for the development of sharpshooting as a national virtue. Seated on the large steamer trunks in the apartment at the Pannónia were such guests as the melancholy, handsome Count Sándor Hadik, who was a crack shot with the pistol, as was the short-statured Count Imre Dégenfeld. Old Andris Kállay, a distant kinsman, arrived from Szabolcs county to propose that duels should be fought with long-bore rifles instead of pistols. Yes, call in Vilmos Clair to reform the dueling code by including the long rifle, lest Hungarian marksmanship be restricted to hunting. Mr. Szemere, in the course of a long peroration delivered in his rhapsodic manner as he sat on his ascetic, pillowless bed, wearing slippers and a red Garibaldi-style shirt, expounded his belief that every Hungarian man should learn how to handle firearms in order to defend not merely personal, but also national, honor.

"Then we should start with the university students!" announced "Pátri" Szűcs, who ever since the days of Kálmán Tisza had agitated for the role of students in national movements.

"Pátri" Szűcs, who held the official position of sergeant-at-arms at the old House of Parliament, had hit the nail on the head. Let the university student body learn how to handle firearms, for some day this might come in handier than their diplomas.

*

Architects were sent out to study the best rifle ranges Europe-wide. Mr. Szemere was so enthusiastic about this project that he even neglected his oldest passion, horse racing, in its favor. And anyway, because of Francis Joseph's decree he was not allowed to visit the Freudenau track in Vienna, the finest in the Monarchy. This eccentric man now came to neglect his usual retinue of kept cranks: the defrocked priest who proposed to reform religion along with the Bible; the failed horticulturist who intended to introduce a Central Asian grass called "Hun's heart" into Hungary, claiming it had been the fodder for the horses of the ancient Magyars on their way to their present land. Similarly neglected was the historian Gáspár A. Zarándy, who had been commissioned to research the genealogy of the Szemere family in case the day came again for electing a king on the Plain of Rákos. Neither was there time for the pirate-bearded sailor who instructed him in the East-Indian art of juggling balls in the dark with closed eyes. Provincial politicians visited in vain, offering their districts to the wealthy and generous Miklós Szemere to represent in Parlia-ment—no, not even the district of Tata did he desire, where his dear friend Miki Esterházy could have anyone he wanted elected. Only the old poet Gyula Erdélyi, known in the household as Sylvester, received an audience, for he had been assigned the task of finding ancient Hungarian names for horses.

"Sylvester, I want you to come up with new Hungarian names for blunder-busses, rifles, and pistols," commanded Mr. Szemere, looking up from his favorite bedside seat.

"How about Hentaller pistols?" replied Sylvester, by way of a humorous al-lusion to the pistols featured in politicians' duels of the day, loaded with breadcrumbs so that no one would come to harm.

Mr. Szemere did not find the joke funny and sent his faithful secretary packing.

*

The lord of Szentlőrinc made sure that his target-shooting competitions were held amidst much hoopla.

Even if we were not familiar with his pamphlets, such as the notable "Fair Play", or with his speech at the National Casino in memory of Széchenyi, which he concluded with the pithy "The Hungarian is not happy"—a phrase that became a catchphrase—we should recognize that he had aimed to be a reforming figure of his age, just as Széchenyi and Wesselényi were in theirs. Alas, he lived in a much less respectful era, and Mr. Szemere, although always the idealist, was often mocked for his efforts. How often had he been carica-tured as the Stüssy Hunter (or Jack of Spades) and reproached for his win-nings at cards and at the races. Even when he was led by the most idealistic of motives there would always be someone who dismissed this eccentric, but deeply Hungarian man.

"Wait and see: he'll end up wanting to establish gambling casinos in Turkey," the sourpusses would say, for at one time this colorful gentleman had indeed entertained such designs.

It was around the time of this target-shooting movement that the noted newspaper editor Kornél Abrányi Jr. received an amnesty for the rest of his prison term by authoring a book about the king. Budapest rumor instantly had it that Mr. Szemere had made his sacrifices on behalf of the betterment of Hungarian youth so that Francis Joseph would pardon his Viennese gambling. According to malicious tongues Szemere had bought up the promissory notes signed by the heavily indebted Katherine Schratt, the much-talked-about Viennese actress who was Francis Joseph's lady-friend and entertainer, only to return them, with his compliments, to the lady. Yes, his tobacco-complexioned physiognomy was always eyed suspiciously—people wondered what this solitary, silent man could be thinking about; and behind his back he was called "Mr. Traktárovich", for in his lifetime he had treated at his table more people than perhaps anyone else in Hungary. Those who did not know him could well imagine that the most important persons in his life were Winkler, the chef at the Pannónia, and Palkovics, the restaurateur at the National Casino; they were unaware of all the patriotic, national ideals this gentleman took to the grave with him.

*

We must hand it to him, he really knew how to throw a party!

There were about a thousand guests at Pestszentlőrinc when he held the first target-shooting competition for university students. Three different kitchens had been set up: the first one was Turkish, in which a cook from Asia Minor was preparing a mutton pilaf, the most famous national dish of the Turks. Mr. Szemere nurtured a deep affection for the Turkish people, ever since he had visited the country on the occasion of presenting, in the name of Hungarian youth, an ornamental sword to Abdul Kerim, "The Lion". A second kitchen was assigned to a Parisian chef imported from Durand's, who concocted various specialties of French cuisine. The stuffed capons served at the Pestszentlőrinc shooting competition were of a size never before seen. Oysters, trout, patés from Holland, washed down by the wines of French vineyards,

53

dispensed from those oversized champagne bottles that have not been seen in Hungary since Pomméry and Greno ceased to be our foremost suppliers. A third kitchen was staffed by the most famous cook from Zemplén county, who watched over her huge kettle of *gulyás* when not squabbling with Mrs. Báló, the connoisseur of fish soup from the River Tisza. Here only Hungarian wines were served, but these were Tokaj vintages from Francis Joseph's vineyards at Mád and Tarcal... And, as legend has it, when His Majesty King Francis Joseph heard that it was his own wines that the exiled Miklós Szemere had served to the guests at Szentlőrinc he relented toward the gambler and soon afterward pardoned him, so that Mr. Szemere, together with his secretary and all the odd specimens retained in the strange court he kept, could once again take up residence in his former quarters at his Viennese inn.

(4 July, 1926)

The Authentic Account of a Legendary Card Battle

1. Miklós Szemere Is Banned from Vienna

Miklós Szemere, who once upon a time was said to be the greatest card player in Hungary, was often seen at Vienna's most exclusive clubs, including the Jockey Club and the Wiener Club, places frequented, in those days of the veritable gold standard, by the "upper ten thousand" among the citizens of the Monarchy.

It was common knowledge that the police, and any other type of authority, had little say about what went on behind the closed doors of these exclusive clubs—all the more so since princes of the House of Habsburg, upon attaining their majority, usually became members of, among others, the Jockey Club, where some of them were habitués. Visitors to the Wiener Club included people such as old Anton Dreher, Francis Joseph's hunting companion, the Rothschilds of Vienna, and Baron Springer, all of whom, by virtue of their name and standing, were unassailable pillars of the social order of the Dual Monarchy.

The constabulary could merely offer a salute when such visitors emerged from their carriages in front of their clubs; no official personage would think of broaching the entrance of these clubs that enjoyed an immunity somewhat like diplomatic extraterritoriality.

Perhaps only once in the Club's history did it occur that the police became involved in the internal affairs of these privileged premises. True, on this occasion the Chief of Police was acting upon the personal command of the Emperor; nonetheless, the intervention had all the exclusive clubs of Europe seething with resentment. Protests were registered by the London clubs and the eminent casinos in France, the National Casino in Budapest and the Club of the Nobility in Rome after the Viennese Chief of Police ordered Miklós Szemere, Royal and Imperial Chamberlain, to leave Austria as a result of a game of cards at the Jockey Club. An unheard-of action!

"Undesirable aliens" who are to be denied entrance to the country have always been listed in the black blotters of the police. Ladies and gentlemen were equally represented on the list. Among the Hungarians already excluded from Austrian soil Lajos Gály, the internationally noted gambler, was the foremost; Lajos Horváth Szentgyörgyi, the amiable gentleman known as "Baron Louis" in Budapest, had also been obliged to stay away from Vienna. Gyurka Berzeviczy, still active at the time of writing, although not excluded was kept under police observation on account of his gambling.

"They were obviously out to get the Hungarians", was the Budapest version.

But the case of Miklós Szemere was unprecedented.

From the gaming room of the Jockey Club, one might say from the side of the most unimpeachable gaming table on the Continent, from the company of the Minister of the Imperial House and Foreign Minister of the Monarchy, Agenor Goluchowski, who was kibitzing at the card game, as were princes of the realm, knights of the Golden Fleece—from this most exclusive atmosphere of the Jockey Club Szemere was summoned to appear in front of the Viennese police, to be told that he was considered an "undesirable alien" and must depart from the city, indeed from the beautiful land of Austria whose spas the Hungarian gentleman had so often favored with his visits.

It was no use asking the Viennese police why exactly a member of the most prominent circles, such as the Wiener Club, had become an "undesirable alien" from one day to the next. The police were not obligated to account for their action. The best lawyers were helpless when the police, at their own discretion, classified someone as "undesirable".

So Miklós Szemere did not ask too many questions.

He packed a few of his things in his hotel suite, the keys of which he handed over to the concierge saying he would be away for a short while. Then he took the next train to Budapest.

The unexpected humiliation had undeniably upset this man who was known for his nerves of steel and his remarkable self-control.

A few days later the Viennese police did not refrain from releasing to the press the hitherto secret details of the order to expel Szemere. Until then only three persons had been cognizant of the affair: Emperor Francis Joseph, the Viennese Chief of Police, and Miklós Szemere himself.

As soon as the "thousand-eyed" press got hold of the information, one of the greatest scandals of peacetime Europe was blown open.

Why exactly had Szemere been expelled?

2. Potocki on the Horizon and in the Horoscope

In those days a young Polish count was sojourning in Vienna, whose elder brother, the governor of Galicia, provided an allowance that permitted a rather lavish lifestyle. His name was Count Potocki, and he had arrived in Vienna equipped with a letter of recommendation to Foreign Minister Goluchowski, a distant kinsman. Goluchowski, who had received the title of "Minister of the Imperial House" on the occasion of the 1896 Hungarian Millennial Festivities, was indeed a most powerful protector. The young count, who hailed from a Polish manor house in the "land of bison", was soon admitted to the Jockey Club and other exclusive circles on the strength of his patron's support—even though his personal bent was for the informal little garden taverns that proliferated in gay Vienna in those days. Young men were always more attracted to gardens where the current year's wine was served than to the easy chairs of a club. But Potocki felt obliged to spend time with his patron Goluchowski.

The Minister of the Imperial House usually spent his evenings at the Jockey Club. He would stroll over directly from his office; he had himself driven there after soirées at court or from his box at the Opera, just as any other high-ranking aristocrat in Vienna.

For the Jockey Club in those days provided a home away from home for the illustrious gentlemen who spent a significant portion of their time there. They dined at the Club, for one could always count on its kitchen. At times some of the more memorable menus of the Jockey Club were transported in court carriages to princely residences, and old, liveried lackeys delivered the daily menu to their mistresses on days when they did not feel like home cooking. Naturally not just anyone was qualified to take out from the Club's cuisine. One needed serious patronage, as in the case of the famous actress Katherine Schratt who had her meals brought in from the Jockey Club in the days when she resided in its neighborhood.

The Club's wine cellars were equally famed.

Word had it that even the Viennese Rothschilds, the archbishop, and traveling heads of state would visit and marvel with envy at this wine cellar stocked with the utmost expertise, where every notable vintage, champagne, and spirits could be found, so that not even the Wiener Club, endowed with such a wealth of ready cash, could compete in this regard, although there had been keen rivalry between the respective chefs and sommeliers of the two establishments. They vied to outbid each other each time a lot of Francis Joseph's Tokaj vintages came up for sale. The industrial magnates of the Wiener Club thirsted for the king's wines as ardently as the counts and princes of the Jockey Club.

Even though young Potocki preferred the wines served at Grinzing taverns he did not disdain the royal vintage on his visits to the Jockey Club—and drank, according to the custom of his native land, from a wineglass that could not be replaced on the table as long as it still contained some wine. As he was naturally something of a connoisseur in the matter of Polish brandies, he took the liberty of criticizing the Club's *sommelier* in this respect. Mr. Potocki always claimed he knew of a finer Zubrowka than that which he was served at the Club.

Miklós Szemere had a rule (which he obeyed to the end of his days) that he always drank his own wine. This meant that in the evening, when, dressed for dinner, he was leaving his apartment, he would always pick a bottle from a corner of his room where he kept his select vintages. At times the bottle would contain champagne, at other times some outstanding domestic vintage. Word had it that this wary gentleman did this as a measure of precaution, for he had seen much in the course of his travels.

At mealtime the bottle would always be opened in front of his eyes.

He never drank more than this one bottle, not even during the oftentimes prolonged drinking bouts at the Club, or in the midst of the excitement of the racetrack. When he was thirsty he would reach for an orange. No matter which famous Gypsy violinist played by his table or which prima donna sang for his ears alone, the party could rage on, but Miklós Szemere stuck to his rule. This was the amount of alcohol that his not altogether sound heart could sustain.

He showed similar restraint with the cigars that he stuffed in his case each evening.

"Only an inexperienced man consumes unknown narcotics," he would gently chide as he smoked, using a long cigar-holder, and took quiet, deliberate sips of his wine while browsing through the foreign and domestic papers as midnight approached.

At midnight he would rise from his table and with slow, measured steps that betrayed no eagerness whatsoever, he would approach the gaming room of the Club where the card game would already have been in progress for some hours, its course observed by gentlemen whose bored expressions hid a certain inner excitement.

3. At the Stroke of Midnight, the Game Began

Opinions vary as to whether Miklós Szemere, known as the most outstanding card player of his day, was a superstitious man.

According to some, being a wise and cool-headed man he scorned all supernatural phenomena, including any superstition.

Others recall that his wisdom dictated the acceptance of certain phenomena that were beyond human understanding.

He did not indulge in such alleged superstitions as rushing home from the casino to put on a pair of ragged old socks that had once served him well in a lucky game of cards; neither would he cross himself, being a steadfast Calvinist; he did not carry good-luck charms in his pockets, nor did he mutter magic spells as was the wont of some players—but he did have certain rituals before sitting down at the gaming table.

He was fond of having his compatriot Andor Péchy present in the room, even though Andor Péchy liked to go to bed early.

Another kibitzer he liked was Baron Zsigmond Ütricht, known for his quick wit.

In general he preferred the presence of those men who were not gamblers but happened to be in the card room by accident and who remained there as interested parties but refrained from play.

One of his longtime favorites was Count Agenor Goluchowski, who had witnessed several of his post-midnight card battles and always expressed his appreciation in a few well-chosen words regardless of whether he won or lost. The Foreign Minister of the Dual Monarchy would never take part in a card game, but he did follow a "well-played hand" with the utmost enthusiasm.

"Card playing requires expertise," the minister would acknowledge, with a touch of grudging admiration. At a dramatic turn of events he would become as heated with excitement and anticipation as if he were a player himself. He especially favored the cool-headed style of Miklós Szemere, whom he considered to be the exemplary card player.

Miklós Szemere never risked more than ten thousand forints in the course of an evening's gaming.

Often enough, upon losing the prescribed amount, he would shrug his shoulders and leave the table with, if anything, even greater composure than the superhuman tranquillity with which he had sat down. Perhaps he acted out his ill-humor only on the objects—such as the small Buddha-figurines—that surrounded him in his apartment. Not infrequently he would toss out some diminutive Asian carving, emblem, or pagan idol purchased recently at the antique dealer's in order to be caressed by his muscular grip so that his stubby-fingered, broad hand would receive the right cards at the right moment. If the figurine proved unhelpful it ended up in the wastebasket. During his last years these Asiatic deities were to be replaced by a pair of diamond cufflinks set in black stone. They brought him a pain-less death at the Viennese racetrack where his often-tested heart was to stop beating.

But at the time of our story he still had relatively few problems with his heart, and his actions were still performed with a hopeful air as if the various "astrologers" who paid him regular visits had predicted eternal life for him. These "astrologers" were mostly long-bearded men who dealt in antiques and brought Szemere news of approaching mishaps or good fortune. At times he would even give credence to cartomancers if their predictions chimed with his turn of mind.

One long-bearded "astrologer" actually named Count Potocki as a man who would cross Szemere's path some day. (A true story!) Apprised of this horo-scope our gentleman, being of a cautious turn of mind, began to pay atten-tion to Potocki's activities. He even went to the trouble of having clandestine information gathered about the young Polish nobleman's background and financial circumstances.

Only in those days of leisure could a gentleman afford "superstitions" of this sort. Just as the clubs examined the antecedents of new applicants, indi-viduals belonging to the upper crust gave each other the once-over before considering closer association.

Miklós Szemere must have received reassuring word about Potocki before he accepted the young count's challenge to a game of cards in the gaming room of the Jockey Club in the presence of several distinguished members, among them Agenor Goluchowski.

4. One and a Half Million Forints Staked on a Single Hand

"May I suggest twelve rounds of *écarté*," was young Count Potocki's proposal to Miklós Szemere, repeated several times.

The Polish youth had by then become too much of a favorite at the Club—in part because of his amiable and obliging behavior and in part because of the distinguished patronage of the Minister of the Imperial House—for the solemn Szemere to consider refusing this invitation.

It was past midnight...and the Polish count may have been in a more than usually elevated mood, having spent the earlier part of his evening in the company of musicians and songstresses in some outlying tavern, but this meant nothing whatsoever since members of the Club were adults deemed fully responsible for their actions.

Szemere reached after the cards with his usual bored expression, as if the game held no interest for him. At times cards came to him like trained dogs, at other times he would turn his back on them, as on an abandoned lover; on this evening he did not scorn the figures on the French cards that kept coming his way in increasingly favorable combinations.

It was as if these cards were imploring his forgiveness for the losses he had sustained recently at the Wiener Club, where Mr. Szemere had been dealing Baron Springer such cards that his opponent laughed in delight, as befitted a well-nourished, cheerful manufacturer of silks. As they would say at the track (both gentlemen owned significant stables), on this evening the red and black was triumphing over the silver and gold. Some had observed a certain glumness in Mr. Szemere's demeanor when, with a tired gesture, he left off playing—as if he had not felt strong enough to overcome the jovial silk baron whose figure resembled a beer barrel.

(Baron Springer, as was his wont, divided his winnings between his daughter Mitzi and various charities; he did not care to keep money won at the card table.)

But tonight the situation was quite different. The cards came with such regularity it was as if they could read Mr. Szemere's mind and were obeying some magic incantation; they arrived with the regularity of figures on a carousel, and they always favored Mr. Szemere.

The young Polish nobleman committed the blunder of doubling the stakes against an opponent riding a winning streak, who accepted the offer without batting an eyelash, as they say. Mr. Szemere merely nodded in agreement, for it was not his habit to retire after winning a hand. He accepted the successive manifestations of good fortune with a solemn, almost reverential air, as befitted one who was capable of appreciating the gift of good luck in worldly affairs.

The last hand would decide whether a debt of one and a half million forints would fall on the Polish youth or on Mr. Szemere.

Mr. Szemere won, and the rest is history.

"I have never in my life been as certain of anything as that hand," said Miklós Szemere when, years later, he discussed this event with the writer of these lines.

His only worry had been losing the good will of Goluchowski, who was present to the bitter end at his kinsman's notorious card battle, which in fact signaled his arrival into the *haut monde*.

The ongoing changes in Hungarian political life at the time brought about a general quarrel with Vienna, the monarch, Count Agenor, and all of Austria, and the opposition coalition triumphed in Hungary. Mr. Szemere was gladly elected representative from Köbölkút, having "pulled off his stunt" in Vienna...

About a year later, the expulsion order having been rescinded, he was no longer an "undesirable alien" in Vienna but a welcome visitor once again.

(17 July, 1932)

One Hundred Years of Horse Racing in Budapest

Could this be true—that horse racing has been around for a hundred years in Hungarian life? It seems as if it all began only yesterday, for the old-time turf heroes, such as Ernő Blaskovics, Iván Szapáry, Miklós Esterházy, and Zsiga Üchtritz are still so close, within living memory. Why, it wouldn't surprise anyone in town to see one of these gentlemen on a spring day riding in a carriage on Kerepesi Road on the way from the races. Nor would it astound us if one morning, as we rubbed the dust of dreams away from our eyes, we were to read on the sports pages once again the names of Kisbér, Kincsem, Tokio, and Rascal—for wasn't it only yesterday that we saw them running victorious races on the turf of the Municipal Park! Nor would it be surprising if, visiting the old-time sporting coffeehouses such as the former Korona with its snuff-colored arcades on Váci Street, or Kincsem Coffeehouse on Kerepesi Road (where the atmosphere was less exclusive, but one would receive the hottest tips), we were to observe, at one of the corner tables, gallants dressed in old-fashioned frock-coats and nankeen trousers arguing over the breeding methods of Bruce Lowe or Robertson. (This is somewhat like the dream of the traveling salesman who voyages on a decommissioned stage coach in the old Dickens' novel.)

So let us take a look now: could it really be a hundred years since horses have been raced along the lines of the English-style system in Hungary?

*

István Széchenyi is generally said to be the founder of Hungarian horse racing, just as he is responsible for the existence of our Chain Bridge. The paintings by Béla Pálik depict Széchenyi in gray pants and black tailcoat, riding his English-type saddle horse on the bank of the Danube, and in the background, behind the count's melancholy visage with the full beard, twirled mustache, and curly hair, we may glimpse the shoreline palazzos of Pest, already as tall as they were by the time Széchenyi was installed for life at the Döbling asylum. (His faithful friend, Miklós Wesselényi, shared the same fate, except that he ended up at the Gräfenberg sanitarium, an institution even bleaker than Döbling.)

It was in the spring of 1827 that the first race meeting was held on Rákos Field near Pest, until then famous only for the National Assemblies held there. Although there is a record of Count József Hunyady holding horse races at Ürmény in the English style as early as 1822, horse racing received its spectacular, truly popular introduction here at Rákos on the day when Count Széchenyi rode out onto the field on his long-maned and long-tailed bay mount, surrounded by a bevy of aristocrats. Archdukes who made the trip from Vienna (where they had not yet seen the like of this, although there was no shortage of horses there) arrived on horseback and in carriages, while some elderly ladies witnessed the scene from sedan-chairs. All the Hunyadys, Esterházys, Károlyis, and Batthyányis were there. Behind them, as if going to the fair, came the people of Pest in throngs; there were hired coaches carrying young fops in tight pants escorting demoiselles wearing bell-shaped skirts and flowery hats. Every carter from neighboring Gödöllő, Kartal, and Aszód, who lay in wait near the Kerepes tollgate, found employment that day. The fixings for barbecues, grills, and wine barrels were trundled out on pushcarts, and the citizens of Buda crossed over to Pest on a pontoon bridge to witness the newest bravura by Széchenyi, the exotic captain of the cavalry, who only a few days earlier had almost drowned in the Danube when his steed shied under him.

*

Although it is nice to hear these century-old accounts, we feel closer to the history of Budapest horse racing as we recall memories of our youth, the names of noble equines and chevaliers that were the talk of the town, when we could glimpse the bearers of these names galloping on the turf in the Municipal Park—while the assembled lovely ladies waved their kerchiefs—or riding in fine equipages on Sugár Avenue, where the loving eyes of public attention followed the owners of popular racehorses.

Oh, back in the sparkling youth of this city many were the dreams evoked by the word "racehorse"!

A racehorse was more than an ordinary quadruped; it was some miraculous apparition with hooves that equaled the horn of plenty scattering glory, fame, and riches not only on its owner but on anyone in contact with it. Darley Arabian, Byerly Turk, Godolphin Arabian, Belgrade Turk, Alcock Arabian: the ancestors of English thoroughbreds whose names evoke the scent of hay at English racecourses, the brisk autumn air of the St. Legers, Doncaster, Oaks, and Epsom Derbies. And the ancestors of Hungarian racehorses: Cambuscan, Büszke, Kisbér, Talpra Magyar, Stronzian, and the Buccaneer-descendants, whose family trees were as familiar in the Budapest of old as were those of their aristocratic owners. (At times even more so!) And those racehorses whose lives and races brought not only glory but wealth to their owners, wealth that was spread around. Kincsem, whose winnings enabled Ernő Blaskovics to build his Kincsem Palace on Reáltanoda Street; while on a more humble scale, a poor waiter could afford to become the owner of a coffeehouse thanks to his winnings on the unbeatable Kincsem. Patience, a Festetich mare, likewise brought a small fortune to those who placed their trust in the endurance of mares, while at the same time she ruined several bookmakers. After Patience's victories old tenements in the Inner City changed owners, since some entrepreneurial landlords had gone halves with the bookmakers. There was Tokio, sold on his deathbed by the Viennese restaurateur Frohner to Andor Péchy and Richard Wahrmann, who, together with Baron Üchtritz, founded the Comp Matchless—and the young lawyer who risked a silver forint on Tokio and won a sum sufficing to open a law office. Ignác, who attained notoriety by beating Tokio when Frank Sharpe, who was riding Tokio, placed a five thousand forint bet on Ignác—a sum that seems enormous in our day. Rascal, hero of the Király Stakes, purchased as a colt at auction by Count Imre Dégenfeld, the most hard-luck player in Hungary, who proceeded to sell him to Count László Teleki—before his phenomenal victories. Rascal, by winning three Király Stakes, had his name enshrined forever in the annals of Hungarian turf; but he is also fondly remembered by the many players who were thought reckless at the time when they placed such large bets on him—they were able to live off their winnings for years. For racehorses are truly beautiful only when they have enabled you to win on them, ever since the globe-trotting Englishmen Walpoole and Miller taught Budapest how to bet on horses.

*

Small wonder that in years past, when Budapest still had faith in the city's own youthful good fortune and fruitful enterprising spirit, far greater risks were taken at the races than nowadays. Everyone in Budapest dreamt of

65

winning, as if the Viennese money-men Lackenbacher, Horner, and Donrin were standing around at the racecourses with their moneybags hanging from their necks for the sole purpose of turning these dreams into cash. Naturally on racing days the traffic at coffeehouses grew in volume. One could not expect the poorer folk to forego this amusement even if it cost them their bedroom furnishings—for this was the day when the famous racehorse they had dreamt of was running! But not everyone had to take their possessions to the pawnshop, for just about every street and every building had its own money-lenders who now became the most sought-out people in Budapest. Uncle Schreiber conducted his business up in the galleries of the old New York coffeehouse, and he was not the least bit choosy in the matter of his clients. But even the redcap who had gotten to know his clients by hanging around some Inner City or Kerepesi Road coffeehouse for decades turned into a money-lender on the day of the races. The red-headed Mr. L. was another money-lender; he could be found in the vicinity of the National Casino or at the kiosk on Erzsébet Square. But he preferred to lend money mostly to young magnates. Many of today's peers of the realm still recall this man's promissory notes. As for the various cooperatives and lesser banks, wasn't their raison d'être the providing of money for the people of Budapest at the spring and autumn horse races? Desk clerks at hotels would keep their safes stocked with cash so that provincial guests or gentlemen from abroad should not be compelled to stay away from the races while waiting for their money to be wired from home. And let us not forget the ever present, ever accommodating headwaiters, who, on the day of the races, after lunch in the winter garden of the Pannónia, would happily empty their wallets to lend some country gentleman the wherewithal for wagers. One might say that in horse-racing season all of Budapest was decked out to play and have fun. Yes, this was once a naive and optimistic city, where it was inconceivable that horses could disappoint the believers.

*

Ah, to have been the owner of racing stables in old Budapest! It meant being a knight of dreams, shining in the dreams of the poor, giving them confidence in their impending good fortune.

According to popular belief the stable owner always wins. If not on his own horse, then on someone else's. Horses need oats; trainers and jockeys need champagne (at the old racetrack, where a glass of champagne cost a silver

66

forint, the winners used to drink champagne); mistresses need new gowns, a box at the Orfeum, a diamond-studded corsage... The Budapest of old envisioned the owner of a racing stables as someone always consuming oysters, caviar, and paté, while accepting wads of money from humbly kowtowing bookmakers... A man enjoying a fraternal relationship with his horse which won at his command; beautiful young women always staring at his fiacre on the street; at the theater the loveliest actresses making eyes at him; at the Orfeum the band playing for his ears alone...for he was lord and master in this town where fame surrounded him and winnings filled his pockets. Well, let us see now, what were those legendary owners of racing stables actually like?

Take for instance Elemér Batthyányi, whose beard, at first black and bifurcated, then gray and full, and finally patriarchal, white, and long, was familiar to everyone in Pest. Yes, the count lived in a beautiful era. Of him the historian notes that Pest was a naive village girl until she made her début at the grand ball of the *haut monde*, escorted on his arm. He avoided politics because of his father's martyrdom after the Revolution in 1849, but horse racing fascinated him all the more, and, in the company of Count Miklós Esterházy he spent more time studying it in England than even István Széchenyi had done. From there he imported his horse Red Hot, the sire of his famous racehorses Gaga, Ganache, and Mindig, and established the Galopin line that runs like a vein of gold throughout Hungarian horse breeding. Well, Elemér Batthyányi gave rise to no colorful legends in the imagination of Budapest citizenry, for our count lived like a hermit in his apartment on Borz Street, from where he left punctually at the same time each day, heading, of course, for the National Casino, and where he returned at the customary hour, again from the National Casino. The noble count was cut from the same cloth as the English club man who leaves his favorite easy chair only for the sake of horses or a beautiful woman. I do not recall a single horse race in Budapest over the past fifty years without his presence, yet his unmistakable figure could often be seen at the Freudenau Derby meetings in Vienna as well as at the lesser racetracks in Hungary—Alag, Megyer, Tata, Tátralomnic, and Siófok—for horse racing had such a following in our country that even our smaller towns held annual races. It would seem that Széchenyi's thunderous voice had had its desired effect when he stated in his tract *On Horses* that Hungarians, for a nation "born on horseback", knew next to nothing about horses. Elemér Batthyányi's lifestyle remains an eternal paragon for Hungarian sportsmen. He never bet on his horses, yet he was all the prouder of them. The popular Budapest myth of his day depicted Batthyányi as some kind of paternal divinity at the racetrack, whose benevolence might enable a common porter to take home after the races an entire roast goose for his family. Those with empty pockets after the last race would also have frequent recourse to Batthyányi's name on their lugubrious march home down Csömöri Road. Only the ladies referred to Batthyányi with unvarying adoration, for it was common knowledge that he admired the fair sex to such an extent that he would order a special train to transport to the Budapest races some beauteous creature from the countryside or even from as far as Vienna.

Among the Batthyányi-era stable owners we must not omit Baron Zsigmond Üchtritz, whose gray beard and wind-swept gray head of hair, always uncovered, were also well known in Budapest. He was said to be the professor of the turf, the greatest connoisseur of horses. This former Veszprém county magistrate was also known for never wagering—he was content with the prizes won in abundance by his horses when he owned a racing stable together with Andor Péchy. He had won Derbies and St. Legers, but his disposition was invariably confident, one might say wise and sunny, regardless of whether or not he brought back the Blue Ribbon from the turf. At the National Casino, at the stroke of midnight, he would take his umbrella, having studied all the foreign papers, magazines, and sports journals, and stroll home to his bachelor quarters on Magyar Street. Thus he did not live on the grand scale that Budapest fantasy assigned to stable owners.

Another member of the "Batthyányi generation" was the "Excellency of Öreglak", according to some the eccentric of the turf. He was Gyula Jankovich-Bésán, the landowner of Öreglak, who also had a reputation for racing his horses as a pure hobby, having no use even for race prizes. During the first year of the war, when horse racing had been suspended, he organized a private race for himself at Alag over the distance of the Austria Prize, having raised a colt especially for that distance. And in fact his colt, named Öreglak, easily left older opponents behind in the home stretch, to His Excellency's immense delight. Gyula Jankovich was also famous for the fabulous presents he bestowed in his old age on a lady of Magyar Street, well known in aristocratic circles for her wit, who read the papers for His Excellency in the afternoons. Only during her readings could he take a truly peaceful nap. He did not like to travel by train and preferred to ride everywhere with his horse and carriage. He was a Hungarian landowner of the old school who loved horses for their own sake. However when deer season began he dropped horse racing and went hunting, for he still had some wall space on the corridors of the Öreglak castle not covered by trophies. Of course, he did not allow his horses to be raced when he was away; he wanted to be there every time they ran. Yes, His Excellency of Öreglak was a figure out of some novel, whom we may contemplate at our leisure while waiting for nightfall to obliterate everything. But at the risk of disappointing the Budapest sports world I must set down that he, too, insisted on moderation in food, drink, and other enjoyments.

And what about that falcon-eyed gentleman with the ancient Magyar face, turning up the lapels of his heavy overcoat even in the summer heat as he speeds, seated in a closed fiacre, from the Hotel Pannónia to the old racecourse, where his bright, observant, solemn, and mysterious glances send shivers through the players who would bet against his colors, the gold and silver? This is Miklós Szemere, who, as a result of his daring bets, did indeed become a legendary figure. One of the most punctilious gentlemen ever to tread on Hungarian soil, when it came to gambling he was as fearless as his conquering ancestors who rushed from the Carpathians with sword in hand to carve out a new homeland for themselves. No one loved sport as much as this man, who appreciated a fine filly more than he did the most beauteous lady in the world and for that reason remained a bachelor for life, as did most men for whom love of horseflesh replaced the love of women. (Horses distract more men away from women than the hunt or carousing, both of which may turn boring in a certain sense, whereas you can never get tired of horses as long as new colts appear each year to please the eye with their playful gallop.) This is how a biographer described Miklós Szemere: "The turf was his salon where he would chat with lady acquaintances, instead of at his chambers at the inn, filled as they were with bachelor curios and his eccentric entourage. He always saved a few refined compliments for elder countesses, paid homage to young beauties, found topics of conversation with gentlemen left over from the *ancien régime*, had some fresh tidbit from abroad for the politicians, a hot tip for demimondaines and actresses, for the bookies ten thousand crowns to lose, as well as a dragon-necked racehorse from his stables, for whose victory old, impoverished countesses recited prayers at the Franciscan Church; he wore a thick overcoat and carried a wide umbrella against the rain." The biographer (not unrelated to the writer of these lines)

69

never mentioned Miklós Szemere's wagers, which he put together as deliberately as an architect designing a tower. When he had a horse he trusted he would bet on it fanatically, with blind faith. Often he would begin placing bets months ahead of the race with bookmakers abroad, in Vienna, Hamburg, and England, where he was well known. There were times when he bet such fortunes that his finances would have been severely shaken had his horses not won. He wagered almost his entire fortune on Eltolins when it ran in the St. Stephen Stakes. The horse won by a nose. He was one of those legendary stable owners who not only kept winning but also had the knack of hanging on to their winnings. He was never satisfied with a little, he always went for broke. And his luck never abandoned him, for he knew horses like no one else. Sports papers of the day were already publishing the detailed results of the racing year and the so-called turf calendars contained the history of each racehorse, but Miklós Szemere trusted no one, only his own eyes, and so, each evening, after his return from the track, he would open his notebook and by the light of two candles enter his observations about his own horses and others he had seen that day. These notes might enable Miklós Szemere, on some later occasion, to wager unheard-of sums on some racehorse that had previously captured his eye. One of his eccentricities was retaining a Polish painter, who depicted in oils each one of his horses, and he had a scribe, old Erdélyi, whose sole task was to invent horse names that had an ancient Hungarian sound. Even apart from all his cleverness and wealth, Mr. Szemere has certainly earned a place in the book to be written about Hungarian eccentrics. But he, too, lived a wholesome life and sidestepped carousals; for lunch always had a small piece of boiled beef with tomato sauce; kept his exercise apparatus in his room; and sipped his champagne slowly so that no one ever saw him tipsy. He refused to add an extra course to his dinner even when he won hundreds of thousands at the races.

And that tall, bony gentleman wearing the old-fashioned top hat, who (without the hat) most nearly resembles a Tyrolean chamois-hunter, arriving at the Western Terminal in Budapest at the start of the racing season to be transported to the Hotel Hungária on its antique coach—who else could it be but Anton Dreher, the "Beer King"? Since those days popular parlance has invented many other kings—Hat Kings, Sock Kings, and Sausage Kings—for in a spirit of democracy the citizen likes to make fun of his own kind. But Anton Dreher was indeed foremost in his own field, the brewing of beer, and his generosity and sportsmanship earned him a sterling reputation among the owners of racing stables. No man had ever seen lanky old Dreher step up to a betting window to place a bet on a horse. But he would leave even the Schwechat hunt, where his guests often included princes of the blood, whenever the May racing season opened in Budapest. Wearing his accordion pants and a short gray overcoat, and sporting a slender walking stick, he watched enthusiastically as his horses ran and spared no amount of money for a good mare or a stallion. His horse Tovább claimed the Blue Ribbon at the Derby. No one could ever say of old Dreher, the nabob of Schwechat, that he lived off his winnings. His lifestyle was the very model of frugality. Since he also bred carriage horses he always rode in his own carriage instead of taking the train to Vienna; in the summertime he rode his straw-hatted four-in-hand to the Kottingbrunn races. We can relate no legends about the elder Dreher, save for the fact that he was the embodiment of generous sportsmanship, as is his son, Eugene Dreher, who took over the famous stables after his father's death.

The hero of present-day sports legends, by virtue of his recently won Király Prize and Hungarian Derby, is Count Antal Sigray, also a sportsman, whose horse Naplopó's winning the top prizes was no mere stroke of luck. This elegant former volunteer Hussar is accomplished in every sport. He has ridden in dressage competitions, ridden to the hounds, and fenced, and is said to be our greatest polo player. As many as twenty-five years ago he already had racehorses worth watching, when Giddy Girl from his young stable placed second at the St. Stephen Stakes. His horse Harsona lost the Derby by a neck; but now, after so many years, those former disappointments have been canceled by the wonderful Naplopó, whose Derby victory is the result of many years' hard work, sacrifice, and sportsmanship. The uninitiated, seeing only the final result, exclaim "What luck!" Whereas in horse racing, just as elsewhere in life, blind luck may at times be replaced by persistence, ceaseless energy, and thorough expertise.

*

Volumes could be written about those notable owners of racing stables in the Hungary of old who would now be cited by lovers of horseflesh as paragons in the sport. The names of Esterházy, Wenckheim, Csekonics, Rothschild, Springer, István Károlyi, Péter Baich, Luczenbacher, Andor Péchy, Béla Zichy, Viktor Mautner, Gazsi Geist, Béla Liptay, and Baron Harkányi were as well known in the Budapest of yore as the name of the phenomenal Prince Tasziló Festetich, who always traveled by special train when his horses were racing at Pest or Vienna. Each of these names recalls a world that we shall never see again. We hear the bells of history tolling the name of the most spirited Hungarian sportsman, Count Antal Apponyi, who was married to Princess Montenuovo. When shall we ever again see in Hungary a princess of an imperial house personally checking the stables at Alag each night to make sure that her horses have received enough fodder, the trainer is not soused, the groom is not smoking a pipe near the straw, and then the next morning making an urgent call to a Budapest bookmaker to wager such and such an amount on her horse in that day's race? Fortunately the name of Apponyi still resonates with the same golden tone in the contemporary history of the turf by way of Count Antal's firstborn son who evinces in our day the same love of the sport, of horses, and of the race as the founder of the stable with the black and light-blue colors did in his own day.

*

Much more could be recounted about the fabled riders of the first hundred years of horse racing here, whose names were as familiar to the public as those of celebrated prima donnas; about the exotics of the turf, savants of horse science, eccentrics, and swindlers—for in a hundred years much can transpire even in the best of families. And many tales could be told about those dear old-time folks who watched generations of colts decade after decade, as if drawn by some family tie, whereas it was only that humans, living longer than equines, are able to recall the sires and grandsires of all those horses...

Surely more qualified pens will some day take up the history of our hundred-year-old turf from the point at which this chronicler, moved by all these fine memories, puts down his quill.

(11 July, 1926)

The Rose of Pest

The Granddaughter of the Old Army Physician

During the middle years of the nineteenth century the birth of a fatherless little girl was registered in the village of Pilis (Pest county): her name was given as Rozália Schumayer.

She was a love child.

Her father was probably one of those jaunty officers in the Dragoons who represented the Emperor's power in the county of Pest during the years of oppression after the Revolution of 1848–49. Perhaps he was a count, or even a prince, this paramour who marched off with a carefree heart to his new post, having seduced the daughter of the local physician. A lieutenant, one Count Stadion, son of the Prime Minister of the realm, was the one who had been seen paying court to the physician's daughter. Subsequently this same Lieutenant Stadion would shoot himself in the head at Nyíregyháza, as a result of another affair.

When his daughter ran away in shame the grieving grandfather adopted his granddaughter. Little Róza grew up in the Schumayer house in the village of Pilis, until she reached the age of sixteen.

At which stage another army officer appeared on the scene.

This was an officer in the infantry, and he eloped with Róza. The naive girl left her grandfather's house, placing her faith in the military uniform, showing that she had not learned from her mother's example.

The old grandparents, left alone in their house and garden, were not able to wait until their granddaughter returned. After Róza vanished they moved on to the cemetery.

The Education of the Lady of the Camellias

Shortly after that time a brown-haired, starry-eyed, delicate-featured new girl started working at the flower shop on Szervita Place in the Inner City and showed great skill in pinning *boutonnières* onto the lapels of gallants.

It was an age when every chevalier worth his salt wore a flower in his lapel. Daily customers included Baron Frigyes Podmaniczky, who purchased his white carnation there; Count István Károlyi, who came for his blue cornflower; Miklós Szemere, who always bought a tea rose; and Elemér Batthyányi, whose choice was a camellia. And many others among the lions of the day started showing up, as the fame of the beautiful new flower girl spread far and wide. The black-bearded, slender young Count Albert Apponyi, leader of the National Party, also dropped in one day, and, of all the Inner City flower shops, honored the Szervita Place florist with his daily custom.

Soon the name of Róza Schumayer became well known at the Arany Sas [Golden Eagle], an inn on Újvilág Street frequented by the gentlemen of Pest county for the board, lodging, and gaiety provided by Mrs. Kommern, the proprietress. Across the street from the Arany Sas an admirer who remained unknown for a long time had rented a ground-floor room for the former flower girl and sent the best French and German teachers and university professors in the capital to educate Miss Róza. An English lady companion chaperoned her to make sure there would be no serious consequences of the serenades that were offered under the window of the mysterious miss by gallants under the leadership of Gullner, the Pest county sub-prefect.

There followed travels abroad, like so many honeymoons spent by Róza Schumayer at fashionable spas of the Continent. Her "admirer" even took her to Lourdes, for besides a worldly education he also wanted to make sure of the spiritual advancement of this "Lady of the Camellias", as the blond-bearded poet Zoltán Ambrus titled the celebrated lady.

Within a few years Róza became a lady of the fashionable world thanks to her phenomenal learning skills and talents—a "most genial creature", as gentlemen of the National Casino said, who had occasion to discourse with her.

"The Butterfly has emerged from her chrysalis!" wrote the author of *The Crimson Coach*, having had a chance to become familiar with her life story.

A Small Palace in the Inner City

The *pied-à-terre* on Újvilág Street soon proved too cramped for receiving noble guests; aside from the poet Gyula Reviczky, whose headquarters were at the nearby Ferenczi coffeehouse, there were other, more significant "poets" who wished to pay their respects to the "Rose of Pest", as this rare lady was dubbed by Albert, Prince of Wales, during a visit.

A house came up for sale on Magyar Street, with a balcony overlooking Károlyi Park. The clever Róza purchased this salubriously located building on a shareholder basis. Each of her patrons, who were invited to subscribe for shares, would be assured daily access to the prospective establishment, where their carefree hours would be passed. The furnishing of the house was undertaken by Endre Thék, a cabinetmaker who sported a French-style beard and loved fine furniture and beautiful women.

"Madame Róza" entered her new home escorted by Elemér Batthyányi, who often enough fulfilled the same role in public. Count Elemér had no plans to marry or to undertake public office, either of which circumstances would have made his affiliation with the "Lady of the Camellias" less than desirable. At the horse races he hurried to greet her as she arrived on horseback, with the same eagerness as he did Mme Rothschild from Vienna, or the famous Daisy. The count paid less attention to a lady's rank than to her beauty and accomplishments. To the end of his life he remained Róza Schumayer's most faithful friend.

Madame Róza had now attained her goal. She had her own home, where, dressed in white, she always received her guests humbly at the foot of the stairs, ready with her French wit and champagne. She was both mistress and slave of her castle. Prisoner of love and mistress of royalty—as the old school had it.

Royal Visitors

Time would pass at the house on Magyar Street as pleasantly and languidly as ever at Mme Du Barry's in the time of Louis XV.

Royalty, sojourning in Budapest under various incognitos, could gain entry to her house at the shortest notice, through the kind offices of the "Nachtmeisters" assigned to them.

Esterházy, during his stint as Officer of the Guard, often acted in such a role by the side of visiting rulers: after the Prince of Wales, he introduced the Persian Shah, who was traveling through, and later Milan, former king of Serbia, whose sojourn in Budapest was more prolonged. At such times Madame Róza was surrounded by a bevy of lady friends, who were as lovely as herself... One of them left for Cairo in the company of the khedive of Egypt. During the golden age of the Népszinház its actresses were often featured at Madame Róza's soirées.

Legend has it that the German Emperor, after his reception at Buda Castle, appeared at Mme Róza's for coffee and compliments—although this is difficult to believe about such a martial poet and puritanical man.

But the wings of the imagination would always soar around the figure of this woman who began to play an increasingly prominent role.

Through her friendship with Kállay she participated in the occupation of Bosnia and Herzegovina. Lajos Thallóczy, fresh from the Viennese cabinet office, would exchange the latest gossip at court for the newest inside information from Budapest. It was she who took down in dictation from Miklós Szemere the words of his famous toast to Széchenyi, which ended with the words "The Hungarian is not happy". This was where the greatest orator within recent memory would rehearse his memorable speeches that were delivered during the parliamentary debate about ecclesiastical policy.

The silver crane that held the visiting cards left at Madame's contained the cards of foreign politicians, governors, and high-ranking officers, who would call here just as they would at an embassy. For this was the embassy of feminine wit and cunning, the plenipotentiary embassy of Venus.

To Die for a Writer

However, Róza could not live without her poets and writers. In this she resembled the Wohl sisters or Lilla Bulyovszky, famous for their literary salons during this era. For she was a creature of feelings who would listen to her heart even in the midst of games of diplomacy.

She had to have a poet by her side who would be the love of her life.

Airing out her rooms after the kings and princes, she awaited the visit of the devotees of the Muse. She herself wrote poems, stories, and novels, which needed to be critiqued by authors. (Later she also gathered actors around herself for her amateur theatricals.)

There were times when her sole confidant was some long-haired poet. The red-nosed Gyula Erdélyi (known as "Sylvester") brought her poets from Buda, while Dezső Malonyai, whose acquaintance she made on a trip to Paris, introduced the more modern writers to her salon on Magyar Street. Toward the end it was a man going under the pseudonym of Pasics—part journalist, part rake—who brought poets from neighboring taverns to entertain Mme Róza.

So there was never a shortage of poets in the house. Usually there was one in permanent residence on the ground floor.

One day Malonyai introduced a young poet to her with the remark that the robust figure of Miklós Toldi on the Arany monument was modeled after this man.

This acquaintance almost ended in tragedy. Róza took her poet to heart and wished to die a romantic death on his account. She shot herself, narrowly missing her heart.

Among the actors, Messrs. Újházi and Szirmai departed from this friendly house with somewhat more lighthearted memories.

Life Is Fleeting

The years flew by over the head of the "Rose of Pest", not even literary laurels could slow their passage—laurels that were attained by volumes she published under the name of Róza Pilisy.

Men-about-town and poets carried around her book of poems for a while until they left it behind somewhere, as Mme Róza receded from the forefront. Her last appearance was under the aegis of Francis-Ferdinand, who, among Hungarians, seemed to favor the fading Rose.

During the war her name became quite forgotten, even though back home in Pilis she turned the renovated old house into a military hospital. Like the noble-hearted, patriotic woman that she was, she took on more than her share of the general misfortune, for hers was a lofty character, of a rare benevolence and philanthropy, as all will testify who enjoyed her sympathy: poor people and poets.

"My life has flown! All my friends wait for me on the other side. My only worry is what will become of Count Elemér..." said Róza to me a few years ago.

She left a beautiful novel behind, that of her lifetime. An era of Hungary filled with pathos, and love, and much refinement; a time when next to the male romantic heroes women strove to be romantic heroines in their living, loving, and dying. No one regrets having known her.

(20 July, 1931)

László Mednyánszky, the Vagabond Baron

On an especially snowy day in the winter of 1901 I was traveling in the Carpathian Mountains. In those days even a man of slender means could afford a Christmas holiday like that; the silver forints in one's vest pocket sufficed for travel expenses.

I was traveling by sleigh, taking one of those contraptions equipped with foot-warmers, stuffed with straw and sawdust, that awaited passengers at the train station of Poprádfelka, from where the big mountain-climbing locomotive turned toward Oderberg; at the time there was no railroad leading toward the Szepesség [Zipser region]. Only the skinny telegraph poles indicated the road hidden deep under the snow, as well as the River Poprad which was not completely frozen over even in that cold but sputtered and cut holes and ravines in its imprisoning coat of ice as it followed the traveler like a faithful dog. Here and there a white church steeple would indicate the places we had to reach to find some warmth.

In those days I did not keep a travel diary, so I forget the name of the village we had just passed through and which looked like every other village in the district. It was a sad place, like old Russian villages in Turgenev's novels. It must still be there, somewhere between Késmárk and Szepesbéla; at its center stands an ancient, mansard-roofed, green-shuttered, two-storey mansion with saltpeter-stained walls, guarded by a fence that must have been new during the reign of Queen Maria Theresa. Above the gate, with its figures carved in stone, a sandstone coat of arms, capped with snow, contemplated this aimless world. In the courtyard, instead of carriage tracks there was only a footpath leading through the snow, and the melancholy garden behind the building contained sad cypresses and mournful evergreens that had grown tired of living long ago. I love such neglected old manors, where, in the middle of winter, one still sees the green shutters of summertime since no one has bothered to remove them; they recall the romantic notions and tales such Highland manors used to be filled with in the old days. Upon clambering out of the sleigh I learned that I stood in front of the Mednyánszky mansion. It was inhabited by a squirrel-faced, agile little old man wearing knee breeches, with eyes as blue as pebbles from the riverbeds in that region. His name was Mr. Czóbel, and as it soon turned out he was the brother of the poetess Minka Czóbel who lived in Szabolcs county. When the doors to the arcaded house were opened, a corridor lined with red bricks welcomed me as I stamped my snowy boots, and a housekeeper sort of woman emerged from one of the rooms, pulling on her slippers as she came out. I was used to this type of Highland hospitality, but not to the corridor that led under the arcades towards the stairway. The once white walls of this corridor were covered with all sorts of gigantic frescoes reaching to the ceiling. Scattered over the whitewashed walls were enormous pine trees, larger than life-sized human forms, landscapes that you could practically walk into, making you feel like a child visiting the panorama at the fair. The corridor was painted along its entire length; in places where the stucco had peeled there were mud-colored gaps—the passage of time had carried off the tip of a nose or part of a tree trunk painted on the wall. These scrambled brushstrokes had a particular magic, the way they covered all available space on the walls in a seeming disarray, recalling a manuscript of Dostoyevsky's that I had recently seen—it was like the scrawl of those prophets who sit all day writing for their own amusement in the solitary confinement of some asylum. These paintings were likewise the record of the thoughts of a strange, mysterious, barely comprehensible human soul that wanted to address us by way of the brush.

"These are the youthful studies of my nephew, László Mednyánszky", said the little old gentleman, who had probably grown accustomed to his visitors (no matter how rare) stopping in front of those paintings. "But why don't we go inside where it's warm?"

Ah, these old-time Highland gentlemen knew how to tell stories when they found a genial listener! Compared to their storytelling the flames crackling in the fireplace (which tell the tales of curiosities glimpsed by acacia trees or reclusive pines from the mountainside) seem like childish babbling. According to the old gentleman, whose face in this light resembled the Stüssy Hunter from the cards, this was the castle from where László Mednyánszky had been stolen in his childhood by a band of Gypsies heading for the Polish border. For Gypsies always love children, even when they have plenty of their own. For years the child roamed with the Gypsies, no one knows in what lands, just as it is impossible to know the trail of the wind. But one autumn evening the boy reappeared at the mansion's gate, recognized by the oldest *kuvasz* who tried to calm down the younger watchdogs, for the boy returned wearing the garb of a wandering Gypsy beggar.

"From that time on he was hooked on the life of a vagabond, even after he became a famous painter," the owner of the Mednyánszky mansion said in conclusion to his tale. And I, hurrying on in my travels, for we had to reach a welcoming inn by nightfall, kept thinking all the way about the old lama who taught a little boy about the wandering life, as described by Rudyard Kipling in his novel K*im*.

Indeed, one of our greatest artists did have the reputation of being a vagabond, for accepted opinion makes no distinction between an aimlessly wandering hobo and an apostle following noble ideals. Even in the way he dressed he did not wish to look like the daubers depicted in fashion magazines, sporting a velvet jacket, a Lavallière tie, and a big palette. Truth to tell, his appearance was often so ragged that his art dealer would exclaim (although the old man was not one to panic easily) "How did you manage to avoid being arrested, Baron?"

His Budapest studio (on the same floor as that of the artist Árpád Basch) was located in Vasvári Pál Street, which was full of second-hand stores where Jews bought and sold old overcoats.

"You ought to see the characters that visit him, straight out of some horror story: I think we'll all be robbed or killed one of these days", complained the wife of the painter next door. Indeed, on that staircase on rainy days one could see the muddy footprints of visitors who, for certain reasons, disdained the use of footwear.

In the tavern across the street there would always be someone waiting for Mednyánszky, while paying for the drinks he consumed by claiming that the "Baron" had promised to meet him there. (The man would possess one of those amazing faces peopling Mednyánszky's paintings of vagabonds.) The tavern was called the Bean Soup, and the topers waiting for the maestro had their eyes peeled on the entrance across the street. For it happened that the painter would return home unnoticed (his oldish, casually dressed figure did not attract much notice as he scurried by close to the wall) and the prospective models waiting at the Bean Soup would suddenly realize that a more alert colleague had pre-empted them and was already hurrying away with bouncing strides from the house opposite, a suit of clothes slung over his arm—a suit purchased for the artist by his dealer perhaps only the day before.

At this tavern countless tales were told about the painter, whose work had attained the highest honors; his landscapes were valued as a national treasure, his dealer took in money by the fistful, yet the artist never had a coat with all its buttons in place. Rumor had it at the tavern that the painter was possessed by evil spirits, that he was unable to control his demons. These spirits would drive him out into the depths of forests, into wild mountains thick with autumnal gloom, unpeopled landscapes that he would observe and paint with superhuman power, recording the metamorphoses of nature, especially in those Hungarian autumns, in paintings that appeared not to have been created by the human hand but by some spirit coaxed forth by Mednyánszky from its lair in a hollow tree.

Artists have liked, since the earliest days, to surround themselves with all sorts of mystery, for art is akin to magic. However for Mednyánszky, our national treasure, there was no need to hide in the alchemistic garb of some renaissance painter or fraternize with Hoffmann's sorcerers; he was a phenomenon of mystery in and of himself, about whom legends would flourish in the coffeehouses frequented by artists and in the salons that were resplendent with his paintings—although few knew him personally. He did not even bother to pick up the gold medals awarded him at exhibitions—he would send his dealer's assistant instead.

"His paintings of autumn are like the melancholy, solitary flute played by a forest faun condemned to wifelessness," wrote one of our art critics about the painting "Autumn World"—and he knew more about Mednyánszky's life of suffering than most people. One thing is certain, the artist reached his philosophy of life in a solitary, remote realm of wisdom where only one in a million have the courage to visit. He had about as much interest in the world that bustled about him as a storm-tossed solitary tree, exiled from his companions, not concerned with the daily news, shut off from the chitchat of the forest shrubs. According to doctors who like to look for health problems in the most remote chasms of life, he was not your normal human being, just as the painter Munkácsy wasn't. Philosophers, who would prefer to pick the whole world up on their knitting needles only to unravel it in their ennui like some stocking, conclude that he was a man of extraordinary wisdom who, after all, lived the way he wanted to live. The tramps at the Bean Soup, who wheedled money from him to carouse in the squalid tavern (without inviting the maestro of course) and who made off with his clothes only to flog them to the neighboring secondhand store (where they fetched a good price, for the art dealer's assistant would redeem Mednyánszky's suits)—the tramps at the Bean Soup thought he was a kind-hearted madman and that there should be more of his sort in Budapest.

But no one will ever know what the "baron of the vagabonds" himself thought, in his solitude.

(5 December, 1926)

The Novelist at the Casino

The National Casino used to have a separate space on the ground floor set aside for smaller private parties: a dining room and a salon on the Szép Street side of the building. Miklós Szemere usually hosted his dinners here, at which Sándor Bródy was frequently a welcome guest. The eccentric nobleman was fascinated by the eccentric novelist, who in those days was also celebrated for his plays. And since Mr. Szemere was one of those old-style gentlemen who preferred meetings over a well-laid table to those at ink-stained offices, Mr. Bródy often received gilt-edged invitations to these small feasts. Granted, the novelist had no say in the selection of the menu (a fact he no doubt sorely regretted), for Mr. Szemere took great pride in his knowledge of cookbooks. This clever gentleman admitted that he tried to do his best to deserve the sobriquet he went by—"Mr. Traktárovich" (since in those days every member of the Casino had such a name, used by friend and foe alike). Yes, "Mr. Traktárovich" was proud of sponsoring dinners that were talked about for days after. (The food served at his Szentlőrinc target-shooting competition had been the talk of the town for months.) Mr. Bródy, having had his dinner outfit freshly ironed by Gyuri at his residential hotel on Margit Island, burst into town, with a youthful shine to his graying hair and with his mustache treated by the wax he occasionally used (although he hated to admit it). Of course his white tie gave him the most trouble for it could not be worn more than once with an evening outfit. Shopkeepers on Lipót Boulevard would at times have to pull up their rolling shutters after closing time to accommodate the tieless author. Mr. Bródy would always be hurrying to another premiere at some theater, for his plays were performed just about every evening; therefore the shop had to re-open to provide him with a white necktie. Bródy tried to apologize: "I've been this way since my days as a lawyer's clerk, always forgetting some item of clothing. Were it not for that, I could have gone far in law."

Naturally Mr. Bródy took a *fiacre* to the Casino. He could always find a cab at Franciscans' Place, with a driver who would know the special approach to the Casino, entering through the gate on Lajos Kossuth Street, pulling up at

85

the red-carpeted stairs, then proceeding around the fountain in the courtyard, to exit by the gate on Szép Street. This is what the etiquette at the National Casino prescribed. Not every Budapest cabdriver was aware of this.

The so-called White Room was staffed by extra personnel whenever Mr. Szemere dined there. In addition to the high-style waiters and footmen, a uniformed hussar with discreetly jingling spurs was indispensable to help with the removal of overcoats and with the pouring of the wine up to the moment at which the champagne was served. After that the hussar had no further duties at the table, for the cigars, for instance, would be brought to the guests by a valet... But let us not rush matters.

Beside the dinner-jacketed host with his impassive Tatar face and his close-trimmed hair and beard, only two others stood by the large, capacious tiled stove. These two were kinsmen of the host and therefore felt duty-bound to arrive early in order to assist with the reception of the guests. The first was the writer György Szemere, who twirled his mustache as if he had just stepped forth from those Biedermeier times when Highland gentlemen still indulged in belletristic pursuits. This lanky gentleman possessed a refinement of soul free of the jealousies that cloud authorial egos when writers meet in the same room. The other kinsman was Kálmán Szemere, a captain in the Hussars, an original, one of the Hussar officers of the old school, with enough adventures to fill a volume of anecdotes.

Mr. Bródy was somewhat self-conscious about his early arrival, but the soft voice of the host hastened to reassure him: "Ah, Mr. Novelist, you did well to join us a few moments early so I can let you know that your inclusion in to-day's dinner party was in fact suggested by that lady of rare loveliness, Countess B., who will shortly join us."

"The dear countess!" Mr. Bródy exclaimed. "There's no finer creature in all of Transylvania."

A round table had been set in the neighboring room, for Mr. Szemere, a bachelor, had no "lady of the house" to seat at the head of the table. Although each guest's place was indicated by a card, the table still had an undeniably masculine arrangement, as if the arrival of the lady guest had been an unexpected honor. Indeed the gentlemen—handsome Count Sándor Hadik, Miklós Bánffy, the intendant of the Opera House, myself, and Baron Üchtritz, a man of peerless intellect, said to be the most learned member of the Casino— seemed surprised when Countess B., tall, slender, and majestic, entered the salon escorted by our host, looking as if she had just stepped out of a painting in the picture gallery of some ancient Transylvanian castle where she had been keeping company with the *grandes dames* of history. She greeted the gentlemen with the conventional smile of old acquaintances, and saved something extra for Mr. Bródy, for Countess B. smiled at him with a wink, almost in collusion, as if meeting the novelist here had suddenly recalled a most amusing incident—some fond memory perhaps, some escapade or youthful folly that makes one smile even after the passage of twenty years.

"Tell me, what happened to your long Russian greatcoat?" the countess inquired, as if that were the sole item, albeit a most amusing one, that she remembered from the past of Mr. Bródy, the former Kolozsvár reporter.

For some reason Mr. Bródy was unable to recall the coat—apparently he no longer cared to be reminded of that Russian-style coat of his. God only knows, everyone gets tired of certain items of clothing worn with such great pride once upon a time.

Now the host invited the company to take their places at the round table, where the black dinner jackets formed a beautiful array against the light upholstery of the chairs; Countess B. was resplendent in her sea-green silk gown. Fresh, bright, and wholesome, she surveyed the company as if she had just emerged from a green forest of pines or the waters of a babbling brook. This unheard-of freshness is a secret known to those very few women who rarely resort to makeup, so that their complexions emanate nature's own splendid scents.

The feast opened with a luscious honeydew melon, of which everyone was served a half, to be spooned out. God only knows where melons like that were obtained with summer still so far away. The iced melon cooled the stomach to the appropriate temperature, for an overheated belly cannot do full justice to the tasks of digestion.

"Tell me, Mr. Bródy, which novel or play do you consider to be your greatest success?" Szemere asked, wanting to come to Sándor Bródy's aid when he saw that the writer was somewhat ill at ease in the presence of the countess.

"I'm not sure about that—my publisher Wolfner would know the sales figures. Pepi Wolfner, that is!" said the writer, somewhat more in his element, perhaps finding it amusing that he could mention the name of a figure of commerce in a room where Wolfner's name had probably never been brought up before.

"He's a book publisher of the modern type," added Miklós Bánffy, as it were to second Bródy, but the novelist refused to go along with the offered alliance.

"As for me, I'd actually prefer my books to be handled by one of those old-fashioned publishers such as Ráth or Aigner; for a book to be truly precious in Hungary it has to be issued by Mór Ráth's firm. The books he published were really substantial—compared to them most other books are of little real worth." (Countess B. was visibly pleased by this statement, for she cast a glance of acknowledgment at Bródy, as if she expected nothing less from a former reporter from Kolozsvár, the capital of Transylvania.)

Mr. Szemere, who was said to be so conservative that he would not even allow his tailor to take new measurements for his suits, which meant that certain garments would have to wait until he gained or lost weight, now spoke up: "Why yes, the fine book publishers you refer to indeed professed a national vocation in their day, for they considered it their patriotic duty to support Hungarian authors' works. But as times changed books have become consumer goods, and book publishers and dealers must be clever and opportunistic to distribute everywhere. I don't like to see Hungarians lacking in commercial spirit, but it seems this is something to which we'll have to resign ourselves."

By now Sándor Bródy was savoring the "Polish soup" which followed the melon. He would have liked to comment on the manner of preparing this soup, for he was a passionate gourmet. But the glance cast at him by the countess suggested that he had better stick to literary topics—for obviously that was what he had been invited for.

"I'm the same way with editors as with publishers. I always regret I didn't stay with Jenő Rákosi, at whose paper I started out. After all, he is the only scribe worth his salt in this country; no one can top him for nationalism, although it is true he goes overboard at times, but that goes with being a chauvinist."

"I don't like Jenő Rákosi so much, not since he became the director of the Népszinház. You can't perform these folksy plays forever," complained Mr. Szemere. At this point boiled beef was served, which was somewhat unusual for an evening meal, but Mr. Szemere's memorable boiled beef could not be omitted from a dinner menu. He was simply the greatest connoisseur of beef in this country. He personally sliced a helping off the huge bone, which he presented to the countess. After that, as the waiter offered the beef around the table, he advised each guest on which side of the bone to cut from. (Only Sándor Hadik continued to preserve his brooding impassivity: not even the most monumental sides of beef could arouse the interest of this exceptionally melancholy person.)

As for Mr. Szemere, he invariably ate his beef with a thin tomato sauce and scallions, for, as he would say, he was a bachelor. But his guests had a rich array of condiments from which to choose. The soup greens were served on separate platters along with the marrow bones, and a variety of mustards, horseradish, and golden saffron sauces were available to those who liked to have a spoonful or two of sauce along with their beef. As an artistic soul who loved all things beautiful Count Bánffy showed his appreciation of the ceremonious presentation of the beef, taking special delight in the crimson of the beets.

(Countess B. cast another glance at Bródy, as if cueing him to continue the literary discussion. As a lady of the Transylvanian aristocracy she expected each man to perform within his area of expertise—just as she expected feats from her steeds and dogs.)

"But while I was unable to turn into a nationalist by the side of Jenő Rákosi—a notion that appealed to me greatly in my youth, for there is no greater delight than an avid Hungarian readership—at least I should have amounted to something at *Fővárosi Lapok*. Of course, this was back in the days of old Vadnai, when he edited the daily paper of Hungarian noble society. Ah, to write for ladies of the aristocracy and arouse the interest of countesses and baronesses. Perhaps the best time to have been there was back in the days of Kálmán Tóth, but alas I wasn't around yet. Back then a Hungarian writer still had some prospects as long as he could tell tales that would please patriotic women. But I never had the honor of having Miklós Nagy, editor of *Vasárnapi Ujság*, strolling up to me to 'squeeze a manuscript' out of me, as he liked to put it. Writers in this country are born to yearn for the bowers of *Fővárosi Lapok*—but Pest, and its editors, spoil them."

Mr. Szemere listened with the same eager attention that he would devote to a highly interesting horse-racing story. This was at a time when there were rumors of his acquiring *Fővárosi Lapok* for "Mademoiselle" (his mistress Adrienne Meszlényi), so that his protégée, the actress, would have her own daily paper, just like certain famous actresses abroad.

89

By now the roast fowl was served, in the form of various pheasants that came with a known provenance, for a pheasant is the kind of commodity one wants to acquire from a familiar estate where special hunters are dedicated to its shooting. Baron Üchtritz, who up till this point had been silent—for not speaking during a meal was one of his deeply ingrained hygienic convictions (as was walking about with his head uncovered the year around)—now inspected the salads served with the roast pheasant and observed that vegetarians do have a point when they extol the virtues of a good salad. (In fact the baron was well on his way towards a vegetarian lifestyle, but he was still undecided about whether he would endorse tramping barefoot in wet grass.)

At the end of dinner Countess B. succeeded, through feminine wiles, in cornering the novelist for a tête-à-tête, and sheltering herself behind her fan—which she wielded like a lady of former times—addressed Bródy: "So tell me what has happened to you since your Kolozsvár days?"

The poor writer replied with a speech such as may be found in one of his works: "Well, I've come down to earth but stand with my head raised high, my shoulders unbowed. I'm afraid I fear very few things, although those who know me can recognize the pedestrian in me. So I might get treated poorly—or what's worse, beyond my just deserts. I am a day laborer—granted a privileged one who doesn't have to sweat—only once have I bitten my lip so that it bled, when my second son was born and I, while my wife was in labor, was obliged to write a lead editorial about city planning for Budapest. I'm not complaining but I'm not really a Budapest person, having remained a provincial all my life. The sad little boy has become a sad middle-aged man, that's all. I've never played the clown for others, I never learned to tell jokes. So I angrily reject the very notion of having anyone ask about my fate."

"Sándor, I have always believed in you," replied the noble countess. "I suggest you pay attention to Szemere. They say he's an eccentric and a madman, but he is the sort who can be influenced to do good. By now he's very wealthy and doesn't have to worry about betting on the horses, although I have noticed that his cardiac infirmity might have been aggravated by his gambling."

"Yes, that restrained, asthmatic laughter of his. And the way he walks. He knows that something is wrong."

"He is the kind of man who could benefit from your attention."

"I'm no good with people who have heart trouble, for I have a heart like an ox's," the novelist replied. "My heart will have to be stopped with an explosive bullet or an ax. For a man like Szemere the best kind of friend is someone as sad as Sándor Hadik—you can see from far off that he's a gentleman beyond desire, he has long ago forgotten desire. Or else Szemere needs a servant, some starveling who'll say yes to every whim of the eccentric gentleman. I am afraid there's nothing I could teach him in this life. He is headstrong and unique, like Ferenc Molnár, who is likewise beyond my powers."

At this moment the approach of the host put an end to the increasingly intimate conversation between the countess and the novelist. Mr. Szemere handed a leather-bound volume to Bródy.

"Since our dinner conversation revolved around book publishing I have taken the liberty of bringing you one of my books which, alas, was not published by Mór Ráth but my humble self."

"But I can see that it was printed by Viktor Hornyánszky. One of the best," said the novelist, taking the book and leafing through it. The hefty tome contained Miklós Szemere's parliamentary speeches.

Mr. Szemere sat down by the novelist's side. "It's typical of me that I hardly know any Budapest writers. I simply never moved in their circles. I know about them by hearsay only, even though I've been wanting to meet writers for some time now."

Bródy, since the countess was not looking, said with a slight toss of the head and a somewhat mocking smile: "Well, your honor can get to meet the gentlemen at the Otthon Club any time. They are somewhat complex people, but they're not that difficult to get to know."

"Well, some night, perhaps," replied Szemere. "Actually, why not tonight, in your company, Mr. Bródy. My cousin György would also be delighted to come along."

The Transylvanian countess gave Bródy another one of her glances.

"I just have to make a phone call, to make sure that none of the card players leave," said Mr. Bródy with the greatest willingness, and he never forgot the grateful look in her eyes evoked by his obliging response.

(16 July, 1927)

91

My Adventures with the Poet on the Crooked Sidewalks
[from Endre Ady's Nights]

The sounds of crowing could be heard at the tavern known as the Three Ravens. It was Zuboly, the learned poet, crowing...

Dawn was breaking in Budapest, in the early spring of 1913.

Why would Dr. Elemér Bányai be crowing, this gentleman widely known (until a Russian bullet laid him low in the Carpathians) by his nom de plume Zuboly?

Zuboly was crowing because this angelically mild-mannered man was angry—frustrated by all the table-pounding during the quest for the plain truth in the company of the argumentative Béla Reinitz, he of the elephantine voice.

Just what kind of a place was the Three Ravens, Endre Ady's favorite tavern?

If you look for it on Andrássy Avenue today it can no longer be found—a common fate of all those institutions, down to the plainest beer halls, where the Saints and Fools had once set foot.

The Three Ravens was frequented in those days by the Budapest Saints during the hours of the night when janitors began their broom-pushing in editorial offices.

Thus Mr. Pál Kéri would be swept out from the editorial offices of the *Pesti Napló*, across the avenue from the tavern. In those days there was no mark whatever on this gentleman's forehead to indicate that one day a Hungarian court would condemn him to death by hanging. No, at the time this young man, who must have been bald even as a child, gave the impression of a poet in the making...

"Red Grajna", also known as Jenő Greiner, had been excused from the Café New York to relocate to the Three Ravens. The son of a wealthy Dalszinház Street landlord, he was an economist by profession, which was not a very remunerative one even in those days: it would be a feast day indeed when he could claim to be the proud possessor of a silver five-korona piece... This red-haired man, too, was infected by the poetry bug, no matter how slyly he rubbed his hands under the table. I would not be surprised if some day we come across poems secreted in various ladies' scrapbooks by this outstanding specimen of manhood, commonly known as "Red Grajna"...

Around the same time Béla Révész was also given reprieve to go forth and haunt, leaving behind the wall of some old monastery from where he had contemplated the events transpiring around him. He entered the smoky room of the Three Ravens as absent-mindedly as if arriving from some distant land, as if he had come to illusionless Budapest from some far-off island resonant with melodies...to search for their distant echoes here at this small tavern on Andrássy Avenue, where from time to time one was privileged to hear the startling hunting horn or solitary fluting of the Weird Stranger.

But the door of the Three Ravens keeps opening again and again, as do all tavern doors oiled by stubborn sorrows and fleeting joys.

And other friends and admirers enter, people who even at this late hour are unable to lay their heads to rest unless they retrace the life history of a poem or some other such trifle.

Hunchbacked Löffelmann the tavern keeper, Quasimodo of Andrássy Avenue, looked on at the company assembling in the back room of the Three Ravens with a certain measure of goodwill, even though his personal acquaintance ran mostly to those ladies and gentlemen whose professional activities tied them to the lights of the nearby Orfeum or Folies Caprice, and who entered the tavern bringing scents of mastic and rice powder. At a corner table exotic dancers would plan their upcoming tour of Moscow, while the actresses at the next table, quaffing brown beer, were augmenting embonpoints that had already roamed as far as Irkutsk and were no longer looking forward to leaving the immediate neighborhood. In another corner we may see Patti, the magician of the Budapest night, whose hairpiece is dyed a chestnut brown, and who, according to local legend, has passed the century mark. Elsewhere superannuated cabaret artists weep into their beer steins about the days when they were the kings of the flying trapeze or masters of sword-swallowing.

And now, squeezing through the door amidst much asthmatic wheezing is the night watchman of old Andrássy Avenue, a man who keeps tabs on every spritzer and bottle of champagne that is consumed, for he exacts his toll in the form of a small personal loan... This portly man is Diogenes Blau, formerly a stockbroker, who now prefers the nightlife in the company of carousing young poets, illustrating his grotesque philosophy of life by pointing out old flower vendors at the Winter Garden from whom nobody buys flowers anymore and complaining about fortune's favorites who speed in fancy equipages down the most scenic avenues, whereas he, Diogenes Blau, can no longer afford the cheapest hansom cab... This connoisseur of the night always inquires about the freshness of the beer on tap, phrasing his query to Löffelmann in his Viennese-accented German, after which he calls out, in an authentic Szentes dialect, to the Saints and Fools conducting their occult rituals in the inner room:

"Boys, the beer's flat tonight. You should drink wine."

*

What were these occult rituals performed in the dead of night in that small room at the Three Ravens by these men who had assembled from the most far-flung corners of the city for the purpose of this daily observance?

As mentioned, at midnight the journalist Zuboly starts to crow like a rooster in order to vent his rage, unable to convince the Roarer of the obvious Truth that, according to Mr. Zuboly, even the greatest idiot in town could see at once. But Reinitz out-shouts everyone else in the small room:

"You are a total idiot!"

And he pounds the table as if preparing to fight, although actually he is dying to find a piano on which he can perform for the benefit of Zuboly, the saintliest of the Saints, the latest song he has set to music.

An unexpected guest, Mr. Hatvany, enters now, also looking for that Weird Stranger who has come to this city via Nagyvárad and Paris, and whose poems offer the strangest notions to the highly excitable local youth, ideas that not even the oldest parrot could pull from the box of fortunes at the fair. But the Weird Stranger has not yet shown his face tonight in the tavern.

"There must have been a soirée at the Vészis," surmises one subdued but jealous voice at the table. It is Mr. Révész, moved to speak just as the otherwise silent cuckoo pops out of the clock striking the quarter hour.

Baron Hatvany, slim in his overcoat, could pass for a figure out of an old English novel about the youth of Arthur Pendennis, and cannot tolerate for very long the redolent sausage, herring, and onion exhalations of the Three Ravens. Besides, he is somewhat taken aback when Red Elek from the Orfeum, the Gypsy bandleader with makeup on his face, sits down at the table among the Saints and Fools and shows great familiarity, as if he had been touring Paris with the young man whose arrival all are awaiting. Nor does the figure of Diogenes Blau, lurking by the curtains separating the room from the taproom, inspire confidence in Hatvany, who is the offspring of a prominent Budapest business dynasty. Mr. Hatvany lingers with dwindling hope, nor is he much encouraged to stay by the loud banging in the bar, where the hunchbacked Löffelmann is thumping on a beer keg.

Journalists are arriving from nearby all-night cafés, with the latest news scribbled on their wrinkled shirt cuffs. News flash from the Café Helvetia: Dr. M., the well-known encyclopedia editor, has just eloped with one of that café's lady habituées who is known to reporters on the night beat by the name of Rosie the Hauler. The elopement took place through a window opening on Ó Street, just as in a novel.

But not even the romantic adventure of the encyclopedia editor can prevent "Red Grajna" from holding forth with dyspeptic venom about absent members of the company—even though he is famous for his splendid ability to unsparingly vent negative opinions about his friends face to face.

And now, bearing copies of *Friss Újság* hot off the press, hoarse-voiced Gyula staggers in, dizzied by the verbal abuse dished out by nocturnal journalists. The pushy news-vendor retires only when he is waved off by Mr. Révész, the paper's editor.

*

At last The Man arrives.

You would think it was a provincial actor bursting through the door to report his success with the mayor's fat wife... Or else you could take him for a young Eugene Onegin, in a fur coat, bored and in search of amusement.

"I've been with Léda, you Fool!" he roars at his best friend and roommate Révész, even though Béla has long ago given up the notion of taking to task his beloved.

He is a handsome young man from the provinces.

Look at his hands: they have the purity of a young *abbé*'s that have been dipped into a basin of holy water only moments ago.

As for his hair, it recalls that hobbled English lord who swam the Hellespont in a frenzy of poetic inspiration.

His eyes reflect the fears of a frightened, sick child whose nanny entertains him with bedside tales of the bogeyman knocking on the door—but in the next moment these same eyes are those of an adventurer greedy for all the pleasures of the road from Nagyvárad to Paris, desiring to ravish the treasure of each and every female body on the way.

These unforgettable eyes!

Their dreamy gaze beamed across tavern rooms sloshed with wine and trash as if the walls had parted for a moment, offering a glimpse of vast melancholy stretches of Hungary.

These eyes cast their provocative, defiant, and fearless challenge straight in the face of mortal Fate, which did not visit him here at the Three Ravens for lack of a cab on Andrássy Avenue—they had all been taken by Painted Women going home in the small hours.

But mostly these eyes cast cajoling and apologetic glances, of an infinite tenderness, as if begging your pardon in advance for all the trouble that they would cause in this country.

Slyly, as if conning you into a crooked card game, these eyes followed the argument between crowing Zuboly and roaring Reinitz. Every once in a while these eyes shot a caressing ray toward Béla Révész, while the poet loudly whinnied into his friend's ear:

"What a deaf Fool you are!"

Meanwhile "Red Grajna" was getting ready for a heroic feat. Being short of money he wanted to start a tab, beginning with his beer and sausage—but the waiter was new. However, he succeeded in accomplishing his stratagem, for the red numerals of the wall calendar still show 1913.

*

But the rest of us windblown word-millionaires, destined to swing from the branch of a tree, could stay on at the Ravens, as well as at the next tavern after the Ravens, a place He always entered with the humility and self-consciousness of a poor boy knocking on the door of a wealthy residence to recite Christmas carols.

But first, before we tour the after-hours bars of the Sixth District (that lie waiting for us like a cat squinting at a mouse), here is the story of the Poet's battle with the Sphinx of the Opera.

In the course of his pre-dawn rambles He had become enamored of these buxom ladies carved from stone, guarding the side steps of the Opera House; women of intransigent heart, whose soullessness surpassed that of the most brazen of fancy females patrolling the sidewalks of Andrássy Avenue. He was well aware that these women of stone cared not a whit about his poems, although in one of his otherworldly trances it was revealed to him that the Sphinx posted forever on the Dalszinház Street side of the building resembled Léda, his lady love. [...]

Having recognized the marble lioness on Dalszinház Street for an embodiment of Léda, He decided to pay homage to the stone-hearted one by ascending the seven steps leading to her pedestal, as if they constituted the sevenfold path of Buddhism. In the course of such greetings his faithful friend would stay back at a distance, for in those days that gentleman scorned both cold ladies of stone and those who had warm flesh and hot blood. Therefore the good friend called out in bored tones in the graying dawn:

"C'mon, Agyibagyi, before they close the Pub."

"Wait!" The poet's voice, perennially hoarse like that of all tuberculars and lovers, commanded from on high. "I must have a word with her."

Evidently He whispered sweet nothings into the Sphinx's ear, inviting her to the apartment at an hour when Béla Révész, the roommate, was likely to turn a deaf ear.

But the Sphinx did not respond.

So, one dawn He became really infuriated.

True, this anger may have also been provoked by the editor Jenő Rákosi's campaign to enlist the public opinion of his "thirty million Hungarians" against our poor poet during the infamous "Duk-duk Affair"—and also by that seemingly harmless light table wine Ady liked so much, and which the Hunchback, being an honest man, did not dilute with water.

On this dawn the Sphinx proved more obdurate than ever, and refused to respond to the poet's entreaties.

"Well, if you won't come, I'm going to take you!" he yelled, and with all the fire of his native Szilágyság region he hopped on the back of the stone lioness.

But the attempt to mount the stone-hearted one proved unsuccessful. The Good Friend standing at a distance caught a glimpse of a hatless body pathetically plunging from the Sphinx's back, so that the beautiful head, peerless in all of Hungary, landed with a dull thud on the steps six feet below.

"Uh-oh, it's curtains for him," muttered the Good Friend, for moments of crisis such as this always evoke the most commonplace response.

For a second or two the Poet lay dead still at the feet of his Beloved.

Then a painful groan rose from the dark steps. "Ah, the bitch!" Certainly the tones of everyday life, if not poesy...

The Good Friend, hurrying over, could only come up with a folksy saying:

"No shame in being kicked by a mare!"

We'll never know if this cheerful maxim had achieved the desired effect, or if miraculous, invisible arms—perhaps an old mother's, praying for him in far-off Érdmindszent—protected the fallen poet... But He bounced to his feet with a laugh, found his fallen headgear, and surged forth fit as a fiddle, in the direction of the misty red glow emitted by the entrance to the pub. His Good Friend followed in amazement. At the entrance to the tavern He turned and shouted:

"Béla my friend, my Saintly Fool, why on earth are you lagging behind?"

And the faithful Révész, his face chalk-white with fright, caught up with him at last.

Daylight's stone-cold sober knuckles were poised to tap on the windows of the tavern, and He was still expounding to the assembled company how the lioness bucked when he jumped on her back... Dr. Lukács, summoned by telephone from the Café New York, examined the poet's head and, unable to find the slightest sign of injury, refused to give credence to the alleged adventure.

*

But it's time to amble onward on Nagymező Street, where the youth of Budapest must have spent at least one-fourth of their lives in those days.

Journalists on a binge, whose shirt collars were not the whitest, would turn up the lapels of their overcoats and stroll down this street once Popovics, the doorman who wore hussar breeches, had put the last lingering drunk on a cab in front of the Orfeum. Sleepy ladies of the night still without a man cast despairing glances after the slender figure of the poet, by this time swaying like a wind-blown reed, supported by Révész, who, on account of his roommate's debilitated state, redoubled his efforts to counteract the effects of the imbibed liquids that medical opinion even back then had pronounced so harmful for the heart. But there stood Kovács, in the doorway of his tavern on Dessewffy Street, with a country-style, hearty welcome for last night's company, still together this morning. Ah, long vanished by now was the scent of French toiletries that had wafted about the poet's face earlier in the night. Instead, there was a whiff of Zuboly's bearskin smell... The poet's slack mouth no longer exhaled the aroma of the toothpaste and mouthwash he favored. By now his breath had taken on the acrid flavor of Béla Révész's ever-present cigars... His wavy hair, fresh from the caresses of some female hand earlier in the evening, was hanging in his eyes by the time we reached Dessewffy Street, and resembled those fly-by-night poetasters who had more or less started to imitate Ady's style... And his white collar also showed traces of the night's events, as if the unworthy words he had dropped here and there had left their imprint on his shirt.

His demeanor, up till then full of friendly blandishment toward one and all, turned wild and cynical on the corner of Dessewffy Street, like that of a provincial journalist with a grudge against his Budapest colleagues.

At this hour in Kovács's tavern the smell of chopped red onions would vie with the odor of raw garlic. The room was stifling with the stale events of the night just passed. Gypsy musicians played cards at a corner table while gaudily dressed wives waited for them with infants in their laps. The waitress was as common as dishwater. But Kovács, the tavern keeper, was all smiles. Placing a bottle of sparkling wine, his version of champagne, on the table, he sat down to listen, leaning on one elbow.

*

Well, the tavern may have been the lowliest in the whole city but this was where the real Ady showed his true colors in front of two friends and an illiterate tavern keeper, who, before encountering Ady's verses, had never known any poems other than the Lord's Prayer and a choice assortment of oaths.

Here, in this dirty little tavern, where sometimes we heard the noontime bells of St. Theresa's Church (for bell-ringers always compete with lamplighters), surfaced an Endre Ady that was never seen by the Vészi girls at their father's polite soirées, and was unknown even to the bright Léda, who had served as a guiding light for the poet ever since his Nagyvárad days, always wanting to point the road forward, whereas the poet's whims at times aimed backward. By the same token the real Ady remained concealed from the company of the Saints and Fools at the Three Ravens, as well as at the Café Meteor where ambitious young lawyers, physicians, and professors would pay their respects to the poet, only inconveniencing him with their homage, rather like schoolchildren crowding to kiss the hand of the parish priest.

100

Here at this pub which no longer exists, among other things we found out that the poet's personality had a quarrelsome and spiteful side. My, he really knew how to scratch, bite, claw, and vent his venom against literary friends and foes alike, loosing on them the two faithful Friends by his side, one of whom sat there with the solemn expression of a Guardian Angel, while the other engaged in literary disputes merely to postpone the hour of having to go home. Contemptuous pronouncements, wicked animosities, vitriolic denunciations that sometimes went back as far as his Nagyvárad days all proliferated here. There was hardly a name mentioned in the Hungarian dailies that the doleful reveler at Kovács's tavern did not have his own say about. Bile, mockery, arrogance, and profound scorn dripped from his each and every word in this grimy little room where the ignorant tavern keeper, like a wide-eyed Devotee, nodded agreement to every word uttered by the "Boy", his term of endearment for the poet. And successful writers, those known as having "arrived", would have had to hang on to their pants on these mornings, had they heard the poet surveying the lineup of Hungarian literature. He had something unpleasant to say about everyone, from old Jenő Rákosi down to the youngest fledgling pen-pusher.

This was the real Ady, the handsome young man from the provinces, wrapped up in hauteur, scorn, and at times even a bit of anti-Semitism— although he was already one of the main contributors to *Nyugat*. In outward appearance a refined, elegant Hungarian gentleman who had been to Paris...

At Kovács's tavern the length of the stay or the quantities consumed made no difference: Ady's coterie had a running tab here, like an account at some financial institution where a large amount has been deposited.

*

And still, during these tavern-studded, pub-crawling times Ady was the most glorious Christmas tree in the park of Hungarian literature.

Regardless of location—at a tavern or at a congenial red-light house—he was a perennially bubbling fountainhead of poems. At his table at the Ravens he would grab pencil and paper to write, without one correction, a new poem as a present to a friend. He would do the same at the Winter Garden, a milieu reeking of cheap perfume and the merchandise of grab-bag vendors—as if his sole aim were to make a night spent in his company unforgettable for his friends.

Like a prince, he was liberal with his gifts.

I am certain that many of his poems survive in the possession of diverse ladies, bestowed as mementos of Venus rising in the sky. Volumes of his poems were being published one after another; he carried the bottle of bromide in his pocket mostly for effect, there was no real need for it back then. The Budapest night exuded an inebriation compounded of French wines, opiate Egyptian cigarettes and women starved for literature. Many of us still remember that poor woman of the night known as Puella Classica, who introduced herself as a poetess at the Café Helvetia, clutching books and manuscripts while provincial salesmen ordered one bottle of wine after another; this daughter of the night would actually read her poems if Endre Ady happened to enter the café.[...]

This was still the blissful peacetime Hungary of old, when Budapest thirsted for culture, especially fine literature, the way wild tribesmen, after their first taste, covet the alcohol brought by traders from distant shores.

The poet, feeling at home ever since arriving in this city, strode down the length of Andrássy Avenue, confident that the *palazzi* would move over to make way for him. After all, some of his poems had already been set to music by Reinitz and had taken flight as song, especially when the composer himself bellowed them in a side room at the Café Magyar Világ. After these concerts I always marveled that the management did not insist on damages for the piano.

*

[...]I will conclude this introduction with an account of my last meeting with Endre Ady.

It is the unwaveringly loyal Béla Révész whom I can thank for this last meeting, and for so many other good encounters with the poet.

Ady wrote me to announce that he did not dare to brave the night alone and would bring Csinszka with him. Because of the lady's presence we could not choose one of our favorite dives, some tavern where cabdrivers congregated and where we had spent so many congenial nights. We had to look for a suitably elegant milieu, although Révész mentioned that the poet would not be able to appear in public, since he was spending most of his days in his sickbed. I happened to be living at the Royal Hotel at the time and arranged for a private dining room accessible directly from the street so that no idle curiosity-seekers would bother the ailing and peevish poet. The so-called

White Room proved most suitable for our purpose, its walls covered by Gobelin tapestries, the tables set with cut crystal and silver and the ventilation system capable of handling even the smoke emitted by Béla Révész's black cigars.

Ady kept us waiting.

He showed up at last around ten, with a carton of cigarettes under one arm, and the other around Csinszka. As always, she smiled while the poet greeted us in mock anger:

"I came only because one must not let down Deaf and Mad people, they're like children. I could hardly drag myself out of bed."

I gave him a closer look. His physical appearance gave no indication that the end was only a few weeks away.

The liveliest thing about him on this day was his hair, not a single strand of silver woven in by all the bodily pain the poet had suffered. His eyes had grown somewhat larger since our last meeting. The corner of his mouth trembled feverishly and he barely touched his food, paying more attention to the bottle of wine. Dear old Révész was unable to conceal his grief. Seeing this, after the second glass of wine Ady resorted to his familiar whinnying voice of old:

"Oh you Madman—you're so Deaf!"

This rowdy, laughing voice of former times was a signal, as it were, for the curtains of the White Room to part and admit the ghostly figures of the past...

Zuboly was the first to arrive, with a bleeding chest wound...

The poet immediately announced that he still did not really believe that Zuboly was dead. There must have been some mistake—all uniforms look alike on the battlefield.

Next to appear, rubbing his hands, was "Red Grajna", fresh from his recently dug grave. For once he had managed to cover the price of the funeral.

"Red hair's always a bad sign on man, horse or dog!" screeched Ady, as if wishing to shoo away an oppressive apparition.

There followed much talk about Lady Léda, who, although not dead, had turned into a funereal wreath in the poet's life.

Then Csinszka gave the quiet signal to leave; all of the wines poured into crystal decanters had been consumed.

The poet stubbornly resisted for a while, as if he had half a mind to saddle up the Sphinx once more... From raging high spirits he suddenly tumbled into the depths of gloom, just as he had tumbled from the Sphinx's back on that other night.

"Maybe I, too, will soon be dead," he said in a voice that cast a chill over the company. There was a knock on the door—not the grim reaper yet, only a waiter, ready to clear the table...

With his departure imminent, the poet drew me close to him and whispered in my ear so the others could not hear:

"Gyula, this woman doesn't let me drink. See to it that there's a two-liter bottle in my overcoat pocket to take home."

I saw to it.

And that was the end of our last supper.

(1 February, 1925)

The Lord Mayor of Budapest

1.

The finest decoration sported by the Lord Mayor of Budapest used to be the tricolor municipal sash worn over his Francis Joseph-style tailcoat each time he conducted a wedding ceremony for some young couple.

Yes, we had arrived at that democratic era when the Budapest Lord Mayor's full-dress outfit was the tailcoat, the same as that worn by any high-school teacher, tax-bureau chief, or elderly mayor of a municipality who wanted to present a dignified appearance. I will not go so far as to claim that the *díszmagyar*, the traditional ornate outfit, was absent from the Lord Mayor's wardrobe, for it was still needed for the celebration of major national festivals when the Hungarian lords, their faces solemn with historical awareness, customarily visited—amidst a jingle-jangle of spurs and clatter of heirloom swords—even those houses of worship that belonged to denominations other than their own. However, the Budapest Lord Mayor gradually abandoned this old-fashioned outfit without which no Lord Lieutenant or sub-prefect would have dreamt of presiding over a county assembly in the nineteenth century. Only the Budapest Lord Mayor and commissioners of education promoted to the rank of Royal Councilor went about without *díszmagyar* outfits. But those whose lucky stars had elevated them to the rank of Privy Councilor, or to the Order of the Iron Crown, third grade, or to the Cross of the Francis Joseph Order of Knights, or, by some miracle, to the Order of Leopold, were inseparably associated with the *díszmagyar* in the popular imagination.

The Lord Mayor of Budapest would have liked to be addressed at least as "Your Worship", but, alas, he was only entitled to "Your Honor".

Looking at the history of the recent past it is worthwhile to consider the diversity of ranks that beautified, charmed, honored, and endowed with value the lives of Hungarians during the reign of Francis Joseph, a reign that spanned two generations...

I have never tried to attain any rank, not even in the volunteer firemen's association, but I can imagine the heavenly transfiguration experienced by a fellow citizen during those prewar, peacetime years, upon reading his name in the official bulletin confirming his appointment as a Royal Councilor! Suddenly new perspectives opened up in judging things and events... New friends and acquaintances arrived, people who had previously blissfully ignored your existence... You purchased a new hat and (after much practice at home in front of the mirror) your greeting would acquire a touch of condescension... The royal grace bestowed a definite new glow on one's face; visits to the barber would become more frequent; one's clothes would be ironed more often (for you never saw a Royal Councilor wearing pants that were shiny in the seat, even in a subsidiary office); one became punctilious about sending name-day and birthday greetings—from now on these would always be reciprocated; and above all, one never failed to congratulate fellow citizens "with seniority" who had received a promotion or decoration. In those days, appointment to the position of Royal Councilor meant the onset of a courtly attentiveness, for in the desk drawer of a Royal Councilor lay a list of personages expecting New Year's greetings, in writing or in person—one of the little obligations that came with the medal. One suddenly turned into a devoted reader of the "Decorations" page in the official bulletin, and learned to browse through the almanac that, even in Hungary, began to resemble the *Almanac de Gotha*, for the names listed under diverse bureaus, national assemblies, and official bodies were always followed by the various orders of merit possessed by that individual. A closed crown stood for the Order of the Iron Crown, while a bevy of abbreviations signified Royal Councilor, Privy Councilor, Order of Francis Joseph, first or second grade, Imperial and Royal Chamberlain, Order of Leopold, Order of St. Stephen... Yes, one could daydream at length about all the lovely honors that awaited you during the long reign of Francis Joseph.

The Lord Mayor of Budapest would usually receive some royal decoration upon retiring. But for the Lord Mayor who is the subject of this memoir the most important decoration was the affection of his fellow citizens.

In his youth he was called Pista Sacher and he made his first mark in society by dancing with as much skill as any of those nineteenth-century gallants who owed their social and professional careers to their artistic renditions of the *csárdás*.

(I used to know a gentleman of the old school who had, once upon a time, at a Regatta Ball at the Redoute, created a stir by performing the *csárdás* with a young lady for a solid hour and a half after midnight. This gentleman never accomplished another noteworthy thing in his life, yet he remained to the end of his days a famous figure in Budapest.) In addition, Pista Sacher was quite musical, for in the old days a gentleman needed a certain competence in the higher realms of music to make his mark in genteel society. (Gone were the days of those country squires who would create a ruckus by bringing to town an ensemble of semi-nomadic Gypsies who played outlaw songs of a riotous nature. Music lovers in the bourgeois salons developed a preference for the saccharine sounds of romantic, Germanic fantasias softly performed on piano, flute, and violin. Some of the younger dandies even took up playing the organ, which had hitherto belonged to the realm of austere, long-haired keyboard players.)

But no matter how heart-warming the old Budapest salon life (details of which were discussed during the noontime strolls on Koronaherceg Street and Váci Street that were *de rigueur* for ladies and gentlemen of good breeding), the real seats of power in city politics were the leather easy chairs at the Vigadó coffee-house, occupied in the afternoons by mayors and patricians. "The Professor", as Pista Sacher was soon nicknamed, voiced his political views in vain during the lulls between the dreamy music and even dreamier dances at perfumed Inner City salons. Some of the young ladies indeed looked deep into the eyes of the blond-haired young man, but missed the drift of his ideas. As for the older matrons, they would try to appease him while pouring a cup of coffee: "When Ráth was Lord Mayor we had law and order in Budapest. People lived out their lives in peace." The pillars of society, burghers who already possessed some royal decoration or who were due to receive one, usually dismissed the young reformer by complaining about the great sacrifices made by the municipality in supporting all those ne'er-do-well teachers, and Janka Zirzen's training college sending even more would-be teachers to sponge off the city. "Why, those women don't even aim to get married, and they don't intend to become nuns; they're after some weird new lifestyle that is morally reprehensible..."

"Men and women teaching at the same school, how would that ever work out? We already have two hundred jobless female teachers besieging the city councilors before the June elections. Do they take the Budapest municipality for a charitable institution?"

But something new is already in the air, very similar to the current of reform that had stirred the hearts and minds of Hungarians in the time of István Széchenyi.

The middle class is becoming increasingly self-assertive—possibly also motivated by the growing labor movements. New civic organizations mushroom in every district. Only the oldest burghers still participate in the antediluvian shooting societies. Political clubs such as the Sasok (Eagles), the Józsefváros Club (headed by grand old Hűvös), and the Andrássy Avenue group (led by Morzsányi and Radocza) are starting to pay attention to municipal issues in addition to the parliamentary elections. This mighty upsurge has sent the self-esteem of city aldermen skyrocketing: the Budapest city fathers now consider themselves as important as members of Parliament. A new note of dignity, self-importance, and confident courage appears at city council meetings. There is something of the manner of old Kálmán Tisza in the way Hűvös and Ehrlich command their party's adherents. Following their leaders, the dairy wholesalers, street pavers, and landlords begin to yield to loftier considerations. The daily press is starting to pay more attention to municipal affairs, often pointing out the ruling system of cliques and coteries. The city fathers show greater resolve in confronting "our officials", "our mayor", "our municipality", although the Minister of the Interior still rejects civic resolutions with a deprecating smile. But the same thing is happening with legislation proposed by representatives in Parliament, where the Upper House dismisses it with a wave of the hand.

But the self-esteem of the city—especially since Francis Joseph has declared it to be his royal capital—is growing from year to year. The table societies housed in small taverns, once so powerful in ward politics, are waning in power and stay alive through charitable activities. Only in the outlying districts and among veterans' groups does the table-society president retain a vestige of prestige. New associations and clubs are thoroughly deflating the authority of these fine citizens who had formerly commanded, even in the dead of night, the respectful greetings of the night watchman. Many new, mock table societies are springing up, especially in taverns of the Inner City, making light of the president and other officers, the rituals, the resolutions, and the minutes of the meeting, all to discredit the old-style societies... Perhaps the only serious table society surviving in Budapest is the one where our Pista Sacher shows up on occasion: presided over by Frigyes Glück, it meets at the Pannónia (until recently the "Griff").

This table society also boasts the monumental figure of József Márkus, the incumbent Lord Mayor.

Even though the old table societies were past their heyday, other social organizations existed where a young man could distinguish himself.

Take, for instance, the glee clubs, those solemn gatherings of citizens devoted to indulging their musical inclinations. Most famous among them was the Buda Glee Club, which won first prize at the nationwide competition held in Fiume. This seemingly innocent ensemble of male voices offered an opportunity to discuss the future of Budapest—whenever the bass baritones paused in their endeavors to go as low as they could go. Men who join glee clubs are usually idealists, and idealists are always willing to consider reforms. Returning home at night they would recount to their wives the program of fine songs performed, not omitting to mention the reform projects voiced by Pista Sacher, who by that time had received Francis Joseph's permission to go by his maternal family name of Bárczy.

In addition, there were the volunteer firemen's associations and also a variety of sports clubs, all of them occasions for important social contacts. Beside the yacht clubs, the fencing clubs played a considerable role, since their membership included many socially prominent gentlemen. The clubs formed at the fencing salle on Koronaherceg Street, as well as at other locations, were dedicated, in addition to maintaining a sound mind in a sound body, to curbing the still rampant street bullies of Budapest. For these rowdies refused to vanish from the streets in the wake of the old horse-drawn trams and carts peddling Danube drinking water. Too often one heard the sound of a loud slap administered at the theater or at a ball; and the famous masked balls at the Redoute not infrequently ended with a knifing. The reform-minded future Lord Mayor was determined to develop his physical strength and courage... One never knew when a man appealing for the votes of his fellow citizens might be called upon to demonstrate that he was worthy of their confidence.

Already back then Budapest was a lovely, charming, smart, and amiable city, but the most respected man at Wampetics' restaurant was still Dezső Szilágyi, the nation's Minister of Justice, Keeper of the Seal—and a fencing champion.

2.

Who remembers those grim and dank old prisons in which the children of Budapest spent their schooldays once upon a time?

I can still recall some of those seedy edifices with the outlandishly creaking gates where the poor Oliver Twists of Budapest entered, to climb the dilapidated stairs... Yes, a stroll in the neighborhood of the old elementary schools on Damjanich Street or Aréna Road definitely brought to mind Dickens' heartrending children. A red-nosed custodian would wave his broom to enforce discipline among ragged and sickly schoolchildren; instead of the dusty, dry, stifling, unwholesome smell of old schoolhouses these places reeked of the sewer; rats would stick their noses out of their holes for the entertainment of these Olivers; the classrooms had bare brick walls, and the teachers longed for the arrival of spring when they would be able to open the windows and give the place an airing.

Enter a building like that and your heart was gripped by fear; surely at night it was haunted by the ghosts of dead children who had contracted fatal diseases there; by day the potbellied headmaster (back then only potbellied men were appointed headmasters) was bellowing when he was not in the act of drafting reports to the board of education about tardy teachers. Periodically this "master sergeant" would visit the city council in person, while a quaking faculty awaited the dread news: who had been reported, or transferred to the far side of the city, or forced into retirement? These prison-like schools of former times each had their evil jailer, whose mood swings terrorized the hapless women who taught there.

To an outsider these classrooms seemed intolerable, with their crumbling ceilings, stoves insidiously leaking smoke, and dim windows denying children a glimpse of the sky—classrooms where a teacher would get to hate his pupils. For the poor man was only human after all, and fallible, and such prisons gave free rein to any dormant evil instinct. Teachers in these old schools were never supposed to be in a good mood—if they felt like being happy they could go to a tavern at night. And go they did, many of them becoming anarchists or canvassers—as often happens with inmates released from prison.

And consider the unfortunate woman who taught there, one hand clutching her diploma, the other her hard-earned daily bread, ever hustling to keep her difficult livelihood, her heart filled with regret for a wasted youth; and with despair, seeing other women contented with their lot. How did she feel in this rat-filled environment, complete with a jailer for a headmaster, teachers unused to courtesy, and schoolgirls with the shadow of diphtheria on their faces? She had probably come from a better family and had longed, with youthful idealism, to obtain her teaching diploma, feeling that her future would be secure and not dependent on some man falling into a marrying mood during an endless bout of *csárdás*. She would be able to afford a seamstress sewing her clothes, to support her old parents, to travel to some inexpensive Highland spa in the summer... And with the passing of youthful hopes, doomed to wilt here, at last she has found employment, but to earn her daily bread she has to languish in prison day after day, declining in health and growing resigned to losing everything that makes a woman's life worth living.

Yes, who remembers these wretched buildings on the streets of the capital, that loomed as frighteningly as the grimmest hospitals, as beggars with running sores, ragged vagabonds, horrifying poverty—buildings that carried the legend "Public School" on their façades? Who remembers their drafty entrances that gaped at you, emanating endless slavery, child abuse, desperate rancor against society, and vapid uselessness? Who remembers the terrors of the father first leading his child into this tenement, and the child's first attack of despair on having to return to the disease, filth, and vermin rife in these schools?

Goodbye and good riddance to these old houses of misery, tumbledown killjoy cages of childhood. There came a young man named István Bárczy (known to older gentlemen by the name of Sacher), to tear down the romance of childhood misery. If Boz, the English novelist, had lived in Budapest at this time, he would have lost one of his main themes after Bárczy's tenure as commissioner of education. After the razing of the old schools, even playing hookey from school lost its stature as a favorite pastime.

The name of István Bárczy, the broad-shouldered man of middling stature with the professorial hairstyle, will long live in the history of happy Budapest. "He should have been a bricklayer," opined those who were not necessarily elated by forever having to go around sidewalks closed off on account of another new school being built.

Well, you had to hand it to the former glee club member, he certainly loved the smell of mortar. He kept insisting that teaching and learning were only possible in clean, handsome, comfortable buildings, and started construction at a rate that assumed each Budapest mother would give birth to at least two future schoolchildren each year. His cheerful, roomy, well-ventilated, many-windowed red-brick buildings sprang up one after another, and seemed to smile at the passerby. Call them palaces if you will, palaces where healthy, happy people spent their lives, new edifices speedily built to invite even adults to acquire letters, science, culture. Such a red-brick structure attracted children in the outlying districts, as would a snowman in the middle of the park, with a carrot for a nose; called out to them as a storyteller, a magician, or a fairground clown would; it summoned children with welcoming arms, ready to embrace and to caress.

"Hmm, these children have it better than we did," the Budapest citizen reflected.

Philosophers have long ago observed that the purpose of human life is to raise one's children and to secure their future by teaching them, if possible, a livelihood.

Well, not everyone happens to share this view, for there will always be adults unwilling to forget the privations of their youth, the sufferings and miseries of their apprenticeship, and who therefore wish to inflict the same on their children, citing the Latin adage "The palm tree grows bearing a burden".

To refresh memories I will invoke some of the responses of contemporary citizens to Bárczy's proposal to build, in each district, seven or eight new elementary schools (seventeen in the Sixth District alone). "My school was so far I had to get up at the crack of dawn if I wanted to arrive by eight," the citizen would groan, adding proudly "...and still, I made it on my own!" Another reminisced that "in the good old days teachers had to earn their keep by teaching both morning and afternoon"; he (as a child) "took lunch (one slice of black bread!) to school, and the teacher did not leap up from his desk when the noontime bell signaled lunch hour. In those times the municipality saw to it that all the money paid to the teacher was money well spent. And anyhow, any old building would do for the few years you attended school..." "Bárczy was really building new schools not so much for the sake of the children who would take wing from the finest birdcage soon enough, but to provide splendid, luxurious palaces for teachers. Small wonder, when he used to be a teacher himself."

"He spends all our money on schools!" exclaimed the citizen, demanding that someone should "keep tabs on the city fathers' expenditures". "Why, even Óbuda has seven schools already, and children there don't even go to school after early spring because they have to work in the vineyards." "Teachers are lording it in the schools, why, some of them go about in tailcoats, and women teachers have enough free time to write novels. Back in our time, that was the sole prerogative of the Lord Lieutenant's wife."

No, the Budapest citizen was not wildly enthusiastic about Bárczy's building program. In those days whenever a new construction was started, the landlords from the neighborhood gathered at the sight to kibitz: "What will they think of next? How much rent will they charge? Who would be fool enough to move up to the fourth floor, or the fifth. No, you can't build Andrássy Avenue-style palaces in every street—where would the lower middle class and the poor people be able to afford the rent?"

The same kind of kibitzing would begin as soon as the mason laid the foundations for a new school.

"Weren't our children attending some school already? And where did we learn how to read and write? I don't see any increase in the business of midwives around here, but there's a new school built every day, it must be for the benefit of all those good-for-nothing teachers. Just so the city fathers can get their nieces a nice cushy teaching job."

Other viewpoints also surfaced in the critique of this "staggering" amount of construction.

"Did you notice how many new schools there are in the Sixth District? The city must pay to support seventeen schools there—of course, it's all because Vázsonyi is their representative. While Józsefváros, although it has the same number of people, gets only seven schools. Where's the justice in that?"

But Bárczy kept on building "as if every day was Christmas", as if the dedication of a new school afforded his greatest joy in life. "Some people are fanatical enough to think of building schools even in the Angyalföld district, where children have better things to do than attend school." The truth is that, since István Bárczy, the cause of education in the capital city has been taken far more seriously.

After Bárczy, Budapest teachers were no longer shocked when parents addressed them with respect, for they knew that their exceptional position entitled them to some prestige. In the roundabout thinking of marriage-brokers a Budapest teacher became almost as good a match as an official of the state, with a guarantee of lifelong security. Teachers grew accustomed to decent clothes, good housing, and educated society, for they were always welcome in the district club, and, if personable enough, received invitations to hospitable middle-class homes where the parents would introduce to them their school-age child. Individual schools began to compete in the quality of instruction, vying with each other to claim the best students, teachers, and headmasters. After Bárczy took over, gone were the old-style teachers who started as village schoolmasters and came to Budapest to become anarchists

113

out of frustration. (Pista Sacher's earlier eloquence in the salons was thus not wasted.) Teachers awoke to the highest desideratum of human existence, which is a healthy amount of ambition. To shine, to excel among the thousand teachers at seventy-nine different schools. The Érsek Street elementary school in the Terézváros district was in pedagogical competition with the Erdély Street school in distant Józsefváros. "Bíró Street has the best faculty," some citizens proclaimed. Others swore by Felsőerdősor. Suddenly people paid serious attention even to oddballs such as Jakab Gábel, who could teach an illiterate soldier how to read in a few hours.

And the "poor teaching staff", in the person of the woman teacher, no longer cursed the day as she hurried to work, although previously a foggy autumn day would have made her wish for an outbreak of influenza so she could have a day off. She became more self-confident once the raging, potbellied headmasters became a vanishing species. She no longer had to depend on the whims of a single individual, for she could make herself heard at the school council. The democratic spirit introduced by Bárczy was first registered by the women who taught, for the simple reason that women are more intelligent than men. And the democratic teaching staff proved more understanding and empathetic with the girls under their tutelage; long-suppressed ambitions resurfaced to be "the best teacher" in town... And if this teacher now felt like writing, her ideal was no longer some aristocratic lady author, but Selma Lagerlöf.

Gone from the new school, along with the ignorant, jailer-style headmaster, was the figure of the janitor who had threatened pupils with his broomstick. Parents now knew that their complaints would be heard if their children were abused at school.

"Ah, they used to cane us at school!" sighed the citizen, a relic of former days. "The teacher would slap us... And still..."

Before the old-fashioned citizen had a chance to finish his say, the Lord Mayor of Budapest drummed a new slogan into his ear: "Next we are building inexpensive housing for poor people!"

"Why couldn't Bárczy become a bricklayer?" the old Budapest citizen grumbled, to himself.

(17 January, 1926)

The Streets of St. Theresa

1.

[...]In those days [1905] Francis Joseph was the ruler of the land; the increases in compound interest made the burghers' sleep restful at night; at the store the greatest upheaval might be the hiring of a new assistant when the old one opened up his own business; people did not work past retirement age and their pensions were as secure as if Rothschild himself had guaranteed them; the citizen knew precisely how much he had to pay in taxes and the exact price of a pair of new trousers, as well as how much he would end up saving at the end of the month and what he would do with his savings. There was enough money around to pay for fine funeral monuments and statues to commemorate the great men of the nation.

[...]

One writer with a penchant for cynicism claimed that the Budapest citizen became susceptible to democratic notions because he had no physical shortcomings, and thus he had time to exercise his mind as well. An even more cynical commentator deemed that the first democrats in Budapest were those folks who had waited in vain for some kind of medal or decoration from the king, and, frustrated by the hopeless wait, gladly espoused the newly arrived, loudly proclaimed democratic ideas. I, however, am of the opinion (having walked about town in those days with eyes wide open) that the democratic movement reached Budapest, like waves beating on a shore, precisely when the time was ripe.

The slogans of the new doctrine began to be trumpeted on the streets of Terézváros, Saint Theresa's district, with the urgency of a fire-engine speeding towards a burning house. By the gentle lamplight of the family circle the young generation debated with the old; the father, dubbed behind his back "an old government-supporter", argued with the son, who proudly claimed to be a democrat. We must admit that the new school of thought greatly increased the citizen's self-esteem, above all that of the so-called petty bourgeois, who, chiefly in the district named after St. Theresa, struggled with daily cares, enjoyed small pleasures, lived and died without ever being led by any higher ideals. This petty bourgeoisie of Budapest was as ripe for new ideals as those simple fishermen of Galilee once upon a time.

So we had the opportunity to be on hand, around the tower of St. Theresa's Church, when the anonymous and hitherto unknown Budapest petty bourgeoisie scored its first exhilarating triumph.[...] Once, in one of my novels, I had traveled about in a red coach, visiting distant horizons and lives. Now I am going to take a quiet, meditative stroll on the streets of St. Theresa, where I believe we shall find a few interesting sights.

2.

Árpád the Swordbearer, the election campaign manager who had been an animal tamer for a while and as such had a penchant for fantastic notions (for example, why can't people be trained just like lions?) often stood on the balcony of the steeple of St. Theresa's, from where he could survey his district. He paid no attention to the dome of the Basilica, taller even than St. Theresa's, rising to the West, for that belonged to another district. In fact he did not even like to waste a glance at the far side of Király Street (which zigzagged like a succession of Z's) beneath St. Theresa's, because that side belonged to the Erzsébetváros district. From that side of the street, from the Pekáry House, bearing a dragon head on the corner, and the Red Cat with its loud brass band, rowdy revelers were taken to the Seventh District police precinct. Terézváros, his own Sixth District, began here at Schreiber's coffeehouse (which boasted a ladies' band), and extended, along Nagymező Street, all the way to Schön's coffeehouse (also with its ladies' band) where the best goose liver was served at dawn, thanks to potbellied Uncle Schön's patronage. Between these two coffeehouses, these two Terézváros outposts, one could see many wonders by looking around from the tower. No, the other districts really did not matter, thought Árpád the Swordbearer as he stood on the balcony of St. Theresa's Church.

"We must make the citizens proud of residing in Terézváros!" exclaimed the Swordbearer, who intended to be a factor in municipal politics, being a restless man devoted to noisemaking.

116

"The Terézváros citizen has everything in the world", the former animal trainer would vociferate in the summer on the terrace of the Abbázia coffee-house, where in those days the loudest and most assertive colloquies could be heard in Budapest." Take for instance the buildings on Andrássy Avenue, these beautiful modern palaces so well built by old Lechner. If you live in one of them, why, you've got credit in this entire district. You have no worries about furniture, tailor's or shoemaker's bills; the butcher's boy whistles as he brings up your order on the service stairs, as if the money paid on Andrássy Avenue were better than elsewhere. At night you don't have to stumble around in the dark. The street lamps give a bright light, the shopkeepers keep their window displays brilliantly lit until midnight, and the stairways are lit up as if there were a ball somewhere every night. No, gentlemen, the citizens of Terézváros have no grounds for complaint.

"As for the shopkeepers of the district, they are the best in all of Europe. Once you enter a store on Király Street you cannot leave without a purchase. Why, if he has to, the storekeeper will give you the goods for free, or at least on credit. Once I found myself buying thirty suspenders in a local shop, although I entered without intending to buy any. Another time, in a small jewelry store no bigger than a boudoir, I had to purchase silver and gold keepsakes for my whole family. On credit, naturally. [...]

"But the ladies of Terézváros, oh God! They are the most educated in all of Hungary. The girls can attend the best girls' schools, either Janka Zirzen's, or the upper school on Andrássy Avenue, which Gyula Wlassics has gradually converted into a girls' high school. Our district has the most elementary schools as well as girls' middle schools. The finest girls' schools are on Bajza, Felsőerdősor, Üteg Streets and Váci Boulevard. Their graduates are trained to be teachers, who will be able to hold their own in the best of company. The Inner City and Lipótváros districts each have only one girls' school; well, you can tell by the ladies who reside there. And we also have two commercial academies for women. It must be an angelic fate to be born a woman in the Terézváros district."
[...]

Having loudly proclaimed his municipal views, the former animal trainer, like a skilled stump orator, changed his tune.

"But not even the citizens of St. Theresa's district are exempt from the fate of growing old and infirm, a fate I hope will be delayed as long as possible for the worthy citizens.

117

"Although we cannot boast a St. Roch's or St. John's, or a Red Cross where large numbers of the sick can be accommodated, we do have an internationally famous Jewish Hospital, supported by the Israelite community. A native of Terézváros could not wish for a better place. But I've said enough, for I see the prominent nose of Vilmos Vázsonyi approaching along the boulevard. He will give you the latest news in local politics."

3.

Bakers always like to take part in public affairs, and this held true in Terézváros as well. Old Man Glasner, whose aromatic shop was the largest among the bakers of the district, grumbled as he strolled past the Abbázia coffeehouse on his way home from Radocza's club on Andrássy Avenue.

"There's that Vázsonyi again, keeping the citizenry up late with his talk," the old baker muttered to himself. Being a proper tradesman he preferred to espouse the ideas of the Liberal Party.

Bessenyei, proprietor of the butcher's shop in the same building on Andrássy Avenue that housed Radocza's club, likewise cast angry, bulging eyes in the direction of the Abbázia.

"All these young lawyers are good for is to complain about the price of Prague ham. That's the extent of their politics. So they should stay away from Prague ham," groused the owner after closing his shop. He easily lost his temper when customers started to bargain about prices.

But out of sheer curiosity old Brauch, the pork-butcher from Nagymező Street, peeked in at the windows of the coffeehouse, although his reputation was founded on offering the lowest prices around. But he, too, shook his head on seeing that young attorney with the Cyrano nose pounding the table inside with youthful ardor.

"The price of pork is going to go up!" worried Mr. Brauch.

[...]Inside sat that young man who had elicited such anxiously disapproving looks from the older citizenry enjoying a certain measure of financial security, while on him were pinned the hopes of small retailers, who in their shops on the side streets could only skim through the daily paper between customers; the storekeepers sitting on stacks of kindling in front of their wood and coal shops, bitterly convinced that hard winters were a thing of the past; shoemakers, who hoped to re-sole each shoe that came their way; fruit vendors who loved street processions because they sold more plums; and those small-time tenants all over the district who hastened home at night before gate-closing for fear of having to confront the concierge who usually delivered rude messages from the landlord... Nameless individuals such as these, people whom no one keeps track of in town, except maybe once in a decade when the census is taken—these were the folks for whom the name of Vázsonyi brought a gleam of hope to their eyes. This was the name cited by Strasser, the installment salesman, who told his clients that we, as Hungarians, should vote for Vázsonyi; also Horváth, the cheese salesman, who did not bother with Király Street in the summertime, for it smelled there as if every store had a plentiful supply of cheese; Uncle Bauer, the bailiff from Óbuda, who consoled the clients in his difficult trade with the promise that if the Democrats won the law would be more lenient...and the umbrella repairmen, who could be seen only on rainy days, when everyone was already soaked to the skin anyway...or those little tailors who patched hopeless trousers from morning till night, until they ripped again...or owners of coffeeshops who had leisure enough to read the whole paper...and chimney sweeps, with whom not even Mihály Táncsics, the first Hungarian Democrat, would ever shake hands.

It was humble folks such as these who first learned Vázsonyi's name, and who would, from time to time, check out its bearer through the windows of his favorite coffeehouse. Yes, there he sat, his fellow citizens could be sure of that. As we have said, he had a large and expressive nose à la Cyrano, but other than that nothing about him resembled the adventurous native of Gascogne. [...] He sat in the coffeehouse and delivered murderous gibes about those who refused him their support or who downright opposed him. It was obvious that this man would either make himself a great deal of enemies or else would have many friends. But the habitués at Radocza's club waved him off with a confident gesture: "In our district small-time grocers don't account for much. Landlords have the upper hand."

4.

The Terézváros district street fair, held on a fine, early autumn day, was always a noteworthy event in Budapest. The crates that Beliczay the candlemaker would bring to his tent on Nagymező Street were larger than those he took to any other fair. For in the evening the candles would be lit until midnight in every tent: the gingerbread makers', knife grinders', fruit sellers', and all the bazaar booths. An old-time, municipal park-like atmosphere took over in front of St. Theresa's Church, complete with swings and carousels... A vast throng would stumble amidst the taut ropes around the tents, including every pretty girl of the district; every young man worth his salt has had an amorous adventure at St. Theresa's Feast.

Well, it was at one of these Terézváros fairs that Árpád the Swordbearer, animal trainer and election manager, first unfurled the tricolor flag that has always signaled election time. The white field of the flag carried the following inscription: Long Live Dr. Vilmos Vázsonyi!

If memory serves me well this event occurred near the tent of Beliczay the candlemaker, who was not a resident of this district but hailed from neighboring Erzsébetváros. Perhaps for this very reason Mr. Beliczay cared not a whit about which candidate the Swordbearer was promoting in Terézváros. In those days the soul of each Budapest district was as remote from the next one as if they were islands in the ocean. The Swordbearer calmly piled some empty crates one on top of the other. The carousel bells were ringing in the neighborhood as frantically as if this were to be the last fair in the capital. The paper trumpets squealed in an attempt to console the impoverished citizens loitering around the tents. Whistles screeched, rattles rattled, drums rolled and harmonicas took turns one after the other. The women acted giddily, the way they like to be at the fair, having brought their pent-up emotions from side streets, lit by gas lamps, that yawned with boredom and ennui. The gallants gallivanting in the crowd no longer examined the assembly through lorgnettes but resorted to the monocle, which was the latest rage. The mild, potbellied burgher stood gawking at the tumult just as he had in medieval times when his pocket had first been picked by a cutpurse. The bawling voice of the clown promised, as ever, hair-raising sights to visitors to his tent. The waists of the vendors were bent like fruit-pickers' by the weight of the accumulated coins in their apron pockets. It was a mild autumn afternoon. The shadow cast by St. Theresa's tower on the pink clouds was as hefty as most women of the district.

In this multitude Árpád the Swordbearer was in his element; after all, he used to prefer to handle rattlesnakes only in front of large crowds in his booth at the Municipal Park. So now he clambered up on top of his pile of crates and waved the flag as if he wanted to conquer the entirety of this Terézváros fair. "Long Live Dr. Vilmos Vázsonyi", the flag proclaimed for the benefit of the giggling, bargaining crowds rolling down the length of Nagymező Street, tired by all the spectacles; for the women nibbling gingerbread, the kibitzers sniffing around the tents that sold roast goose, as well as for those who could afford to have the right chunk of barbecue weighed out on a slice of bread from the fast-food booths set up in Érsek Street.

[...]Well, in the cloister-like reserve of this little side street one day soon there would be a tumult to surpass any Terézváros street fair. In this usually quiet street a palisade was erected as in some great county fair where the bulls have to be kept away from the cows. On the Nagymező Street side of this fence milled all those who wanted the attorney with the prominent nose as their district representative, and the other side was reserved for those who insisted on the incumbent, János Radocza, whose dome was beginning to go bald. The school on Érsek Street was the designated polling station where the two groups of voters now lined up: on one side, the landlords whose tenants dreaded meeting them; the wholesalers, who threatened the retailers with cutting off their credit; all those pillars of society whom everyone was eager to greet politely on the street...

But on this side of the palisade, where the archangels of St. Theresa's, the stone saints and otherworldly potentates watch over the poor people who cross themselves, stand all those who sigh with the deepest sighs that come straight from the heart; those who, when they hang their worry-laden heads do so not just to deceive the tax assessors, and who, when they dare to smile on a holiday, regret it for weeks. For how can a man be cheerful when he has nothing else to his name other than a large family? Here are the forlorn shoemakers from Aréna Road, who hammer wooden pegs into boots without any particular hopes; the small grocers from Bajnok Street who always pay the price when some long-time tenant moves from their street; the laundresses from Felsőerdősor who have no time to put on a fresh blouse; the little tailors from Gömb Street, who have resigned themselves to a shortage of clients; and the coal dealers from Izabella Street of the lovely name, who always complain that winter comes much later to their completely built-in street than, say, to outer Andrássy Avenue; and from Szív Street all the small tavern proprietors who joined the opposition because of the severity of police inspectors; the shopkeepers from Váci Boulevard who look down on those from the opposite side of the street belonging to the Lipotváros district, for they were obliged to vote for the government-party candidate... And with that, the fate of the election was just about decided.

Never had there been a street fair like this one in Terézváros. The stone dragon's head on the balcony, having guarded the Pekáry House for a century, now dropped off in panic; luckily no one was injured by its half-ton weight. The prophets and saints guarding St. Theresa'a Church turned to stone watching the hubbub down below, where instead of the pious chants of yore now rose the strains of the election song:

> ...He's the right one,
> a real Democrat and a true patriot.

This was sung in honor of the young attorney from the Theresa District, stormily and cheerfully, whenever the campaign managers appeared with loud news of the election in Érsek Street.

5.

Even though Vázsonyi was elected as representative from the Theresa District—why, greater miracles have happened before, griped the sour old Liberals—streets and buildings refused to move from their places, the tower of St. Theresa's did not collapse, nor did the landlords receive beatings from their tenants, as had been feared in the club on Andrássy Avenue. [...]

"These Democrats have grown awfully insolent. Now they have their own daily paper. One of these days they won't even give us the time of day..."

There was some truth in this comment made at the Liberal Club table, for all over town it could be observed that the coal merchants sitting on stacks of firewood in front of their stores were no longer reading Lajos Bródy's paper, The Journal, and Képes Budapest [Illustrated Budapest] had also lost its public; well-dressed young men were carrying brochures under their arms to distribute to the so-called Democrats all over town. Új Század [New Century] was the name of these brochures, edited by Dr. Lajos Báttaszéki, not very fortuitously. This old editor wanted to keep his periodical at an academic level that proved incomprehensible for the dry cleaner or grocer who was otherwise ready to

122

go through fire for the Democratic ideal. When old Báttaszéki was reproached for this, the saintly editor shrugged: "Alas, I am not able to write on a commercial level. That was why my former paper failed in Békéscsaba..."

Well, New Century did not take long to kick the bucket, even though it was just starting a series of articles on democratic movements in ancient history...

This was when the Budapest Democrats, ever active and eager, launched their new daily, A Polgár [The Citizen], with its editorial offices on Nagymező Street.

For they had to have a press organ. As anyone with any sense could realize even then, it was not without reason that Tihamér Kohányi, dressed in traditional ceremonial Hungarian outfit, was touring the United States at the time for the benefit of the Hungarian press. Likewise, back here in Hungary, Gresham Insurance and the publishers of Egyetértés [Concord] had their reasons for sending Ferenc Kossuth on national tours. So the Democrats, whose ideals had recently done so well, thought they would be able to support a newspaper that would reassure the Budapest faithful they had nothing to fear as long as they subscribed.

The Budapest Democrats could be confident all of a sudden, observing how their youthful ardor had the old-fashioned bourgeois on the run, retiring behind the screens of impotent mockery and feeble scorn instead of giving battle in the open field... Pepi Wolfner, the book publisher on Andrássy Avenue, still strolled down the sidewalk with the dignified bearing of a Venetian senator on his pre-prandial promenade, but now for health reasons he would do so with his head bare, holding his hat in his hand so that he would not have to greet people, since the old-time political machine of the Sixth District had failed so ignominiously at the elections. And the newfangled Democrats could hug and pump each other's hands amidst loud greetings as if they were still preparing for election speeches on Andrássy Avenue—nonetheless they did not succeed in quite conquering the city. The goose-dealer on outer Andrássy Avenue, and the butchers, still saved their best cuts for their former customers, no matter how loudly Vilmos Vázsonyi's speeches were applauded. And in the neighborhood of Bajza Street, have the concierges, grocers and tenants ever really changed their ways? The concierge, even if he secretly voted for the Democrats, still kisses the hands of the tenants; the delicacies are still supplied by the large Inner City markets that deliver supper ordered by telephone and willingly provide credit. In the salons the word "Democrat" is still pronounced with a certain overtone... "He's a Democrat," says the society

123

lady of her discarded lover, or the bourgeois referring to a dropped acquaintance. A Democrat could be the baker's delivery boy who brings the fresh pastry for breakfast, or the domestics' employment agent (if he dared to be); the barker at the fair could be a Democrat, or even that misguided young lawyer Vázsonyi, who seemed destined for better things with all his brains...

But here on Andrássy Avenue, where a certain upper-crust restraint is still observed, one can't really expect a Baron Géza Fejérváry, Grand Master of the Order of Maria Theresa, or for that matter even the industrial baron Miksa Schiffer, suddenly to just join up with the Democrats.

Thus in St. Theresa's district the Democrats, in principle, triumphed, but remained as poor as back in the days when enthusiastic members offered up their penny-ante winnings for party funds. The periodical *Új Század* gave place to *A Polgár*, to see what it would be able to squeeze out of the right-minded petty-bourgeois of the district. Spirited young journalists conferred till the wee hours about what they should write so that the grocer on Aradi Street would not only cheer Vázsonyi but also pay for a subscription to the party newspaper. They sent out canvassers for ads, but these returned with sweaty brows to report that the wholesalers refused to advertise in the Democrats' paper, for the Democrats were not their clients anyway. In his coffeehouse Vázsonyi waxed perhaps even more satirical than ever before. The gibes he now made would have frightened off some of the meeker provincials. But the Budapest folks knew he acted that way only because he could not afford to finance his party's newspaper. This is how matters stood for the Budapest Democrats after that memorable Terézváros street fair, when the habitués at the marble tables of the Abbázia would have liked to believe that they had conquered the whole world.

6.

[...]If you had walked each morning down the length of noisy Theresa Boulevard, and had seen every day the Cyrano of Theresa District as he made his way on foot from his law offices toward the banks of the Danube and the House of Parliament (in those days no attempt was ever made against him, that only happened later, after he started going by automobile)...you could testify that the streets of St. Theresa have undergone great changes over the past decades.

For instance, that young attorney who was once upon a time chaffed—for in those years of the distant past jokes were made in good spirit and were not taken with such bloody seriousness: some called him "the Pope of Theresa District", others "The Rabbi of Theresa", or "The Tancred of Theresa", or "Saint Theresa's Jew", or "The Wise Man of Theresa", just as once upon a time Ferenc Deák had been dubbed "the nation's wise man"—oh, that attorney with the prominent nose after a while no longer walked the streets so that every wood and coal dealer could shake his hand on the way, the shopkeepers' hefty wives greet him from the doorway, and each citizen wish him a good morning. No, the once pedestrian representative of the district now rode in an automobile, and a ministerial one at that. [...]

The quondam young lawyer was now a minister, unprecedented in the history of the Jews: a Minister of Justice, or, as the anglophiles put it, "Lord Chancellor". Therefore that particular government automobile appeared on Teréz Boulevard, which, ever since Kálmán Tisza's famous pair of grays in the last of the ministerial fiacres, has been changing its passengers so frequently. [...] No, not even the most daring astrologer would have predicted that the road from St. Theresa's streets would lead all the way to Francis Joseph's chambers, the title of Excellency, the halls of the Ministry, and the velvet seat that was one of the highest offices in the land. Árpád the Swordbearer and the other early Democrats who, out of eccentricity, defiance, or more likely sheer spite rather than the force of their convictions, joined the flag unfurled at the Terézváros street fair, did not live to see this final great turn in the road. They were Aarons, who tired upon reaching the promised land...

But the stone saints and guardian angels on St. Theresa's Church, who always watch over the faithful of this district, lived to see the great turning, this never-imagined triumph of Democratic ideals. "One must believe!" echoes the remembrance of former days.

Whatever your religion, denomination or party, there is one thing that will bank the twisting and turning roads of fate, and that is an honest faith. As may be seen from the example of the Cyrano of Theresa District.

(16 January–20 February, 1926)

Kossuth's Son

What do you see in the expression on your face, you, nineteenth-century Hungarian, when you glance at photographs of yourself thirty-odd years ago, having dug them up among the odds and ends of the past?

Glorious youth, triumphant young manhood radiates contentment on that face from your long-gone past—for that was around the time when "Francis Joseph gave permission" for the sons of Kossuth, the saintly, reclusive exile of Turin, to return to Hungary...

We must return to our youth thirty years ago to recall that marvelous feeling which for a while added a sparkle to daily talk in Hungary, making all hearts beat faster, and kindling historical lamps in eyes that had grown dull. For by then most hearts had come to resemble our springtime farmlands, accustomed to producing the predictable profit thanks to the unstinting use of fertilizers by the thorough, purposeful husbandry of the Liberal Party, until it seemed that old Lajos Madarász remained all alone on the far left, no one else wanting any part of the Independence Party ideals, of March 1848 and the dethronement at Debrecen... The Athenaeum Press was selling fewer and fewer copies of Kossuth's books, his memoirs from exile... Not even in dyed-in-the-wool Independence districts were death-threats issued any longer to supporters of the government-party candidate... Dániel Irányi, the last Hungarian patriot, was nearing his end, and soon he would be dead in Nyíregyháza, the last stronghold of Hungarian Independence... Sickly and languishing was the great oak planted by our Prince Ferenc Rákóczi, under whose boughs the Hungarians of old instructed the younger generations in the sacred teachings of independence... When Lajos Kossuth breathed his last, and the Hungarian of the Century returned to meet his maker, he sent out a sigh that turned into a roaring wind, a springtime tempest as it reached his beloved homeland. Now the Hungarian soil shakes itself, after having been lulled by the bewitching round of *csárdás* danced by Gyula Andrássy; the Budapest asphalt quakes, after having been rolled smooth and rid of any revolutionary wrinkles under the boot heels of Kálmán Tisza. This spring, next to the blond maidenhair fern of the Hungarian meadow lands there spreads a melancholy veil of mourning; instead of violets the soil sprouts black boutonnieres, and a mighty expansion stretches the chests of those imperial-style coats so fashionable in Hungary among the generation that came after the Coronation. Kossuth may be dead, but his sons are coming home.

Ferenc Kossuth spoke an idiom resembling that of an encyclopedia translated from English by someone using a not always reliable dictionary.

As a cub reporter I heard him speak at the "Golden Bull" in Debrecen, on his nationwide tour. After the speech Károly Rácz, the blond-haired Gypsy violinist, had his band strike up, instead of the national anthem, the popular song of lament that goes "Yoi, that German's such a rascal...". While Lord Lieutenant Count Dégenfeld cast a look of consternation toward the musicians, the Budapest journalists who had accompanied Ferenc Kossuth on his tour were already kicking their chairs away in their rush to the telegraph office, with Győző Pichler leading the charge, shaking his reddish lion's mane[...] For an earth-shaking event had just taken place in Debrecen at the "Golden Bull": after Ferenc Kossuth's toast of loyalty to the Crown, the Gypsy band had struck up, instead of the national anthem, a song that harked back to the agonizing imprisonment of revolutionary patriots at Kufstein and Olmütz.

We provincials, however (with the one exception of the Lord Lieutenant), would never have dreamed, in our mellow post-prandial glow, that some crotchety old night editor sitting at a desk in Budapest could magnify into a scandal of international magnitude the mere fact of a Gypsy band playing "Yoi, that German's such a rascal..." at the banquet for Kossuth. After all, one heard this song played during the mildest entertainments, where not a hair on anyone's head would be hurt. No, the officers of the Dual Monarchy's army would no longer leap from their tables to rattle their swords when some carouser had the Gypsies play this tune, after the Rákóczi March and the Kossuth-song. Actually, the citizenry of Debrecen had resorted to duels under the severest conditions to dissuade these K.u.K. gentlemen from interfering with their merrymaking. Historians of Hungarian dueling still remember the name of Debrecen's mighty champion Mandel; local newspapermen such as Polczner and Gallovits would ask for satisfaction at the mere hint of a slight, and the blood of journalists and officers mingled freely on the Debrecen parade grounds.

So at the time the Gypsy band did not create much of a stir in the banquet hall of the "Golden Bull".[...] As for Ferenc Kossuth, he had not the least idea of what was implied by the song played by the Gypsy band after he concluded his toast.

Had Ferenc Kossuth arrived here incognito, on the rattling omnibus of the "Golden Bull", he would not have stood out among the other guests at the hotel. [...] Just as the innkeeper was able to recognize at a glance whether a guest required French mustard or preferred the horseradish from Pthrügy that could wake the dead, or craved red-hot paprika with his roast, in the same way the Gypsy bandleader could also guess what the guest's favorite song was. Why on earth did Károly Rácz think that the foreign-looking Ferenc Kossuth's song was "Yoi, that German..."?

For he was foreign-looking indeed; it was hard to believe he was the son of the Lajos Kossuth who reigned supreme in Hungarian patriots' dreams. (Indeed, old residents of Debrecen discovered no resemblance in the son to that soul-shaking phantom who had once upon a time, in the neighboring church of Nagytemplom, proclaimed the dethronement of the House of Habsburg.)

Even the cut of his clothes seemed foreign... Although the suit was made of fine-quality wool it appeared to have been purchased ready-made at some Milanese emporium. (Hungarian gentlemen in those days preferred to follow the London fashion in clothes.) [...]

His drooping mustache brought to mind one of those British colonial majors whose portraits could be seen in the London weeklies. His large, round, brown eyes recalled Italian ladies familiar from paintings that evoke the scent of orange groves and seaside *osterias*. [...]

Could he have heart trouble, I wondered, as I observed Ferenc Kossuth in that Debrecen inn, noticing the remarkably distended vein at the side of his neck, perhaps as a result of being unused to the extraordinary ovations he received each day. Could he be that new comet on our horizon that we had talked about so often at the house of my grandfather, the eldest Krúdy, who disdained both the smallpox vaccine and Pasteur's serum as possible cures for Hungary's gradual abandonment of the Independence Party's ideals? Could this man be the stardust that would cure all those inflamed, near-blind Hungarian eyes? Could he be the remedy for all our troubles? What had he brought with him from Italy? Was it one of Garibaldi's bloody shirt fragments, such as were peddled about in Hungary, or was it perhaps a chunk of radium to clarify the minds along the Danube and Tisza rivers? Would he be able to rejuvenate Hungarian hearts tired by the long wait, to make them beat again with a youthful throb? Was he a magician, an alchemist, or an agent? I watched him with the fiery eyes of young colts at springtime.

As I listened to him speaking, I wondered what language he thought in. [...] You could tell by his accent that he had lived abroad for a very long time. Although he did not commit any howlers, it was still obvious, from the speeches he gave during this first nationwide tour, that he had attended foreign schools and had gone to a university abroad, that he was widely read in foreign languages and had much international experience. But he was nowhere near the magician of the tongue that his father was. Still, he brought tears to the eyes of the old men who heard him here in the Hajdú and Nyírség regions.[...]

After Ferenc Kossuth's speech, what right did Károly Rácz have to play that song, so notorious, and heartfelt, since it had sprung up from the very soul of the nation?

That was the assignment of the day. Dueling swords, pens and minds were exercised over such questions not only in Debrecen but all over the country. Back in those days Hungarians had nothing better to do than to grapple over issues like that. So the war was on... Only Ferenc Kossuth was unaware of why everyone was embattled around him. He had never heard that mocking song at the house of his father, the grand old exile of Turin, although it would have been most appropriate there, of all places.

(The explanation of the band's peculiar musical choice was as follows: a local journalist, Gyula Rudnyánszky, had paid the Gypsies in advance to play that song...)

Two days later I met Ferenc Kossuth in Nyíregyháza—at my grandfather's residence.

Those who arranged Ferenc Kossuth's tour did so along the lines of the traditional rules of political campaigning. The pattern set by the electioneering candidates of former times established the model for Ferenc Kossuth's tour on his return to Hungary after the death of his father. After arriving at a provincial town he would pay his respects to the mayor and other local notables. He was most cordially received everywhere, although the womenfolk were not overly enthusiastic about him, for he never asked the hostess to take a turn around the dance floor, even though word had it that he was an eligible widower. Yet to achieve anything in Hungary you must first of all con-

130

quer the "distaff side" for your cause. At least that was the way of doing things whenever delegates ran for office. In the course of his nationwide tour not once did Ferenc Kossuth dance with the women, even though there were plenty of wasp-waisted maidens and matrons raring to be given a whirl. But Ferenc Kossuth, being a dignified and scholarly individual who, in addition, bore the burden of a great historic name, paid visits to men such as my grandfather in Nyíregyháza, men who were past being of any interest to women, save for one or two corpulent matrons who still hoped that, out of respect for past memories, the nonagenarian would be dotard enough to lead them to the altar.

But my old grandfather, in spite of his advanced age, still carried himself as straight as a pipe stem carved of Turkish cherry wood, and had been elected president of the 1848/49 Honvéd Association of Szabolcs county because, among the surviving former officers, he was the most accomplished at swearing.

"So, young man, how's it hanging?" he asked Ferenc Kossuth, when the latter paid his visit at this escutcheoned house, but refused to light up one of the cigars offered (even though this "Virginia" cigar had been smuggled from the special lot manufactured in Hungary for the personal consumption of Francis Joseph.)

My grandfather sat wearing his red-piped, ash gray housecoat with a tasseled red belt, as was the fashion among Hungarian gentlemen at the time. His outfit was completed by a pair of slippers and a Turkish fez, in honor of Abdul Kerim, the "Lion of Sebastopol", to whom a delegation of Hungarian youth had not long before presented a ceremonial sword.

My grandfather's eyes measured Ferenc Kossuth, who wore his usual suit. "Son, I do believe if you wore a traditional Hungarian-style outfit you could easily beat our incumbent representative, Miksa Beniczky."

Ferenc Kossuth announced that he had no intention of running for office in Nyíregyháza. "And why on earth not?" asked my grandfather, his eyes round with amazement. "Is it because Francis Joe won't allow you? 'Cause here in Nyíregyháza we do what we feel like. We're not afraid to let the world know that Kossuth's son is our representative, no matter what Francis Joseph says!"

Ferenc Kossuth gently proceeded to calm my grandfather. He explained that he did not want to pick a quarrel with Francis Joseph.

"That's too bad," the old man grumbled.

Ferenc Kossuth went on to explain how awkward it had been for him when the Budapest press created such a hullabaloo about a certain song being played by the Gypsy band in Debrecen. During this speech my grandfather just about chewed up his cigar. At its conclusion he leaned closer to his guest, eyes flashing, and asked, in a voice quavering with indignation: "Tell me, son, didn't you come home to start a revolution?!"

His hands seized the hand of the younger Kossuth.

"Peace must prevail—my father made that clear in his messages," Ferenc Kossuth replied.

In the meantime the local choral society, tracking Kossuth's itinerary, had quietly assembled under the windows of the house on Orosi Street and, at a signal from the leader, Santroch, broke into the old revolutionary recruiting song that begins "Lajos Kossuth sent a message..." The watchmaker Mayer, who would be crowned the nation's top basso at the Fiume singing competition, was leaning against an acacia tree while his voice descended deeper than any cellar in town. The tenor Kubacska took delight in making the windowpanes rattle in their frames. Townspeople flocked from near and far, women left off kneading the bread dough and stood with their children out at the front gate to see the famous man.

In his room, the air thick with cigar smoke, my grandfather still clutched Ferenc Kossuth's hand while he asked him, in a voice on the verge of tears: "So there won't be a revolution in Hungary?"

(29 March, 1925)

1. Gyula Krúdy with his son Ádám,
   Budapest, 1908

2. Market place in old Pest
   around 1890

1.

2.

1.

2.

1. Baron Frigyes Podmaniczky
    around 1870
    Photo by Borsos and Doctor

2. Gábor Baross around 1875

3. Ferenc Kossuth around 1900
    Photo by Mai and Co.

3.

1.

2.

3.

1. Francis Joseph I in 1898
   Photo by Károly Koller

2. István Tisza around 1915
   Photo by Szenes

3. Mihály Károlyi in the 1910s
   Photo by Erzsi Landau

1.   2.

1. István Bárczy around 1920

2. Miklós Szemere in 1896

3. Endre Ady in 1908
   Photo by Aladár Székely   3.

Photographs by courtesy of the Hungarian National Museum

Francis Joseph's Wine

"Our old king stays in such good health because he drinks a bottle of Tokaj wine each day", they used to say in Hungary, back when Francis Joseph, in the course of his long reign, became the stuff of so many anecdotes, fabulous tales, and legends. (In Hungary even in our day a tall tale does more to establish a reputation than years of hard work.)

Well, let's take a look at this "Tokaj wine" which, along with our Gypsies, has for centuries spread the fame of Hungary the world over.

Indeed, Francis Joseph owned a wine cellar in the Hegyalja region: a cellar of such size that a pair of carts, each drawn by four oxen, could easily pass each other under those arcaded vaults. There were hogsheads in there so large that they could not be moved: coopers had had to build them stave by stave on the spot. Of course, there were also smaller kegs, such as those used by travelers to warm their feet in sleds on long journeys for which flasks would not suffice. And yes, the barrels were all filled with wine of a world-renowned vintage. But real Tokaj wine does not like to be cooped up in casks for long, because there it cannot receive the meticulous care it has come to expect over the centuries. This wine prefers to reside in a special kind of bottle that is not quite half a liter but more than four deciliters. In its youth, after its union with the wine, the bottle is virginal, almost colorless; but with the passage of years, while the wine waits as silently under its seal as a genie in the *Arabian Nights*, the bottle grows tawny and darkens as it ages, like a tree trunk left behind by the woodsman's ax or a man who somehow manages to evade death. Spider's webs love such a bottle of Tokaj wine and will seek it out in the most obscure corner of the cellar, to claim fame for their insubstantial wisps by settling on such a bottle. (Old László Mezőssy, himself a Tokaj wine-grower, was most jealous of Francis Joseph's wines and insisted that stewards in the royal wine cellar bred spiders on purpose.) When the bottle reached the right age and acquired the appropriate patina of bygone years it would set out on its journey around the world, like some eccentric old man who refuses to die at home and keeps traveling to dodge death. Francis

133

Joseph's wine went on to Gödöllő, Buda, Vienna—but its finest travels came around Christmastime, when bottles were sent as presents to foreign princely courts. Francis Joseph, who was not without reason called "Europe's foremost gentleman", kept track of those he owed a favor. In the Lord Chamberlain's office (as legend has it) there was one clerk of bibulous visage whose sole task all year long was to make up the list of those personages who would be sent Christmas presents of wine from the Hungarian king's own preserve. Francis Joseph would put on his eyeglasses when this list was handed to him as November came around. While he rarely emended state documents, on this important list he always found something to change—mostly by adding more names.

Now that scholars are doing research in the Imperial Archives and turning up more and more documents in Francis Joseph's handwriting—his barbed, army officer-style script still show after the passage of nearly a century, the influence of the captain of the Imperial army who had taught Francis Joseph to write—a manuscript-collector has acquired one of these Christmas-present lists that bears, in addition to the rotund letters of the ruby-nosed clerk, Francis Joseph's annotations specifying the personages who must not be omitted from the round of wine shipments. Naturally Queen Victoria, the grande dame of England, occupies first place among those who must receive a sample of Francis Joseph's wine. The "grand old lady's" life span had to be prolonged at all costs, for her survival was a guarantee of continued European security. (Actually, no one would have supposed the Prince of Wales to be disposed to carry on a lengthy war, he who had not long before been tossing champagne bottles while sampling Vienna and Budapest nightlife under the guidance of Colonel of the Guards Esterházy.) Also receiving wine was Pope Leo XIII, since the King of Hungary owed eternal gratitude to His Holiness for the Crown of St. Stephen. The king's wicker baskets, made by wickerwork specialists for bottles of Tokaj wine out of white osier with colored withies forming the Hungarian coat of arms, were sent by priority diplomatic pouch to distant St. Petersburg to the czar of all the Russias, for Hungarian physicians had long known that Tokaj wine was the best cure for the Siberian flu. So much for the kings and princes on the secretary's list for the annual distribution of wine (old László Mezőssy, in his capacity as wine merchant, oft bemoaned the fact that he was unable to compete with Francis Joseph in the lavishness of these promotional gift packages); let us now see who, among the Hungarians, received these signs of royal attention. First on the list of Hungarians was Baron Géza Fejérváry, about whom it was rumored that he had permission to be seated in the Royal Presence, as an old soldier who had lost the resilience of his legs on the battlefield. According to the list a shipment of wine was sent to Kolos Vaszary, the Esztergom primate, as well as to the other Hungarian cardinal, Lőrinc Schlauch, bishop of Nagyvárad. (Although popular wisdom had it that Francis Joseph's wine cellars could not measure up to the quality of the most reverend prelate's, these gifts of wine were nonetheless gladly welcomed by the episcopal household.) As long as Kálmán Tisza was alive, the king's Christmas baskets never failed to arrive at the Geszt manor, and likewise at Kismarton, addressed to Prince Esterházy, although it was common knowledge that this gentleman had the grandest vineyards in Badacsony. (But it made no difference; the pope would send golden roses to queens, although they possessed more gold than the Vatican. Even so did Francis Joseph favor his faithful followers with wine.) Among the Knights of the Golden Fleece Count Nándor Zichy received his Christmas wine along with all the archdukes.

We gain a closer glimpse of Francis Joseph's figure, which has by now assumed mythological proportions, when we read, added onto the list in the royal hand, the name of the Unitarian bishop of Transylvania, who also happened to be called Francis Joseph. And among those honored by the gift of wine we also find a woman's name, written in Francis Joseph's hand: that of Frau Katherine v. Kiss-Schratt—who is none other than the renowned entertainer Katherine Schratt herself.

Thus it becomes perfectly comprehensible why old László Mezőssy (who never went on a visit without sticking a few bottles of his own home-produced Tokaj wine inside the lining of his fur coat) would complain back home in Nyíregyháza: "Now what am I supposed to do with my wines? I don't have the wealth of my neighbor, Francis Joseph, to give away my Tokaj left, right and center. I must sell my wines to Polish Jews in kaftans, who never receive free samples from the king. This is what Francis Joseph forces me to do..."

(Let me add that nobody felt worried on László Mezőssy's account that his chagrin over F. J. would prove fatal, as was often the case with otherwise healthy Hungarian gentlemen in the old days, over whom death seemed to have no dominion. Why, he was older, and in ruddier health, than Francis Joseph himself; the Szabolcs county physician Andris Jósa kept his cheeks rosier than the king's were kept by the court physician Kerzl. Not even influenza bothered Mezőssy, as it did the owner of the neighboring vineyard. At seventy-five he remarried and his youngest son, Béla Mezössy, eventually became Hungary's Minister of Agriculture. In the old days our countrymen who were approaching their seventh and eighth decades generally compared their age to one of two men. The first was Lajos Kossuth, "the hermit of Turin", and the other was Francis Joseph. As long as Kossuth the nonagenarian remained alive, his surviving contemporaries could rest at ease. Likewise, Francis Joseph had his coevals who, as a peculiarity of their old age, tended to fall in line with Francis Joseph's state of health. It was said of Géza Fejérváry that he would at once take to his bed in his Andrássy Avenue villa in Budapest when he read in *Pester Lloyd* the news that, with the early onset of winter in the Viennese Burg, Francis Joseph had caught his annual cold. And what about all those invisible legions of Hungarians who were the same age as Francis Joseph but survived him? No telling all their worries, anxieties, and complaints when their renowned contemporary breathed his last at Schönbrunn...)

In clear weather one mountain is visible from the Nyírség region: the Kopasz at Tokaj, which, like a benevolent creature, appears to have slipped away from the company of its grim confreres just to please the Hungarians of the lowlands, who would otherwise never have known what a mountain looked like.

Kopasz is indeed as bald as its name would indicate, and the students, tourists, and merry picnickers who climb its steep paths think they can see from the rocky mountaintop as far as the twin towers of distant Debrecen. But back in Francis Joseph's time, before we got acquainted with the vine-pest phylloxera, the sides of Kopasz were decked out in the finest green skirts in all of Hungary. It was a more precious vestment than that worn by the Badacsony mountain, on whose top the bishop of Veszprém planted a stone cross as solace for storm-tossed fishermen on Lake Balaton, and more sublime than Gellért's Hill, on whose rocks Professor Kerékjártó was the last to harvest the "Gellérthegyi Hand-Picked", as the vintage was described in golden letters in the old catalogue of the Royal Hungarian model wine cellar. In the minds of our countrymen the Kopasz mountaintop rose higher than even the Lomnitz peak in the Carpathians, for it stood for a point of national pride, the wine of Tokaj. It was truly a royal pastime to own a vineyard in Tokaj. It was costlier than most other pastimes, for the vines diminished year by year; not even old László Mezőssy could find a remedy against the devastation, although this merry old rascal's prime preoccupation, besides actual ladies' skirts, was dressing the skirt of the grapevine. Word has it that Francis Joseph put aside the reports of army maneuvers when someone dared to report that a smaller harvest was expected at his Tokaj vineyard than in the previous year. Would there be enough to send Christmas gifts to the Queen of England and Empress of India?

Not to worry, some clever personage remarked, the Tokaj cellars are so richly stocked with bottles of earlier vintages that we can put up with years of phylloxera infestation... And at once work began on compiling a sort of *Almanac de Gotha* for classifying the wines of the Hegyalja region by vintage. The birth-dates of the wines kept in the cellars were recorded with greater care than those of humans. In keeping such a register of vintages Francis Joseph's cellars led the Tokaj vintners, even though the ruler paid little heed to his Tokaj wines except when it was time to think of Christmas presents.

"It's all an illusion, I tell you," roared László Mezőssy, for once again he could not keep up with Francis Joseph. "Why would 1820 be a better year than 1830? Was there a comet reported for that year in the National Calendar?"

But he had to abide by the judgment of the professional oenologists. After all, Francis Joseph possessed the oldest vintages in all of the Hegyalja region. The wine-merchants, who transported barrelsful from here to distant parts abroad by the cartload (for one never knew, on a train the helpless barrels might be tampered with), also carried with them news of the register of Tokaj vintages. Bygone years and certain old vintages came to be revered, as were gold ducats minted at Körmöcbánya for special occasions such as a coronation.

Although this does not strictly belong to our story, I must mention a certain perfidious steward of the king's wine cellar, who might have been the only one among the king's household officials to be jailed for fraud. It happened at the time when the king's favorite daughter Maria Valeria was again expecting. She requested His Majesty her father to send her some of the same 1820 Tokaj vintage she had received as a present during her previous confinement, even though it was not Christmastime. Francis Joseph responded to her request with promptness and the courier was dispatched at top speed toward the Hegyalja wine cellar—after all, it was the least F. J. could do for his unborn grandchild. The courier returned to report that not a single bottle of the 1820 vintage was to be found, even though the register showed eighty bottles left. Francis Joseph became seriously irate.

"I don't care if they steal my wine, that's what it's for—but I will not tolerate them stealing from my daughter," he is reported to have said to Hieronymi.

Thereupon an inquiry was begun, and it led to the royal cellar keeper Z., about whom it was also learned that he gambled away in the casinos of Nyíregyháza and Debrecen considerable sums from the royal treasury.

"I don't care about that," F. J. told the Hungarian Minister of the Interior. "But I must know what he did with my wine!"

"He drank it."

"Imprison the scoundrel!" F. J. commanded.

So goes one of the many legends surrounding the wines of Tokaj.

(18 July, 1926)

Francis Joseph I, the Foremost Gentleman in Europe

To tell every detail about him one would have had to be a ghost haunting the Buda Castle Hill...ascending the secret stairway to Buda Castle from the Vérmező side, back in the days when this field still went by the name of the "Generals' Meadow". (In Francis Joseph's time this hidden passageway saw use on two occasions: once by Lujza Blaha, the beloved "nightingale" of the old Népszinház, who, for some unfathomable reason, had been "summoned for an audience" at the midnight hour by the Father of Nations; and the second time by a Danube otter which, in the middle of one winter, nimbly clambered up the steps all the way to the study of the greatest lord in the land, giving the servants a hard time before they managed to eject the uninvited guest.) Yes, one would have to have been a knight entombed within those regal walls in order to be able to give an accurate account of what kept F. J.'s cheeks, even in old age, as ruddy as some unusual leaf encountered on a walk in the Buda hills—whereas by that time even his ubiquitous portraits on thalers were beginning to fade into yellowing memories... Or else one would have to have been a flesh and blood guardsman outside the king's bedchamber, back when this late descendant of margraves tossed and turned on his army cot under the coarse military blanket, because the margravine, the one from Wittelsbach, refrained from gently opening the door leading to her bedchamber in order to inquire about the wherefore of her lord and master's insomnia... Yes, one would have to have been anything but a journalist in F. J.'s time, for this gentleman had the lowest regard for even the most influential of editors, who had the power to persuade theater directors to groom the daughter of a janitor into a star... Two specimens of this prestigious species were known to this faithful reader of the Viennese daily *Extrablatt*, which was not above printing horror stories: one was a strapping, red-mustached Jewish man, inclined to obesity, who tended to look on from behind his pince-nez with a certain sense of superiority even at the famed military exercises of the old Austro-Hungarian Monarchy, and might possibly have muttered to himself the usual comment passed by editors on manuscripts bound for the wastebasket: "Worthless."

This red-mustached journalist was personally banished by F. J. from the areas where His Majesty delighted in observing the maneuvers of his superbly imposing infantry and his gorgeous Hungarian hussars, the stuff of fairy-tales. (The doyen of Hungarian reporters at the time, Izidor Barna, whose name is still often mentioned in histories of Hungarian journalism, returned to his boss, the solemn Jenő Rákosi, with a heavy heart following his banishment. Fortunately this former director of the Népszinház was well enough acquainted with the ruler's other human foibles not to take a tragic view of his reporter's banishment from the military grounds.) The other Hungarian journalist personally known to F. J. was a gentleman named Futtaki, who edited a mimeographed news bulletin in Budapest, a position that was not highly esteemed in the capital in those days. Futtaki and his colleagues were responsible for collating the lists of those in attendance at funerals, balls, executions, and other formal occasions. Dyed-in-the-wool newspapermen back then did not hold such journalistic work in very high regard, for every cub reporter knew how ready the participants at funerals and other public functions were to assist the member of the press busily jotting in his notebook, to make sure that their names were spelled correctly on the list of those in attendance... Well, Futtaki never left out anyone worthy of mention among those at the scene of a fire or a Danube flood... His merits were recognized accordingly. Francis Joseph ordered a horse to be assigned to this man, to enable him to report accurately about the progress of the army exercises. The story has it that the good editor was not overjoyed by the horse, which threw him more than once from the saddle and also bit him without cause. (On the other hand, F. J. refused to recognize the existence of Kornél Ábrányi, Jr.—even though the latter wrote a book about him. But that was after his imprisonment for *lèse-majesté*.)

So only these two gentlemen were known to F. J. from the Budapest middle class, the so-called press corps, which at night, at the Café Fiume or at Princi's newly opened New York coffeehouse, was beginning to consider itself the leader of Hungarian intellectual life. Far from it. Francis Joseph, the ruling monarch, was the leader of everything here, secure in his reign with the security of his horse-hair helmeted Burg gendarmes strolling about the premises of the Viennese Hof. They never had to draw their ornately hilted swords at the well-mannered Viennese public, who were as well groomed as the neatly trimmed shrubs in the Imperial Gardens, while the equestrian statues of gen-

140

erals and other military commanders standing in the various courtyards of the Viennese emperor's residence proclaimed the glory of the House of Austria till the end of history.

I would now like to describe to my son how we, the fading generation of the nineteenth century, remember Francis Joseph, the king who maintained the strongest grip over the hearts and souls, as well as the sword-bearing arms, of his Hungarian subjects, who were wont to be a rambunctious lot, much given to daydreaming about brave deeds of old.

Thackeray, whom even his detractors held to be the finest London journalist of his day, wrote a book about the Georges that readers received with hosannas both in England and on the Continent, at a time when these former British kings no longer had anything to do with anyone. Surely Francis Joseph will some day become a similar topic for Hungarian writers in the future, a challenge for the imaginations of the finest journalists and novelists. Therefore it will do no harm to note down our personal impressions about this gentleman of the ruling House of Austria, so that generations following us will have an even better picture of him than what is available in the paintings of Gyula Benczúr.

He was not a man of tall stature, not even back in the days when Hungarians had their first glimpse of him, traversing the eastern plains in a four-horse carriage, in regions where only recently Kossuth, the lawyer from Zemplén, had been stirring up the flames of revolt, and prior to that the outlaws of Sándor Rózsa had run wild. As observed by loyal court portraitists (who, if they had their way, would paint a royal canvas every day), back then he was of a rather willowly and slender physique, and the red sash across his chest produced a dashing impression... Above the white coat the face may even be said to be dreamy, reminding one of the unfortunate young prince who was the subject of Rostand's drama—for they were related by blood, as were all offspring born to the hefty Austrian princesses, although malicious posterity dares to question the facts of paternity. The curly chestnut locks harked back to the times when his ambitious and determined mother Sophia had caressed these curls at the Lainz Palace. As yet the reddish mustache was not quite thick enough to befit a supreme commander, and according to tradition did not win the approval of onlookers among the roadside shepherds of the lowlands, who recalled Kossuth's manly beard and Sándor Rózsa's tallow-smeared mustachio... Not long after this Alföld journey the court barber received orders to contrive to make the youthful Austrian emperor's face look older. My uninitiated mind to this day cannot fathom how in the world that black beard managed to sprout next to the reddish mustache, to be referred to, by fifty million subjects, as the *Kaiser-Bart*.

I could go on about his physique in as much detail as a court photographer, for as a young journalist I had plenty of occasions to see him. Back in those days I was so familiar with the receptions that awaited F. J. on his arrival at the railway terminal that I could have written "off the top of my head", without leaving my table at the café, my dispatch to the paper about who was there to receive F. J. at the Eastern Terminal... It was always the same civil and military officials who dared not pass away for lack of royal permission.

"His Majesty descended from the train with buoyant strides", wrote the quondam journalist, as he had learned in the trade.

Well, I could say a thing or two in my memoirs about the buoyancy of those strides, for in my day, alas, F. J. no longer quite possessed the flexibility we associate with an acrobat. In earlier times, when Gyula Andrássy the elder, he of the swaying, swinging stride, not only dictated the Monarchy's foreign policy but was also constantly in the royal presence, the elegant, foppish, light-stepping Highland style of this pockmarked gentleman in all likelihood made F. J. take the stairs with a more sprightly step. At the Pest manufacturers' and businessmen's ball, when the king and queen first met the local taxpaying citizenry, F. J. made a splendidly virile impression, although it is true that his faithful Andrássy was equally prominent as the chief master of ceremonies at the ball. But the white-haired widow of a piano manufacturer on Koronaherceg Street, whom I often assisted in winding her yarn, repeatedly mentioned that the women of Pest had all marveled at how much taller than the emperor the slender empress was. "There was as much as half a head's difference between them", I can still hear her say. But by then F. J. had become broader in the shoulders, just like any army officer who joins the general staff at an early age, and he had come to feel at home in majestic poses, having learned how to bestow gracious glances at his subjects, although most of the time he still preserved a stern aspect, rather in the manner of an officious cavalry cadet who is determined to shine in front of unseen superiors by being extra hard on the troops and observing service regulations to the letter.

But who could have been the superior of F. J., who was toasted as the Supreme Commander at military banquets by army officers with a clink of their spurs? His superior was every single man in a military coat who wore Francis Joseph's sword knot, for he felt called upon to set an example for them with his own behavior, as well as for any peacetime sub-officer who aspired to win some day that most solemn goal in life, the golden star of the commissioned officer.

A few more words about F. J.'s physical appearance while we are on the subject, for this is what is most conspicuous about any man, whether he lived in the enthusiasm-filled nineteenth century or in the disillusioned twentieth.

Although he did not resort to high-heeled boots, as do some who wish to seem higher than their fellow men, he did favor "form-fitting" suits, for the tight trousers faithfully revealed those muscular thighs and sturdy knees that were the result of much horseback riding. The close-cut military jackets, although at an advanced age they hinder proper digestion, did contribute to a dashing appearance, for in that age of colorful, splendid military costumes every man strove to have a photograph of himself in some house, preferably on a wall not far from some young maiden's bed, showing him in a hussar or army recruit's uniform. Such photos could be purchased ready-made at the fair, into which one's portrait would be glued. Ah, those innocent times!— when the most popular picture of the poet Petőfi showed him in the brown braided tunic of General Bem's revolutionary troops, with the caption "My Homeland!" written in blood floating before his eyes.

In the nineteenth century a uniform was practically a must if you wanted to be taken for a man of consequence, when the king himself forsook his military tunic only at the time of the royal hunt at Bad Ischl. In those days the red-bearded Tiller, tailor of uniforms, greeted all of Andrássy Avenue with a wave of his hat as he turned the corner, and provincial shoemakers' apprentices dreamed of being admitted to the volunteer firemen's association, merely to get into some kind of uniform. Ah, glorious times! The ladies would rush to their windows on hearing the clinking of sabers instead of waiting for the strumming of the poet's lute.

F. J. had a prominent role in bringing about this fashion for uniforms, perhaps for the very reason that, being "half a head" shorter than his spouse, the Bavarian princess, he wore military uniforms exclusively day after day, year after year. Although F. J. may have had his faults, for which some day he will have to answer to bunion-footed historians, I can only praise him for not neglecting his masculine good looks, his "deportment" as they used to say—although the very lady he would have most liked to impress in the entire Monarchy spent much of her time traveling, as if she were fleeing from something that was waiting for her at home.

...In my days as a young reporter I often stood in the courtyard of the Viennese Burg, in open-mouthed reverie like some half-baked poetaster who is only interested in the affairs of royalty, until the kindly gendarme pointed me in the direction of Kärntnerstrasse. In those days I witnessed the second period of F. J.'s manhood when he began to wear those so-called officer's caps that we have come to associate with old balding army officers. This cap was tall and rigid as the irrevocable paragraphs of the Army Regulations. There were mysterious little air vents on the side of this cap, no doubt to allow the balding skull under the heavy cap the benefit of youthful little breezes that accost even the aging regimental commander on his ride toward his pension. Such an officer's cap was large and ample, its golden braids reached down to the ears and the nape of the neck, as if to symbolize the Monarchy's military might that extended to all of its territories. At times this stiff, oversized officer's cap seemed to me to be a cousin of the top hats worn in the Austro-Hungarian Monarchy by balding gentlemen who still cared about the dignity of their appearance. Meanwhile, as Francis Joseph's stature shrank from year to year, the clever military tailor compensated by heightening the style of the cap. But among F. J.'s old friends none needed it: not Prince Lobkowitz, the commander of the Budapest army corps; not Géza Fejérváry; not the gigantic Count Paar, who spent most of his life in F. J.'s immediate vicinity.

As the cap on the Monarchy's head grew taller year after year, the emperor's stature diminished. He was still universally regarded as "Europe's foremost gentleman", for Wilhelm II's deformed arm disqualified him as a masculine ideal and England was ruled by that elderly lady, after whose passing the populace in the City of London still preferred the old Victoria gold pieces to the new sovereigns bearing the portrait of Albert, the former Prince of Wales, now going by the name of Edward. Francis Joseph alone remained unchanged, even though the royal crypts were opened and resealed during his reign with the same frequency as in any other period of history. F. J. was unalterable Destiny himself, and only a provincial journalist who saw him infrequently would have noted that although the army officer's cap grew from

144

year to year, it could now barely be seen over the top of the back seat in the court carriage. His facial features assumed the still permanence of a souvenir album bound in red leather, filled to the brim with memorabilia. It was bruited that the doctor no longer allowed him the "Virginia" cigars that were made especially for him by the Hungarian Ministry of Commerce, while young medical authorities recommended that the shipments of Tokaj wines sent from the royal wine cellars at Mád ought to be checked by Kerzl, the court physician, now that His Majesty was approaching seventy... But the journalist would still pronounce the king's appearance "sprightly". Although the silver forints—especially the old two-forint coins—were by now remarkably worn, so much so that the fine, bearded, imperial profile could barely be distinguished on these Körmöcbánya products, the king himself would still display a rosy face when his carriage passed in front of the Emke coffeehouse on his way out of the capital. (His sagacious master of ceremonies saw to it that F. J. usually arrived at the Western Terminal and departed from the Eastern one, so that all the streets of Pest would have the pleasure of seeing F. J. ride by in the carriage drawn by those beautiful grays, although he responded more and more feebly to the startling hurrahs of the shoppers assembled from the outer districts, the storekeepers of Rákóczi Avenue, the journalists with their press badges, and the secret policemen with their nightsticks. I myself have often stood at the intersections to observe again and again Europe's foremost gentleman, for in his day he was the most interesting visitor in town.

There I stood and greeted him, although I do not think F. J. bothered to notice me, not even after I had mentioned him in some of my novels.)

...And so F. J., with his cheeks as red as the winter sun, rode on toward St. Stephen's Church and was seen no more from the windows of the Emke coffeehouse. The dignified court hunter's feathered cap was waved for the last time from the box of the royal equipage. One last time F. J. returned the smart salute of the excited district captain standing at the intersection—and the next time I saw the foremost gentleman in Europe, whom I always regarded with a kind of superstitious awe, was at St. Stephen's Church in Vienna... He had departed without making me a prince.

F. J. received the final homage lying in a small black casket, not much bigger than a child's, covered with the finest black silk. At the funeral service my colleague M. L. and I were swept by accident into the vicinity of old archduchesses who knelt and wept into the tiniest black-edged handkerchiefs that would not have been enough to receive the tears shed over a broken trifle. The outfits worn by these imperial ladies reflected the reddened, bleary-eyed labor of blonde seamstresses working through the night. Nearby a colonel stood wearing poppy-red pantaloons, his head hung in meditation about his future assignment. Outside, the warriors from the front awaited the spectacle about to emerge from the church. We had to hurry to catch the afternoon express to Budapest.

(25 January, 1925)

Ida Ferenczy, the Queen's Lady-in-Waiting

...Ida Ferenczy's lot was a rare one for a lady of the Hungarian lesser nobility, and in the Hungary of old she was talked about as often as her friend, Her Majesty Queen Elizabeth, who already in her lifetime had become more or less sublimated into legend in the small country manors and palaces where fabulous tales find devoted listeners. When the season of long evenings arrived in Hungary, making the lighting of lamps inevitable (although folks believed that breathing the effluvia of oil lamps was most unhealthy), there would begin the round of feather-plucking, corn-husking, and cabbage-shredding, accompanied by cartomancy and story-telling (for one had to find occupations that would not strain the eyes), and in those quiescent country houses hardly an autumn evening would go by without some mention of Queen Elizabeth, to whose name Ida Ferenczy's would be linked as inevitably as Castor's was to Pollux. The queen liked to spend autumn—which at the Castle of Lainz was as solemn as the novels of Miklós Jósika, and winter, which boded nothing but court ceremonies, receptions, and balls at the greenish-yellow stuccoed Imperial Palace in Vienna—as far away from her domains as possible, like some bird of passage seeking warmer climes at the change of seasons. The newspapers published the official communiqués issued by order of the sovereign, reporting where Her Majesty was spending her melancholy days, and these reports always contained the name of Ida Ferenczy, a lady of the Hungarian lesser nobility. Without this Dame of the Star Cross Order, who had been promoted to the rank of personal friend, the autumn days in Corfu would have been unimaginable, or the mild winters at the French coast, or those summers spent touring and mountain-climbing in Switzerland or in some other mountainous region. It seemed natural that we would always somehow feel closer to Ida Ferenczy, who was blood of our blood, than to the melancholy princess from Bavaria, about whom all that we could gather was that her ever-present sadness was not relieved even when Francis Joseph I, a man toughened by solemn duties, went out of his way to woo her with endearments. As for Ida Ferenczy, we were not absolutely convinced that she, too, lived only for mourning

147

(although she led the languid life of old maids); therefore we dared disturb her with missives and petitions for all kinds of royal leaseholds, permits for tobacco cultivation or distilleries, or else a decrease of taxes. Especially after word got around in Hungary—for news of this sort spread like wildfire throughout the manor houses of the impoverished petty nobility—that there existed an invisible fairy godmother of these country houses who could secure the support of a charitable foundation for those ladies of good family who, due to whatever circumstances, were unable to find husbands.

Was Ida Ferenczy really a savior of Hungary while she accompanied the grieving wife of His Majesty the King on her anxiety-driven peregrinations? Although the queen did not take an active part in matters of government (which would have been a difficult achievement alongside Francis Joseph), still she had at least as much influence as Madame Blaha, who on the stage of the old Népszinház once beseeched Francis Joseph (seated in the royal box) to commute the death sentences of the thirteen Hungarian hussars who had hacked to pieces their cruel sergeant in Galicia. The queen did not interfere with governing the ship of state, even when she stayed under the same roof as her husband at the Burg in Vienna, or at Lainz, where the castle, deep in the gloomy woods, had been built by Francis Joseph expressly to suit Elizabeth's melancholy moods... I have seen the chambers at Lainz Castle that Elizabeth considered perhaps the most bearable of all the palaces in her realm. The queen had three adjacent rooms, in the last of which there was a bathtub behind a screen, such as one might see in certain country mansions in Hungary. Only her bed was, possibly, remarkable for its size and majesty, like a Russian Orthodox altar carved of wood, replete with gilded, colorful angels and ornamented with peacock feathers and garlands of artificial flowers, somewhat like the bed that had belonged to the martial-minded Empress Maria Theresa, that was big enough to accommodate all of her large family and which was formerly on display at the imperial court museum. Queen Elizabeth's bed reminded one of those pious persons (chiefly from the Highlands), who, even in bed, liked to think they were in church, and spent hours praying for relief from the misery of some lengthy affliction. On the small table by Queen Elizabeth's bedside lay diminutive, ornately bound volumes of the works of Heine and Byron—although these could have been placed there by the reverent museum staff for the benefit of the latter-day visitor, for it is unlikely the queen would have left the works of her favorite poets behind at Lainz when she departed from there.

148

A Biedermeier salon connected the queen's apartment to the king's somber, forbidding chambers that contained his iron bedstead and faced northwest, from where the nastiest winds could be expected. This salon, where perhaps no visitor had ever sat, hardly saw any other traffic than Ida Ferenczy's crossing it periodically, for, among others, one of her nerve-racking tasks was to convey the queen's messages to Francis Joseph I, messages that would predictably add a further touch of severity to the king's face, which as a rule was not known for an expression of easy-going cheer.

"Majesty, the queen would like to travel," announced Ida Ferenczy, a maiden from the Hungarian lesser nobility, stopping at the threshold of the door to Francis Joseph's study and bedroom. At the window stood the small desk covered with ink-spotted green baize, such as one might find in a provincial chancellery; in the corner, a wash basin fit for the office of an assistant clerk where colleagues wash their hands before marching off for their noontime stein of beer; a revolving chair at the desk, such as old storekeepers might sit on after interposing an inflatable rubber cushion... And the dreary bed that could have been a grenadier's in the time of Frederick the Great.

"Where does the queen intend to travel? Is she perhaps not feeling well here in our company?" asked Francis Joseph I in that icy, scratchy tone that men acquire in the autumn days of their lives.

(At Perbenyik Castle in Zemplén county where she was a frequent visitor of the Counts Majláth after the death of the queen, Ida Ferenczy would often speak of this voice which she could not forget as long as she lived—for some voices, not necessarily the most melodious ones, have a way of haunting a person to the end of her life.)

Ida Ferenczy mustered a heroic reply: "Her Majesty the Queen wishes to travel to Greece... To the Villa Achilleon on Corfu."

Francis Joseph stared straight ahead, as if he could already see the coming winter days of grim solitude he would have to face once more, and replied, feigning indifference, to the Dame of the Order of the Star Cross: "The court courier will prepare an itinerary. But I insist in advance that the itinerary be strictly adhered to and that you wire me from everywhere."

(Among modern inventions Francis Joseph I valued only the telegraph. He refused to travel by automobile. Why should he, when he owned the finest Lippizaners in all of Europe to draw his carriages?)

At the Castle of Lainz a gilded, narrow, winding staircase led from the queen's apartments to the castle garden, and court etiquette restricted the use of this spiral stairway to the queen and her children. But Ida Ferenczy, as soon as the redeeming fiat had been issued from the king's mouth, rushed down these secret stairs to notify Her Royal Highness, who was taking a walk in the garden or in the woods, that the king had been merciful toward the bored ladies of the royal household... Autumn was coming, and soon the Lainz Castle would be emptied. The servantry in the court stables, hunting lodges, and kitchens that were decorated with the heads of horses, oxen, and deer executed on a scale harking back to antiquity, would soon be off to the Viennese Burg with its thick walls, leaving only a handful of useless old game wardens behind to smoke their pipes all winter long.

The queen was taking a walk in the woods that stretched for miles, where in the valley clearings one could glimpse the stag ambling toward the stream and hear the wild boar crashing through the overgrown thicket. It was not easy to locate the most melancholy of queens in the gloomy wilderness, but Ida Ferenczy managed to accomplish the task, as she regularly did in the service to which she had dedicated her life.

"Majesty, we're off!" she shouted from afar on the embowered trail, and waved her kerchief.

The queen turned her eyes, which so few had ever seen light-hearted, upon her favorite lady-in-waiting. "I knew right away you were bringing good news, because I have just fought off a snake that wanted to bite me," said Queen Elizabeth, and pointed at the carcass of a gray and white striped viper she had killed with her hazel-wood walking stick. Ida Ferenczy looked on in dread at the venomous serpent that thrived in the fallen leaves of the sultry woods...

"Help me, Ida, to thread the snakeskin onto my walking stick so I'll be forever safe from poisonous serpents."

So said the queen, and proceeded to thread the snakeskin onto her hazel-wood walking stick, which she henceforth always took on her travels, along with her other lucky charms.

But the walking stick covered with viper skin could not protect her against the sting of the most venomous serpent, the human one... The anarchist caught up with her in Geneva and stabbed her in the heart.

150

The white-haired Ida Ferenczy, speaking in her old age about that trip to Geneva, had tears in her kind, loving, healing eyes, for she still blamed herself, evoking this forever burning wound...

"We were to blame for the death of our beloved queen, because we did not observe to the letter the exact itinerary we were supposed to follow, handed to us by the Lord Steward's office in Vienna. Neither my lord Esterházy, the queen's major-domo, nor my lord Berzeviczy, the queen's courier, were insistent enough in their protests against stopping, on the way home from France and the cloister of St. Bernard, at Geneva, a place always full of unstable individuals because of the permissive local freedoms. We agreed to let the queen stop over at Geneva, even though this was not on our itinerary... Ever since then we have all fallen out of favor at the Viennese court."

...And the provincial gentlemen, who had been used to thinking of Ida Ferenczy as Queen Elizabeth's friend and the charitable benefactress of the Hungarian nation, let out a sigh. It was a sigh laden with bitter regret and pain for the sad queen and her tragic fate, as well as the nevermore of all those would-be distilleries, royal leaseholds, low-interest loans from Viennese banks, and even provostships and bishoprics that the benevolent Ida Ferenczy's intercession had so often secured in the past that she could veritably be blessed for remaining an old maid. While faithfully accompanying her royal friend on her melancholy peregrinations, she never forgot to open all those letters from faraway Hungary that had followed her to lands in all parts of the globe.

(3 October, 1926)

151

Baltazzi, the Agent of the Prince

Princes never had enough money, and our Crown Prince Rudolph was no exception; the first-born son of perhaps the richest sovereign in Europe oftentimes ran out of cash. Edward Albert, Prince of Wales, son of Queen Victoria, heir to the crowns of Great Britain and India, had the empty-pocket blues even more often. These two hereditary princes were frequently beleaguered by money troubles and had to consider their financial options with wrinkled brows, just as any other contemporary man-about-town who had spent his allowance. The heir to the British throne had his yearly allowance voted by Parliament, in a rather tight-fisted manner, for the members were well aware of the prodigality of the Prince of Wales. A spendthrift usually receives less cash than a thrifty person. Rudolph received only a slightly larger allowance than most other archdukes with no private fortune of their own. Francis Joseph gave his son twelve thousand forints, justifying the amount as the equivalent of a minister's salary. (But in actuality more money went through Rudolph's hands than a mere minister's salary.)

What did gentlemen in those days do when they ran out of spending money? They turned to moneylenders, whose raison d'être has always been to assist young men who are broke.

Both heirs apparent received frequent loans from Baron Hirsch, whose name once upon a time was known the world over. In his old age he devoted to charities part of his enormous fortune—which derived from constructing railroads in Turkey and from other successful ventures. Beggars the world over who preferred to seek charitable gifts in writing sent their importuning letters to this man's address in Paris. In the editorial messages column of Hungarian newspapers the name and address of Baron Hirsch appeared daily. But the Prince of Wales and our Rudolph did not exactly need the papers to know where to find Baron Hirsch. One of the Baltazzi brothers—Aristide—had already insinuated himself into Rudolph's confidence. Who exactly was this Aristide Baltazzi? For a while he was merely a kibitzer at the Jockey Club; later he became an owner of racehorses. A gambler and man-

153

about-town. A man of the world and a horse dealer. At times the color of the rainbow; at others, darkling as the man on the moon. He had traveled all over Europe and met everyone who was anyone from the Bosphorus to England. He was a man of short stature whose eyes flashed formidably, who liked to fight and who was a horseman of devilish skill. (It was because of his exceptional horsemanship that Queen Elizabeth took notice of him at a Gödöllő hunt and called the chevalier of Greek descent to her son's attention. How could the mother have known in advance that by introducing the curly-headed horseman she had led her son to meet his Destiny?)

Aristide Baltazzi laughed it off when Rudolph confided that both he and the Prince of Wales were in such embarrassing financial circumstances that they would have to curtail their nightlife.

"I think I can help", said Baltazzi, who in those days was still primarily a horse dealer, buying racehorses for Barons Springer and Rothschild, the ho-telier Frohner, and the Jockey Club. "I myself haven't the money, nor can I ask my friends for a loan on behalf of Your Highnesses, because sooner or later it would reach the ears of His Majesty Francis Joseph. But I have an acquain-tance in Paris, a certain Baron Hirsch, who was a partner of my father's in building the Turkish railways. He is a clever man who knows how to keep a secret. He will be able to lend Your Highnesses as much as is needed."

The Crown Prince had misgivings. "A loan like that might be costly."

"In all of Europe, only His Majesty Francis Joseph is able to advance Your Highness money without interest," the little Greek replied, knowing full well that that was the one "source" to which Rudolph would never turn.

Baltazzi traveled to Paris. Soon his message arrived. Baron Hirsch would be glad to oblige Their Highnesses. There would be no interest, but he did have one small request. Would the Prince of Wales, upon his return to London, put him up for. membership at the local Jockey Club. (Membership at the London Jockey Club meant a guaranteed welcome at exclusive clubs and casinos the world over.) The Prince of Wales hesitated a moment.

"He's asking a lot. I happen to know that only last year the French Jockey Club rejected Baron Hirsch's application for membership."

In those days the heir to a throne was expected to know about such things. But the loan was urgently needed. Pest was never more attractive than in the spring of the Prince of Wales's sojourn here. What a pity it would have been to leave here and to travel on, following the itinerary, to Calcutta! Rudolph was secretly glad that Baron Hirsch did not ask for membership at the Budapest National Casino, for then he would have had to go the extra mile. Pest was beautiful, and the telegram was sent off to Baltazzi in Paris, with the Prince of Wales's promise to obtain membership for Baron Hirsch in the London Jockey Club.

As for our poor Crown Prince, what kind of interest did he have to pay for the loan negotiated by Baltazzi? His part of the bargain would prove the costliest. Baltazzi, on his return from Paris, told the Crown Prince that all he asked for his efforts was that his niece, who would turn sixteen by the time of the next carnival, should be presented at the Viennese court following the customary protocol. Although Rudolph had not yet met Mr. Baltazzi's niece, Baroness Maria Vetsera, who was still a boarding student at a convent at the time, he had no objection to the stated condition. After all, the baroness's uncles, the four Baltazzi brothers, although their father was only a Greek banker, were well known for their liberal and gallant ways in Viennese society. Miss Vetsera was the daughter of a Moravian general who had married the only Baltazzi girl. No, there would be no problem in getting even the most punctilious of Viennese court chamberlains to accept the girl's credentials. Actually Rudolph had a low regard for the formalities of court etiquette. And in addition the Vetsera girl had aunts such as the Countesses Stockau and Ugarta, who had been ladies-in-waiting to Queen Elizabeth and who had married the Baltazzi brothers from the vicinity of the throne, one might say. (Countess Stockau was married to Aristide B., Countess Ugarta to Hellior B.) And so a year went by until the time of the interest payment rolled around. The Prince of Wales had still not returned to London to make good his promise to Hirsch; and Maria Vetsera was still under the supervision of the nuns.

The day of the interest payment, no matter how distantly it looms, eventually comes round. The day of the creditor arrives! One day Rudolph received an invitation from the widowed Baroness Vetsera, kindly requesting his presence at the tea-party for the sixteenth birthday of her daughter, who had recently graduated from the convent school. The general's widow lived in a small side street in the Inner City, not far from the Jockey Club and not too far from the Viennese Burg which she regarded with awe as the residence of no mere mortals. The Crown Prince met Baroness Maria at her sixteenth birthday party. The table was set with a light blue cloth, Altwien china, and old silver, as befitted a general's widow; the apartment on the ground floor was serenely

155

bourgeois. There were oleanders in planters in the courtyard; in the windows, potted cactuses and geraniums; an overweight pug in the widow's lap. On the walls were photographs of unknown men arranged in fan-shaped configurations, with a general's portrait in the center. On the corners of wardrobes were ornamental bouquets à la Makart, Indian statuettes from the bequest of Count Stadion, who had been a friend of the general's. The windows were open, one could hear the footfalls of passersby in the side street; incense was smoking on the stovepipe. This was where Baroness Maria Vetsera lived with her mother, and her dream was to be presented on the occasion of the carnival reception at the Viennese court—in the absence of the empress most likely to Archduchess Stephania or Maria Josepha. Rudolph's first visit to the Vetseras was soon followed by a second one.

It was as if the Crown Prince had happened to stray into that side street by accident. Wearing civilian attire he used to roam the streets of Vienna, paying a visit to Sacher's (where, legend had it, there were more archdukes than waiters in the dining room), dropping in at the Jockey Club where the Greek gentlemen calmly lounged under the Gobelin tapestries; or else he would wander sunk in thought, usually ending his meanderings in some small tavern on the outskirts, for the Crown Prince was becoming enamored of love songs and wines that heightened love. He always had his unmarked *fiacre* drive him to his favorite tavern after leaving the Vetseras' apartment.

The image of the Greek girl with her thick head of hair and eyebrows that met over a face with a chalky white complexion took up residence in the Crown Prince's heart, tick-tocking with the persistence of a pocket watch. No matter how much we wag our heads, certain affairs of the heart will always remain incomprehensible. The news of Rudolph's love affair sneaked in through the keyholes of the Viennese court, where everything that happened in the city and in the Monarchy was known. The office of the chief Lord Chamberlain simply struck the name of Baroness Maria Vetsera from the list of those invited to be presented at carnival time. They say that even Queen Elizabeth's intercession and Rudolph's entreaties were in vain.

"I will not receive my son's paramour," said Francis Joseph as a matter of course; for in addition to his duties as ruler of the realm he was also a paterfamilias.

Much has been written about the tragedy at Mayerling, where Crown Prince Rudolph killed first Maria Vetsera then himself; but this alone could have

156

been the sole acceptable cause of his suicide. On one side the Baltazzi brothers were pressuring him to keep his promise; on the other side towered the immovable figure of Francis Joseph. It was no longer possible to live on honorably, to go on with the blissful, sentimental afternoons in the Inner City apartment furnished in bourgeois taste, where no one paid attention to the canary's song any more, for the poor baronesses cried all day, not knowing what to do after their disgrace. They planned to leave Vienna, as did one of the Baltazzi brothers (Alexander), who immediately left for Paris, or Henry, who from then on never came to Vienna from his villa in Baden. Only the unhappy Crown Prince wandered, solitary, about Vienna; his father Francis Joseph did not even deem him worthy of being confined to quarters, a sentence he occasionally passed on one of his higher-ranking army officers. Rudolph was free to do as he pleased, not even the court chamberlains cared about his comings and goings. This was the greatest punishment that could have been meted out on the proud Crown Prince for his involvement with Maria Vetsera.

This makes for a dry story, next to the fantastic tales invented by the popular imagination about Rudolph. But this had to be the course of events that unhinged the Crown Prince's psychic equilibrium. It could not have been true that Francis Joseph struck his son—he was a greater gentleman than that—and it is untrue that he threatened Rudolph with confinement. He simply did not say another word to him. By the time he could have relented, the Crown Prince was dead.

(31 July, 1927)

Letter from Pest

10 May 1914

Madame,

On Kossuth Street, where at noontime in May both respectable and demi-mondaine ladies seem to pass by in a reverie, their shoes and hats dazzling, their cheeks the color of apple-blossoms, the perfumes wafting in the wake of their fluttering skirts convincing us that only the most refined ladies show themselves on this promenade and that the police have no business whatever with the professional standing of some of these faery-like apparitions, such as would necessitate a written permit, usually carried in a garter—oblivious to all else I observe this Vanity Fair from the doorway of a hotel. It is the same as it ever was: the professionals outnumber the amateurs. Fifteen or twenty years ago, strolling about with an old relative who served in the police vice squad, I was appalled to learn the real profession of some of the princesses we encountered. Maybe those elderly ladies in the provinces are right when they express their scorn for the women on the streets of Pest. Springtime in May, and the horse races, seem to revive certain ladies who take a professional interest in love. One could say that every other woman here carries the Chief of Police's permit in her garter belt, and the rest offer their sacrifices to Venus without police permission. I wonder where the respectable women of Pest are to be found?

The hotel, which recently opened its American-style doors to the public on Kossuth Street, went through two frightful days after opening, before raising the siege laid to it by that segment of the Pest *demimonde* which aspires to be *haut monde*. One might say that every secret prostitute in Budapest had suddenly developed the burning ambition to open up shop in the lobby, café, or restaurant of this elegant new hotel. The place appeared auspicious: it was opened by Americans, who probably would not be familiar with local conditions, so that those ladies whom the waiters in the cafés of the Ring Boulevards serve with condescension envisioned making a dignified and respectable impression here. And so they came, they flew, they flocked here from all over town. Actresses both unemployed and active, women and girls used to a modest little snack at a corner table of a café, now seemed to blossom into countesses in the advantageous light. Ah, to appear respectable, refined, unapproachable: this is the dream of every Budapest dame who has ever gone astray. It was as if they all wore new clothes—the robes of public esteem. As if they had all simultaneously agreed to forget that only yesterday they had accepted the solicitations of a stranger who had accosted them on a side street. Mincing, haughty, and supremely confident, they "descended" on the new hotel, counting on its location near the aristocratic quarter and the exclusive clubs to gild their tarnished plumage. Loud and pretentious old battle-axes settled into Louis Quinze chairs, and notorious tarts, lately refused service at the Café Tarantella, now strutted their stuff on the sumptuous carpets.

But the English-speaking proprietors withstood the assault. They fought tenaciously, courageously, a fight to the death, for their most precious commodity, their reputation was at stake. The waiters responded to the siege with frosty stares and a granite calm, failing to fulfill orders; one might say that a secret sign, an unspoken message greeted each of these ladies, so that smiles, threats, bluster, and rage were all in vain—they had to retreat to the street, back to their old haunts, the hidden tables of dingy little cafés. Madame, I observed this rather strange warfare at close quarters. I think this happens every time a new hotel or café opens in Pest; the first guests are delivered courtesy of the so-called demimonde, for whom setting up business in new environs means a promotion. Too bad the campaign was over so soon, the siege raised, the halls emptied; ladies of suspect character no longer displayed themselves in the windows and slowly the first timid and cautious harbingers of genteel society appeared, taking their places in the well-aired halls.

(10 May, 1914)

Winter Campaign

Dedicated to the quiet, humble Hungarian looking on at the World's Fair, challenged to a wrestling match by the flashy showman...

Life is an unfriendly and chilly old play; the war, had it found me in my ardent youth, would probably have done its share to change my way of life and thought, my present world-view and bitter frame of mind. Perhaps I would have gone and redecorated my house with weapons and armor, replacing Biedermeier furniture and paintings. But today's warfare no longer resembles the stuff of our storybooks and traditions. War has turned into a giant factory; scientists, mathematicians, and engineers control the machines—at the push of a button a hundred thousand men go forth from the trenches; pull a lever, and a hundred thousand men disappear underground—this is the victory of the bureaucrat's jacket, worn out at the elbows, over the proud leopard-skin dangling from the warrior's shoulder, the triumph of almighty science over human disposition and spirit. We are nearing the utopian age when it will be machine against machine, the way today's armored trains, trucks, and airplanes do occasional battle.

Modern warfare has, as it were, curtailed the role of individual bravery, along with the clash of shining, glorious swords. Siegfried and Attila appear without their swords, Hunyadi without his broadsword; Wallenstein's ostrich-feathered, ornate warriors have discarded their vaunted, almighty short swords, and the earth-shaking charge of Hungarian hussars with sabers extended, our gorgeous national fantasy, is devastated by miserable pitfalls and hidden trenches before the points of those sabers can get near the enemy's skull...

This war, which not so long ago still seemed a panorama of illusions, dreams, and fervent fantasies (seen from the distance through the astronomer's telescope, the poet's frenzy and the imaginings of young men), has by now manifested its actuality: creaking peasant transport carts, uniforms devoid of gold braids; gray or improvised winter wear, felt boots and wrist warmers; underground caves, machine guns; highways turned into muddy mires in Serbia, floodgates in Flanders, impenetrable fog on the Polish and Russian fields. In place of shining medieval knights, clangorous

161

Valkyrie-helmeted superhuman beings, Godefroy of the Holy Land and Richard the Lionheart, fearless and irreproachable knights—whose stone-carved effigies we have seen in so many old cathedrals—we now have infantry soldiers equipped with entrenching tools, crawling through the mud, lit up by the searchlight beams of human eyes watching from a great distance.

This is a war of plain, gray uniforms, straightforward technologies and dusty statistics. The horrified, screaming terror caused by blood-red comets in the sky and the scary darkness of the eclipsed sun, cities clad in black, the stoppage of the usual course of human affairs, women insane with grief, orphaned children wandering the highways along with stray dogs—these medieval images of war that have survived in our imagination are nowadays not glimpsed first-hand. Armies march through the city, trains crammed with recruits rattle by, the walking wounded trudge past us; we learn the names of towns and villages from wire dispatches; the war correspondent tells us how many kilometers have been gained; nowhere a desperate charge that would decide the course of the war, nowhere a thoughtless mistake to tilt the balance one way or the other. All we see is an endless series of laborious, thoroughly weighed actions. Every army has by now learned these new tactics; even if though there had been enthusiastic, prodigal expenditures of blood, acts of bravado in the first phase of the war, now on every front we see only diligent, persistent, cautious endeavors that resemble the work of boring an artesian well or solving an endless series of logarithmic equations: such are the events of war these days.

This is a war of industriousness.

The command *Kard ki, kard!* ["Draw swords!"], which sent our souls into a spin at military parades during the peacetime years; the legendary shout *Előre!* ["Forward!"], leading the superhuman bayonet charge of infantrymen storming and crushing the enemy, are rarely brought to a climax in the currently running play. Miklós Zrinyi's death-defying sally, the eagle-like swoop of "Blind" Bottyán's *kuruc* cavalry, the siege of Buda Castle and Görgey's winter campaign in 1848–49—all the heroic acts composing the military flourishes of Hungarian history—we witness as they assume new shapes in our days.

The emblem of this war will be the monotonous, tireless, and overpowering labor of the steam-hammer. Present-day armies are like those tools of awesome power that hammer cannons out of blocks of steel. Troop movements are calculated to the second like the strokes of a vast machine. The hammer never fails to strike its target. The blow is perfectly aimed, like the infrequent shell fired by the 42-cm mortar. Armies, as it were, fight shy of superfluous and aimless tasks. They retreat without hesitation or a sense of defeat, if that is what the steering wheel of the machinery orders, and advance without delay if that vector of exertion is deemed expedient. After all, for a military commander retreat is almost as difficult as advance. In fact, orderly retreat consumes more energy than an all-out attack on the trenches. The charge takes but a limited amount of time, whereas the length of the retreat depends not only on the commander but also on the pressure applied by the opposition.

This war will be won by a cautious, gradually increased but never overextended expenditure of energy that takes into consideration all variables. This war is fought by the captains of industry.

This war is not defined by the intoxicating din of fanfares, oak-leaf-crowned physical jousting sung by poets, the thrill of a wrestling match or sword fight, the clangorous parade of helmeted heroes sporting feathers; it is a war of soldiers wearing the plainest, most inconspicuous uniforms, dug in and alertly watching, advancing an inch at a time, engaged in a lengthy series of diligent moves and industrious hammerings. The hero of heroes is the sniper, firing infrequently but always hitting the mark; the recruit, equipped with pickax, who undermines enemy trenches and blows them up; the supply train that negotiates impassable roads to deliver ammunition and food; and the sleepless infantryman huddled for days on end in rain and cold, only to advance at the right moment a few steps closer to enemy territory.

Our nation's pride, the world-famous Red Devils so dear to our hearts, descendants of the Hadik and Lenkei hussars, who, faithful to their glittering historical traditions, earned resounding worldwide acclaim early in the war, have now retired in their red breeches into the nation's pantheon of legendary heroes. But at a word of command they will again show up on the currently impassable battlegrounds and gallop on their magic steeds over the triumphal warpath of the Milky Way, where their heroic deeds outnumber the stars.

*

And yet, if we glance over these soldiers' caps as they disappear into trenches, at all the nations whose sons are girded for war—the tough British troops garbed for winter sports, the defenders of France whose remarkable energy far surpasses their poor reputation, the German infantry in their leather trousers, their Herculean strength burdened by the combined load of national pride and the promise of a prosperous future; the Russian armies raised in arms and steeled by one war after another in Siberia, Turkestan and the Caucasus—if we glance over the fancy battleground of this international meet where the champions of various nations march forth with earth-shaking steps, conscious of their wealth and sporting the badge of national grandeur on their breasts, eager to do battle, we see on the sideline, smiling quietly with a humble, inner pride, and marveling with naive wonder at all this commotion, the Hungarian peasant wearing a hat with a bit of feather grass, loose shirt and wide trousers. He is wondering how he ever got to be the comrade of these splendid lords, friend of all these rich folks, center stage in the eyes of the world? Humble and soft-spoken, simple and silent Magyar, how did you ever get to be here, where extinction dwells alongside tomorrow's wealth and glory, when you had no ambition whatever for glory or riches? You bear no grudge against anyone; your peaceful nature prefers the lark's song in the blue sky above your plow; all you want is to raise your little children, keep things in good order in your home, your granary, and around your house; you want neither the seas, nor colonies, nor new territories, for you do not covet what belongs to others; you have never hurt anyone, with sword or word, at the most you have bashed your brother or your chum on the head when you were in your cups—and suddenly, all at once on a midsummer day here you find yourself smack in the middle of a world war. Cannons are roaring, foreign troops are massed on your borders threatening the safety of your small home, your wife and property, your livestock. You did not even notice that you were involved in a war, defending your home. And it was as if you had never done anything else but sharpened swords, handled rifles, dug trenches: you have defended your country and secured your borders, for an unbelievably long six months you have resisted millions of Russians and Serbs in the north and south. Hungarians—whose repute once more shines in the eyes of other nations as do the stars above the Carpathians; Hungarians—looked upon with amazed appreciation and respect by friend and foe; Hungarians—who had never prepared for any

164

war more serious than electing your representatives—what a prodigious war record you have in stopping the enemy and persuading him that you are two-fisted, armed, and courageous.

You naive, humble, silent Hungarian, you poor, careworn, unhappy Hungarian of unfulfilled national yearnings: you are the sole real hero of this war. The hero of honor, duty, and manly responsibility.

We muse over Petőfi's line:

"...Only the poor love their country."

[...]

(24 January, 1915)

A Budapest Gentleman Who Had Stepped Forth from an Old Woodcut

"Oh springtime, love's season, your return once more makes me sad!" We sighed, quoting Pushkin's line, not long ago, perhaps last year, as we dawdled on the riverbank; the sound of church bells from Buda's steeples came floating across the Danube in the wind, and actually we had no other plaint save for the absence of the beloved that each of us had, once upon a time, clinging to his arm at the spot where St. Gellért's Hill is reflected in the river the way in an oil painting an armored knight of yore catches a glimpse of himself in a cobwebbed mirror. Springtime, the rebirth of violets, the pictures in the calendar, and the way various poets have sung vernal songs in our ears ever since we learned how to read, have always promised some wondrous change with the turn of the season, for every one of us would like to change his life—an act that winter's one-note song of somnolent, silent snowfall never inspires. Springtime arrives—and sorrow departs. We go for long walks, or leave town and travel far, far away where we may meet someone, man or woman, whose voice will redeem us, calm and harmonious, so special, renewing our outlook on life, a voice so wonderful to hear. One who will tell us what we are here for, how to be happy, where to go, what to think, how to be good... (Chances are this person will be a man, for women rarely strive to set your mind at rest. On the contrary: your sleepless nights serve them like a sorcerer's apprentice in casting their spell.) Zuboly, that strange, reclusive man who often hid behind a droll exterior, carried in his bag many such voices that had the peculiar effect of making me forget the aimlessness of my life. There was something in his dear person, in his playful, childlike, witty, and sparkling way of speaking, his broad, almost naive smile, the way he would run his hand over his bristly crew-cut and address you with his old-fashioned "At your humble service, and how is your worship today?" clutching his manuscripts and books under one arm, his stride lumbering, bear-like—something that made you feel like living. His kind was the rarest in Budapest. Perhaps it was the infinite goodwill you could sense in his person...or perhaps because he knew precisely how worthless life was, that it wasn't worth sporting a gray *boutonnière* of sorrow on its account...or because of his supreme confidence in his knowledge of people...or his utter lack of knowledge of them: anyway, in his company, in our typical midnight debates in the by then silent café, his person would radiate some splendid compound of hope and confidence, emanations of the sun that would surely rise at dawn.

"What a funny man," I would reflect, with a certain sense of contentment as I ambled home. And I would forget to call for a priest and give up the notion of doing away with myself that night, as long as a man as fascinating as this one, who didn't seem to belong in this place, lived in Pest.

Whenever I caught sight of Zuboly at a table with his small handful of friends I would think: There sit the holy men.

Let's see now, what do I really know about him, although I know just about everything? Was there some secret in his life, as there is in every man's, something that one does not talk about? What were his innermost thoughts when he talked about someone else—wasn't there some furtive suspicion lurking behind his sunny, resigned smile? Once, seeing him talking to a certain lady, I became jealous. For anyone he was chatting with would inevitably fall in love with him. Who was she? She was that certain lady from long ago. A few days later Zuboly looked me in the eye on the street, without saying a word. I grasped his hand and felt ashamed. Another time—a headachy, grim day it was, a day on which, a few generations ago, my ideals, the romantic men of the past century, would have shot themselves in the head—I suspected him of duplicity, imagining his childlike smile was a lie, his idealism a cover for depravity, and that in the delicate, nearly virginal soul of this man the same evil owls perched behind dark curtains as may be found in any of the ivory towers that we proudly label human souls. Whereas in truth everyone cheated in Pest and Zuboly alone was true. He was the most intelligent man I knew—I dare not call him friend, he was so much better than myself. He was too squeamish to tell lies, too dignified to mask his feelings as actors do, and never bothered to learn that fluty voice employed by everyone, dissemblers all. He presented himself as he was. The premier gentleman in Budapest.

Others know him better as the refined, the learned, the best of journalists; all I know is that it was quite natural that Zuboly fell in battle. For he enlisted to do what he did all his life: his duty. His duty was to defend that pass. Zuboly defended that pass until a bullet fired by one of Pushkin's countrymen hit him. My God, how strange that it should turn out to be one of Dostoyevsky's and Chekhov's posterity and kin, the dreamy, melancholy Russian whom we deemed worthy of our sympathy, who killed Zuboly in the Carpathians! A fatal carnival night, when brother stabs brother at the masked ball. Zuboly the revolutionary, the idealist, the enthusiast, consoler of the soul-sick, high priest of justice and humaneness, the best of men, as we imagine those Russians who sang of freedom and were transported to Siberia: Zuboly felled by a Russian bullet. Did the drops of blood that fell on the snow tell the passing Russian that they spurted from a heart that had ardently burned for every poor, oppressed Russian, for every victim of oppression? Those drops of blood in the Uzhok Pass chant a strange refrain. And under the snow lies Zuboly, gentle and forgiving—probably thinking to himself that Dostoyevsky was still a great writer.

And now, past the first convulsions of grief, the clenched fist, the curses, it would appear to me that Zuboly's death on the battlefield superbly complements the style of his entire life. The unvoiced question haunts my mind: Who else should fall in battle if not Zuboly, the saintly, the gentleman, the scholar? Who among the most upstanding men in this country would have deserved this most romantic and beautiful of deaths on the field of battle? To fall in battle is not for the worthless, the cowardly, or the insubstantial. Only decent men die in war, as I wrote not long ago. And destiny nods in agreement. The most decent of men is gone. Zuboly, with his foresight and phenomenal intelligence, must have smiled to himself when last August he left town without farewells to join his regiment. He would play a trick on Budapest, he must have thought, and leave without causing his friends any pain—and so he smiled, while we waited for him in vain. He would leave without farewells, not wanting to cast a pall over the picnic. And he might even have given a sly wink as his train left the outskirts of Pest behind.

"I wonder who Dr. Mikes will argue with now?" he may have mused. And maybe a smile lit up his kind, dear face at the thought of the mysterious doctor now left "high and dry".

I hereby induct Zuboly among those beautiful men of old whose portraits I carry in the innermost chamber of my heart. Ah, one must first die to actually become the hero of a novel. But Zuboly, the way he lived, alternating weeks of lethargy with wild, superhuman spurts of activity when he worked night and day and then slept for days on end; the way his nonchalant nobility never cared about his own person, his constant easygoing, friendly readiness for

169

any sacrifice, his grand-seigneurial scorn for money and riches: here was a living romantic hero walking in our midst. If old Jókai had known him...he would have made him the hero of a novel.

And now, as I say farewell to Zuboly, I see him again as I first glimpsed him in the Museum garden, where the relief view of Sümeg is seen on Himfy's lute and Károly Kisfaludy's sightless gaze looms in marble. In those days he worked at the Museum. And passing in front of these lyrical evocations of the nineteenth century Zuboly seemed to be a strange, poetic figure himself, who had stepped forth from an old woodcut, someone we had read about in a beautiful volume in our youth when all of us were heroes of romantic novels.

So now Dr. Elemér Bányai, of the nom-de-plume Zuboly, has truly become a lovely old woodcut, he who has walked among us in the Budapest night dressed in the Pest fashion. Whereas in actuality he should have lived only in a beautiful book.

(18 April, 1915)

Women's Hands

A long time ago, before the war, the so-called women's movement was watched with a certain anxiety by pessimistic men. Women were restless all over the world, demanding justice and equal rights, including the right to vote, and there was as much table pounding at their meetings as at election time in their book clubs. Truth to tell, I found this sort of thing attractive, the way one fancies a colorful skirt of an exotic cut on a strange woman, the somewhat mannish hunting hat on a dear provincial dame, or the man's suit on a woman teacher whose brow is clear and whose conduct is saintly...just as I favored those rare and splendid women who have more character than men and stronger wills, women who never tell lies and who are never seen crying... A woman may always count on a man's interest if she sports a few masculine feathers in her hat or heart. For every tired, lazy, world-weary man would like a woman to do his thinking for him, as our mothers did when we were little. The learned and renowned Dr. Sándor Ferenczi, with whom long ago, before the war, we had profound and exciting discussions about women, feminine moods, feelings and dreams, and managed to solve some nearly unfathomable cases and histories, once declared that women would win their ultimate victory over men when we all become children again—as some of us already have. The fifty-year-old man and the twenty-year-old youth secretly, latently always look for a mother's love in seeking the love of a woman. There is no man so masculine, or young man so tough, that he does not yearn to be cuddled and caressed at times, and to be loved as a baby. (It is possible that I have not reported the prominent psychiatrist's words with complete exactitude, for the discussion took place long ago and I have in the meantime added some of my own reflections. I can only hope that army doctors nowadays have no time to read the papers.)

Thus back when the feminists had reached the point where no one laughed at them any more, old gentlemen nodded in solemn agreement at young ladies' lectures (possibly out of sheer craftiness or politeness, for old gentlemen generally like to nod their heads in the direction of young ladies); youthful sociologists began to address the "feminine question"; the most charming Mrs. Sándor Teleki demonstrated at the National Casino; and patriotic women of the old school (as they were featured in humor magazines—elderly ladies from outlying districts, decked out in black, sporting cockades in the national colors in honor of the revolutionary martyrs)—were completely relegated to the background by the latter-day apostles of feminism. It is a pity that our feminists, in the course of their propagandistic work, insisted it was beneath the dignity and seriousness of their cause to deploy their Venus-like charms in the combat against patriarchal society. It is possible that for this very reason their movement gained our marked sympathies: no one ever saw them flash a white skirt-frill, and legend had it that their leaders went about in leather jackets. After all, plenty of men had, in the past, made use of ladies' garters to hang themselves, and traditional ladies' associations were known for sending their younger members to solicit contributions for the various charity balls... While feminists refused to kick up their heels in the promotion of their sacred cause, glittering pince-nez were worn by women just as they were worn by surgeons, and I cannot say that I ever heard Miss Glücklich address anyone in tones a shade warmer than is customary. Yes, the self-effacement of these ladies decidedly commanded our respect as they labored for the distant future and struggled against ignorance without ever breaking into song either in the manner of Saint Cecilia or of demimondaines. We respected them and therefore forgave some of their errors. I can't imagine anyone seriously condemning them for striking Lord Asquith or for their offense against King George's racehorse. They acted passionately, for they are, after all, women. They acted thoughtlessly, for they are, after all, children. And anyway in Budapest they have never beaten up a man, even though it would have been most amusing to see them clawing one of their adversaries on Váci Street. But no, they progressed toward their goal in a solemn and dignified manner. None of them was seen leaving a rally with hat askew and hair disheveled. Their demands have been decent and reasonable. They ask men to grant them merely certain human rights, and not their entire lives, as those frivolous, non-feminist little ladies—or women in general—tend to demand.

Thus before the war the seeds sown by prophets and reformers were beginning to sprout green shoots. Learned men, and many an Excellency, sat in the front rows of the audience when the feminist proselytizer took the podium and almost everyone in town gave their approval, so that I began to think that when I turn into a frail octogenarian who is no longer noticed by the society beauty in her theater box and never encounters a yearning pair of eyes at the ball any more, before joining a monastery I will look around among these well-read, erudite women to see if I can still make use of what I learned in childhood about well-mannered behavior from the dancing-school instructor, who was a Polish émigré. Ah, an old man does not have much of a choice among life's pleasures. And one should not scoff at a chance to attend and applaud the debates carried on by cultivated, spirited young women in the heat of their noble passion.

For women are more intelligent than men.

Then came the war and the men stepped forth. Suddenly the indispensability of men became blatantly obvious.

The poor feminists had to simmer down. Who has time now for women's rights when we must make our stand and defend the Carpathians? Society, family, and clubs lose their priority when blood flows in the field. Women are nowadays expected to mourn and to nurse, give their sons to the fatherland, and see their husbands or fathers off to war with a smile. To economize in the kitchen, to lead the blinded soldier across the intersection, and to conceal their sorrows. Their Excellencies no longer have time to attend the meetings of the hapless feminists, who have scattered like a flock of birds frightened by gunfire. The most educated ladies, whose brows radiate intellect, learning, and philosophy like sunlight reflected in a cooling spring, are now engaged in changing the dressings of wounded soldiers and accomplish this often most demanding, and at times far from dainty, task with resignation. Yes, they have to wash dishes, they who dreamed of the Ministry of Culture and Education. They disinfect woeful, repulsive wounds on the holy, afflicted extremities of unfortunate soldiers, they who had intended to dedicate their lives to the flights of the spirit, to the most refined manifestations of culture. It is wartime now, hearts are in agony, suffering sweeps the chambers of the soul. And for quite some time we shall hear no more about women's right to vote, their noble intentions and beautiful projects, the blessings of peace and quiet, for destiny keeps a tally of dark-souled men and of rosy nails. There are still too many wicked men on earth who compel hapless soldiers to march toward death. Our dear feminists, the kind, bright ladies will have to work on bandages instead of legislation. The attention of the public, the not always comprehensible trends in vogue, nowadays turn away from the bloody realism of

173

everyday facts, from the wavelengths where actual life is found: rights, justice, the body politic; Uncle Tom's Cabin and a world-redeeming socialism that would end human sufferings. As if in these days when each event has the impact of a shell landing in our midst, the frightened fashions seem to escape toward things that have long dropped from memory.

Naturally religion is making the greatest gains.

Everyone is religious again. Eyes are turned toward heaven.

And literature shows a predilection for the more ethereal styles of former times.

And if we take a closer look around us we may note with amazement that a peculiar, broad-skirted lady with a sweet, dreamy smile is promenading all over town: it is the Biedermeier style, which has actually never departed but has turned her post chaise around at the city limits. Old volumes by Jókai and the Romantics take the place of books by Zola and Mikszáth. And women's fashions for the spring follow the loose, old-fashioned styles. The pianos play fewer American tunes and all sorts of tender, sugary melodies play hide-and-seek in people's hearts, as if the whole town were hopelessly in love. The old bandleader, Marci Banda, who in the course of his long life has learned what kind of music people like and when, has never played as many pieces by La-votta as nowadays. The world wants tenderness and sentimental anguish.

The only difference between old-time *weltschmerz* and today's is that now everyone has an equal claim to the greatest grief, sorrow, and weariness. Meditations on life and death were never more justified than now. At the theater not only housemaids weep copiously during sentimental scenes. The bugle call sounds in the Carpathians and people at home sigh with anguished hearts in the abandoned bower, like the swains and diary-keeping misses in melodramas of bygone ages.

And I do believe that after the war is over, when this endless suffering comes to an end and our minds have a chance to calmly digest the events of these days, the feminists will turn out to be right. Women will achieve their long-sought rights.

They will have been earned by mothers who gave their sons to the homeland.

(11 April, 1915)

A Hungarian Village After Sundown

The village I visit in Somogy county must have been inhabited by Tatars once upon a time, for the name of the place, Kiliti, sounds positively Kirghiz—especially as pronounced in almost Asiatic accents by Grószberger, the village carter. We go past Sió, with its mostly Catholic population, where a roadside saint watches over Our Lady's cart-drivers. Now we approach a red-tiled steeple from which the star of the Calvinists points at the sky; a rooster carved from stone stands on the chimney of a peasant house; calm, quiet watchdogs stare in silence after Grószberger's cart as if they were asserting around the house the serene, dignified comportment of their absent masters. We stop at the tavern where a jaunty Jewish man with a typical Hungarian face, wearing gray trousers and a shirt, asks if he can be of service...

This is a good-sized, prosperous village with a broad main street. The children standing around the newly arrived cart accept the offered candy only after some persuasion, and even then they have to think it over; a bearded Gypsy with an aguish visage stands leaning against the wall, waiting to be called; from inside the dark tavern the words of a song sung by an elderly voice float out: "I'll come home wearing medals..." Above the aspens the summer sun has set, the dust raised by the herd returning home assumes a grayish tone, fat cows and hefty white oxen (belonging to the Veszprém chapter house) go past us, as if we were in a land of fairy tales. Suddenly, for no reason, I think of the horse dealers and butchers of my childhood and their likable, hearty market manners; I can see lame old Stern the famous cattle dealer winking at these wondrous cattle, old Stern who would slap the sidewalk with his hands as he danced at the end of market day. These splendid cows with their udders full must have fattened themselves on biblical grasses all day long, these mellow-eyed moo-cows, spotted Swiss and smaller, white Hungarians trudging home with an almost housewifely tread, their udders swaying; next the broad-backed village bull, followed by a herd of stampeding swine as if all the ham in the country had come to life here. Such a multitude of pigs' trotters, and, in all the roadside puddles, of white ducks, with fat

175

geese treading on green grass with a stride worthy of some grande dame who sponsors the flag dedication—the unexpectedly substantial wealth found in this obscure village is so astounding that it merits thought. Hungary will never be starved out. The larders in this country are full. Our cattle are as fat as the stooks of wheat harvested in the field. The sparrow and the passenger pigeon will always find their feast following a grain-laden cart on the country road. Nothing has changed in the past twelve months in the Hungarian countryside. The seed sown has again brought a handsome harvest and by the amount of our livestock you would not be able to tell that the army cooks have to feed millions of soldiers. Why, each and every warrior could feast on roast goose should the army high command think it desirable.

The strapping tavern keeper addresses me with his hands in his pockets:

"Yesterday I shipped lime blossoms to a pharmacy in Budapest. That brought in eight thousand korona. The wheat harvest will be next; these days I'm more of a broker than a tavern keeper. No one comes to the tavern. All the men are at the front."

And indeed, we have not seen a man, no sign of one; the men of Somogy county—the famous 44th regiment—have all met the military standard. The magistrate strolling homeward is the only man left in the village to oversee the women. But these women know how to take care of themselves. They are lively, smart, and articulate.

"How much is a goose?" I ask a girl who is herding them home.

"They're not for sale. They're barely two weeks old. They've got to grow some more."

"But for the right amount, and if I ask you real nice, wouldn't you sell me one?" I tease the young woman, whose eyes seem to reflect the campfires of distant Asian steppes.

"Well, they're s'posed to be eight forints apiece, but you can have one for seven."

Grószberger the carter can't let this pass without a comment.

"Your prices have gone up! Yesterday the Siófok notary's wife bought geese here for five and six forints apiece."

"That was yesterday. You yourself have aged since then, and my geese have got fatter."

Grószberger, who is indeed getting on in age, jumps off the box in a huff and picks up a gew-gawing goose. He weighs it in one hand.

"This one's not even ten pounds yet. Take my word for it. I can tell the weight to an ounce."

Now he shifts the goose to his right hand.

"Eight pounds, at most," he says deprecatingly.

But he turns to me and adds, in German:

"It's worth the money, your Honor!"

Alas, this is not the time to buy a goose, and I call Grószberger back to the driver's box.

"Let's try to be back in Siófok by nightfall."

But Grószberger's arrival has roused the village. He usually brings buyers to Kiliti. Women—everywhere it's the women—show up at the front fence of their yards.

"I have eggs," says one of them.

"What're you asking for'em," asks Grószberger, starting to bargain out of habit.

"Six kreuzers. I've got about eighty."

"Too much," replies the carter and smacks his horses to move on.

"We have chickens, too," says the young woman.

"How many?"

"About forty."

"Not enough for us," fibs Grószberger.

"There's twenty more over at the Göczöls'."

The carter waves this off.

"Still not enough."

Now another young lass steps up, adjusting the scarf knotted under her chin.

"Are you buying ducks, Grószberger?"

"Yes, if the price is right."

"And why shouldn't it be," snaps the young woman.

She picks up a duck from the dust and Grószberger weighs it, shaking his head.

"Woman, you'd have the heart to sell this little duckling?"

"Three forints. We've got a dozen like that."

Grószberger feigns indignation.

"Are you out of your mind, woman?"

But he flashes me a look under his rusty hat that has a duck feather in its band.

"It's worth the money. Let's buy it."

"Let's get going, Grószberger," I tell him. "It's getting dark."

At the next fence we are offered a calf for sale...

"We don't want anything," the carter calls out, but he stops his horses.

"With your permission, I sometimes do a bit of dealing. I wonder what they're asking for that calf," he mumbles into his mustache.

The village philosopher, the dealer in lime blossoms, still stands impassively, hands a-pocket, in front of his tavern. He approaches me with slow, sauntering steps while Grószberger bargains for a calf he has no intention of buying.

"This going to be a long war?" he asks, or states, with one eye shut, as if deep in thought.

"If it lasts much longer," he goes on, meditating aloud, "it'll be the end of *egyke* in Somogy county."

"How so?" I ask, to keep up my side of the conversation.

"Well, these obstinate folks never heeded the Lord Lieutenant, or his deputy; the preacher preached in vain; it was no use putting the midwives in jail—these people to this day refuse to give up *egyke*, the practice of having one child per family. Each couple always has only one child so the family wealth will be handed down intact and whole and grow unhindered. So the wealth won't have to be divided up between siblings, and parents won't have to take time from work raising all those children. Nothing could change their ways. Why, the law would jail any young wife caught in the wrong, some got as much as two years—well, she'd just do her time and go home to keep on doing whatever she did, or didn't do, before. No one's had a second child around here as far back as anyone can remember."

"My goodness," said I, shaking my head (thinking "Where can that scoundrel Grószberger be?").

"Well, the war came," the tavern keeper went on with a meaningful wink, "and they took away the men, young and old. You couldn't claim exemption, as before, for being the sole support or an only child or God knows what excuses people invented to avoid the army in the old days. This time they took everyone, and those precious only sons are now falling on the battlefield. They get killed or are missing or come back maimed. Now the women realize how foolish they've been with this practice—the ones with grown sons are the most woebegone for it's too late for them to hope for a second child to replace the older one who's died a hero's death, a second little son to work, create wealth, and inherit the goods. Yes, these women are wailing all day long, left alone, widowed, without a man on hand to help out with the

178

work. What a blessing a second pair of hands would be now around the house! E*gyke*'s had it in Somogy county."

"Are you sure about that?" I ask the village sage. (By now Grószberger could have purchased a whole herd of cattle!)

"Yes sir, I'm positive, because whenever a soldier on leave or convalescence comes home and stays awhile, well, after he goes back to the front the wife checks out the cradle of their only child, which had been retired to the attic, and has it repaired by the carpenter. The soldier husbands come home and have serious, cautionary talks with their wives, the ones you can have a serious word with. Another child would be a good thing around the house and the whole country needs the extra hands to help out those who fight and work nowadays, to replace the arms shot away and frozen off at the front..."

So in eight or nine months' time the registries of birth will again be opened by the priests in Somogy county. Miracle of miracles, a second child will be born to families that already have their one son. Older women, whom no one has looked at lately, will be going out with their skirts shorter in front. Those poor only sons, many of whom never came back from the Galician front, will be replaced in a hurry in Somogy. The best thing the government could do would be to give the regiment two weeks' home leave... Although it's all the same now. From now on, no mother will teach her daughter the sinful practices of old when she gets married.

"Where have you been, Grószberger?" I ask the carter. He starts scratching his salt-and-pepper beard.

"I was in one of the yards, your Honor. I'd never seen anything like it. This unbelievable abundance around here. They had geese, ducks, laying hens, calves, heifers—mostly yearlings; they've got life insurance, crop insurance, you name it—got everything except for their man, who died in the war, and a baby, although there is one on the way, in four or five months."

"Yes, every house must have a new mouth to feed..." grunts the local philosopher. "In this neighborhood the women are all expecting babies to replace the fallen sons. That's the sign of the greatest wealth for the local peasantry. These young wives wouldn't mind if the stork arrived as soon as tomorrow. Although," he added as an afterthought, "across the Sió, over there in Zala county, things are different. That's folks for you: as long as they're alive they all want to be different, but once they die, they're all alike."

We left this rural Hamlet to his meditations.

The cart rolled on in the twilight. The old man's crooning, like a contrabass from some distant wedding, followed us from the tavern: "I'll come home wearing medals..."

*

We passed a cemetery.

Village cemeteries can be weird at night. As if a dead man stood behind each tree trunk. Gravestones loom white like so many crouching women among the shrubs.

Behind my back the wide-open eye of the moon stares rapturously over the landscape. The moon rises slowly, as it did in the old Nyíregyháza theater where amateur thespians used to pull it up on a thread. Midnight-blue is the silhouette of forests and copses, as if they were so many theatrical props asleep during the summer break. Now the moon lights up the graveyard. In there, the trees stir, take a step forward, stop, move again... As soon as I turn my eyes away the white shapes squatting over the graves quickly rise up. Unhappy souls hop around by the ditch, like toads; but they, too, stand still as soon as I start watching them.

But the dead are on the move. Step by step they are coming closer to the village.

*

A campfire glows red past the cemetery, as if it were some portent. Dusky-faced wanderers lie about the strange hues of the fire, as if they were con-spirators or robbers incinerating the evidence of some great crime. I watch the fire stealthily, giving those little toads a chance to continue their journey in the cemetery ditch unseen by human eyes.

I hear a drawn-out sigh in the fields—perhaps a woman, perhaps the moon-beam.

"This is a fine land," I would write in my travel diary were I a foreigner, "where children are sown and harvested like the wheat or rye; the soil can be relied upon to make an unfailing return."

(1 August, 1915)

180

The Coronation

"At least I was here to see it", said this Tom Thumb on the penultimate day of 1916, when, after forty-nine and a half years, Hungarians were again getting ready to crown a king. It was one of those wet winter days when you must rise betimes to catch the sunrise...

The Royal Meteorological Institute had predicted fog and precipitation, but on this day, on either side of the Danube within sight of the Matthias Church spire, no one dressed for the weather. As winter clouds scudded their dripping extremities over the Buda hills, up yonder, where the first villas dot the hillside, the sleeping, dark windows began to glow with red lights not long after midnight. And up on Buda Castle Hill (where it's never the dead of night anyway, if and when the Hungarian king happens to be in residence) lights were showing both on the east side facing the Danube and on the western side where the king's bodyguards were quartered. You cannot get up too early on Coronation Day. This was the shortest night as far back as anyone could remember, and Budapest, the city that never quit before midnight, slept only an hour or two. Gas and electricity bills for this night must have run higher than for Christmas Eve, since there were tenants in every one of the city's twenty-five thousand buildings preparing to look their very best at the coronation in the morning.

During the war years nurses' whites and Red Cross uniforms began to be seen on women of fashion. After Francis Joseph's death the volunteer-nurse outfits were displaced by mourning. Women's heads were adorned with snug-fitting round hats with white flounces and black veils to make each Budapest lady appear, if not a close relative, then at least a lady-in-waiting to the deceased monarch. Actress and countess alike affected this fashion, which gave them the appearance of ladies wearing the insignia of the Order of the Star Cross. Violet de Parma was dabbed on diminutive black-bordered handkerchiefs in homage to the new queen's connections with the House of Parma. Women were beautified and made more modern by black mourning worn for the late ruler of the empire who had been called the Father of Peoples in all

181

lands where Moravian yarn was sold. Therefore, on this dawn in late December, many Budapest ladies elected to don black instead of festive coronation colors and gold, since barely a month had passed since Francis Joseph's interment in the Viennese Capuchin vaults.

*

Count Miklós Bánffy was the master of ceremonies for the coronation of the Hungarian king. Prince Montenuovo, Lord Chamberlain under Francis Joseph, master of High Spanish Court etiquette, had retired to a Franciscan monastery in Spain, according to hearsay.

Count Bánffy, a Transylvanian gentleman, had begun his schooling at the Kolozsvár theater, published short stories under an assumed name and joined the Journalists' Club, and, after his appointment as Intendant of the Hungarian Opera, designed stage sets à la Ludwig of Bavaria... Bánffy, the descendant of an ancient house, master of pomp and spectacle and an expert in theatrical lighting, was ideally qualified as master of ceremonies. (Francis Joseph, who had always attributed more value to money than it deserves, had been much plagued by parsimonious officials both at his coronation and during his long reign.)

The writer of these lines had the good fortune to see King Charles a mere step or two away, in that small arched niche by the holy water font to the right of the main entrance of the church. This niche had been designated to receive the king and the queen for the few moments after their arrival until the beginning of the ceremony. (Not even Bánffy the opera director could plan for each second, although he had meticulously paced out and measured every inch of ground in and around Matthias Church to estimate the time it would take for Charles, from the right wing of Buda Castle, and for Her Majesty and little Prince Otto from the opposite wing, riding in the coronation equipage, to arrive at the main entrance of the church. The other members of the royal family would use the entrance on the sacristy side guarded by the chief of the Budapest plainclothes police force and his frock-coated assistants, who made sure that only family and clergy were admitted.)

Only the bare-headed Charles, and Zita leading her child by the hand, entered the niche near the main entrance for a few private moments before the coronation while organ music filled the church. (Outside, on Trinity Place, a fanfare had already announced their arrival.) From the front entrance to the

182

main altar each and every participant had their assigned place in which to stand during the ceremony. The members of the royal escort: the king's officers and the queen's ladies-in-waiting (bedecked with decorations, diadems, necklaces and pearls) lined up in front of the niche after Queen Zita's train disappeared over the threshold. After a short while King Charles reappeared, in the uniform of a general, his youthful, rosy face showing signs of emotion and his hair damp with perspiration. He set out on the long red carpet leading to the altar, lined on both sides by Hungarian lords, loyal subjects of the Holy Crown, in ceremonial garb.

The king's unforgettably youthful bearing seemed destined to mark him to appear forever young in the doom of history, already looming in the wings. His bared head raised high toward the heroes and saints of Hungarian history in stained glass up above, he marched with hands clasped in front of him across the flag-bedecked church under the solemn, anxiously expectant, emotional eyes of the assembled lords of Hungary. His steps were light, confident yet reverential, in the manner of one approaching the finest moment held in store by fate, as he made his way toward Prince-Archbishop Csernoch who was waiting up by the altar. This king about to be crowned was almost a head shorter than most of the bearded, sword-bearing magnates, and could have passed for the son of many a hoary-headed representative. He appeared lost and orphaned in the course of his long walk.

His forlorn solitude lasted until the moment when, up near the altar, to the right of the prelate, the gaunt, bony figure of Count István Tisza appeared, clad in a matte black Hungarian-style outfit. Solemnly peering through his eyeglasses like a Calvinist churchwarden, he sized up the attendants at the coronation before bending his head, as if from this moment taking under his sheltering wing the young king who had lowered himself to one knee on the altar step. This was the most glorious day in Count István Tisza's life.

For as long as Francis Joseph, that monarch of most prepotent will, reigned, István Tisza could never achieve the predominant position of mainstay to his king and emperor. Francis Joseph was a solitary, solemn, diamond-hard individuality...around whom other members of the ruling family stumbled like bit players in the closing act of a drama whose author had no more lines for them. By now, gone were Count Andrássy (the elder), Baron Fejérváry, Kálmán Tisza, and old Archduke Joseph. Thus, in the empty royal antechamber, István Tisza was left to inquire, anxious and offended, when the day of his audience would arrive—the day when Francis Joseph would not only hear him out but also heed his counsel. That day never came, and Tisza's figure receded from the ruler's vicinity.

But on this occasion Tisza loomed as sole friend and future support to King Charles (dubbed Plötzlich, "the Sudden"), to guide him out of the labyrinth of Francis Joseph's weighty heritage. An elder statesman who had not been swept out with the old furniture after the former ruler's departure; a stalwart figure whose position was actually strengthened by Francis Joseph's demise. It was only natural that King Charles IV would try to anchor his storm-tossed boat to this rock of stability. ("Even though he's a Calvinist", said Queen Zita.)

This was the zenith of István Tisza's career, when the church elder from Debrecen stood on the coronation dais, relegating the archbishop to the role of mere assistant in placing the crown on the head of King Charles. It was Tisza's sinewy, strong hands that adjusted the crown on the uplifted, flushed forehead, and it was his arm that reached out when, under the weight of the thousand-year-old relic on his head, the king swayed momentarily as he rose from the kneeling position.

"Long live—the King!" Tisza's voice boomed out suddenly, to make way and to clear the air of stifling expectation.

(31 December, 1916)

Charles IV, Our Ill-Starred King

1.

What was Charles IV like?

Had you not known that he was the king...

You might have taken him for a forester—were you to meet him in those woods that belong in the legends of bygone kings, past Gödöllő, where the road turns in the direction of the church of the Capuchin monks in Máriabesnyö; there, you might have taken him for that young forester who was always the paragon of kindness and honesty and about whom books were written for the young, chiefly by German authors like Grimm and Hoffmann. This was the young forester who guided home lost children in the woods; he was the one who stepped from behind a tree to rescue screaming ladies from the clutches of brigands. He had the open and regular forehead of those young men that mothers dream of for their daughters.

But you might also have taken him for a junior officer who had accidentally donned a colonel's uniform; someone who, even in the ominously gray war uniform, was simply an obedient son who had been raised by a pampering, loving mother to be the support of her old age, an elderly widow with no one else left to chop her kindling in the morning; a son whose duties would also include holding up the yarn on his two hands while the mother wound it into a ball—and whose curly hair betrayed traces of those oldest of curling irons that we call the caress of a mother's hand.

Seeing his mustache, you might have thought that he was fresh from the military academy and had recently joined the troops, where a mustache was grown out of consideration for the master sergeant.

His complexion was as rosy as a boy's for whose sake his mother kneels in prolonged daily prayer on the church flagstones, begging the Lord to spare him from the eternal foe of all young men—the "Wicked Woman". Also in the background of this pink face there loomed a pale shadow of the past, the father's face, tormented by psychic pain, a face so ravaged by mute suffering—horrors comparable to Job's afflictions—that it was no longer recognizably human. (Archduke Otto was the name under which the Imperial House's registers recorded this hapless father whose fate was the stuff of horror stories; historians discussing the early death of Charles the Ill-Starred must not ignore the circumstances of the demise of Otto the Ill-Fated.)

I saw him in Vienna when he was still a young officer, at a time when, at the Ballplatz and the Hofburg, the court functionaries and servants who had grown old in the service of Francis Joseph could not have dreamed of the nightmare that a change of rulers brings about in hearts that have grown as stiff as a soldier left forgotten on sentry duty...or as hardened as crystallized preserves stashed away on some high shelf covered with cobwebs of uninterrupted quietude.

Behind those Burg gates, guarded by giant caryatids of stone, no one had been aware of the calculations and combinations regarding the future new ruler that were spun at the Hotel Sacher by lords who could not attain recognition under Francis Joseph's long reign: lords such as Szemere, Pázmándy, and Counts Kinsky and Hadik... There was a separate little Hungarian mission adjacent to the Imperial and Royal Ministry of Foreign Affairs, that followed the steps of the young heir to the throne with a far-seeing, extraordinary attentiveness and great expectation. On the first floor of the Sacher, in Mr. Szemere's chambers, the gentlemen warming themselves by the porcelain stove were aware of such details as: the fact that the previous night at the Burgtheater the future Charles IV had smiled his irrepressibly childlike smile at such and such a scene; whom he conversed with during a carriage ride in the Prater; and what Francis Joseph told him the last time he was received for an audience, right after the visit by the prince-archbishop of Vienna.

"What should I send him for a present?" Mr. Szemere would ruminate, sitting by the stove in his wide Turkish-style pantaloons, the so-called lucky pants he always wore at home to forfend evil spirits. (Every single patch on those pants—and there were plenty of them!—was sewn on to commemorate some happy meeting or lucky visit.)

"I wonder what this boy would like..." Count Kinsky continued in the same vein, for he secretly aspired to be the director of the court theaters under the future new ruler—if for no other reason than because of his liaison with the Hungarian operetta star Ilka Pálmay.

"I wonder why he doesn't like the French," said the all-knowing Mr. Pázmándy, wagging his head, for he would have liked, via the new king, to regain

186

the favor of the Habsburgs, whom the Hungarian Diet, in session under his father's chairmanship, had dethroned at Debrecen in 1849.

Mr. Szemere's forehead showed deep wrinkles and crow's-feet as a result of his meditations. He decided that at the next meeting at the Freudenau turf he would serve up a hot tip for the heir to the throne of the Austro-Hungarian Monarchy; not long ago the blonde Baroness Rothschild of Vienna had listened to his expert opinion at the Fillies' Stakes.

Only the handsome Sándor Hadik sat impassively, for he was not looking to accept any appointment either from the old, or the future king. It was all the same to him, more or less.

...Meanwhile the author of these lines, pervaded by an emotionalism that was unprofessional and verged on the provincial, left these dinners at Mme Sacher's (the menu, as long as Mr. Szemere was the host, always included a joint of boiled beef, as well as tomato sauce), to go on long dreamy walks in the streets of Vienna, in the course of which he would note the speeding carriage transporting the young man who wore an officer's greatcoat and, out of necessity, even though it made him look so old, the same type of officer's cap as worn by his uncle the emperor... While his face, as youthful as a cadet's, was always flushed pink, just as the face of a junior sales clerk who takes the young lady he considers his betrothed on Sunday excursions to Mödling... It was a heart-warming face that would have carried, in one of those Grinzing garden restaurants that had accordion music, the promise of a perennial bridegroom for the buxom young milliner who prattled away seated at a green-painted table and who wrote her name and remarks on the paper fans set out by the thoughtful host and dared not think of Monday morning when the proprietress would probably throw in her face the misshapen hat she had made for some old princess. In short, the bridegroom-like looks of the young heir to the throne were easier to imagine in almost any other context than on the fortune-telling cards consulted for their calculations by the dry-as-dust old gentlemen at Sacher's. For this reason I had always looked on with a quiet emotion at this young Viennese man whose bearing suggested Eastertime and the season of Pentecost, and who nonetheless was not free to get out of his carriage in front of those shop windows on Kärntnerstrasse displaying the photographs of the most fashionable Viennese actresses appearing in current hits; nor could he stop off in one of those crooked little streets of the inner city aged cynical by centuries and redolent of sewer smells, where the single-storey houses were as narrow as candles and where the janitor, when he opened the front entrance, did not register surprise even at letting in a live archduke, for this was a street frequented by numerous young ladies whose colorful skirts fluttered, as did the blue veils of their little hats.

"There goes Otto's son!" the elderly dames would say, pointing their umbrellas after the speeding court equipage.

How could these shopworn creatures have known Archduke Otto? For their eyes had long ago forgotten those winks that make a man enterprising until he is on his last legs.

2.

Henry the Fowler, Charles the Bold, "Dobzhe" Ladislaus, Andrew of Jerusalem...kings whom posterity has endowed with an appropriate epithet, as if to place a wreath on their historical sepulchers. Charles IV, whom nowadays many people call the "Ill-Starred", back in those early days was always referred to as the child of fortune.

...He ascended the throne when he was still a mere general of the cavalry, at a time when Francis Joseph, only a few weeks before, had still been appointing field-marshals. In the full flower of his youth he showed no evidence of the so-called Habsburg jaw, a deformity that made one shudder on encountering portraits of former Habsburgs in some ancient gallery. This was taken as a good omen by soothsayers in the know, as evidence that Maria Josepha's prayers had been answered and her child would avoid that tragic constellation under which so many Habsburgs of late (Maximilian, Rudolph, Otto) seemed to have been born into misfortune. And if anyone dared doubt that the "white lady of the Burg" and other ghosts had indeed been laid to rest when the mesdames at court rushed to Maria Josepha's aid in her hour of travail—well, that person only had to come to Buda in the Year of Our Lord Nineteen-Hundred Sixteen, at year's end, one day before St. Sylvester's Eve, in order to ascertain that at long last a fortunate young man was riding the heavenly cloud-quilts of bliss. On this day Charles IV was the most handsome man in all of Hungary, in whose honor the ladies of our land all wore their finest. (My favorite was Countess Károlyi's outfit. It was made of crimson-purple velvet, aglitter with gold, and the gold-brocaded, fur-lined pelisse over her shoulder evoked the finest periods of Hungarian history. For the same occasion Gladys Vanderbilt, Countess Széchenyi, donned a clasp a foot long and a hand's breadth wide, studded with diamonds the size of hazelnuts. Today its worth would probably buy half of Hungary.)

It was getting near the end of the year, high time to show one's face in church—especially for the sake of this most congenial young man of whom I had become so fond from a distance (I am sure he was unaware of this)—and so I once more got up at dawn, as early as when I had been a student at the Jesuits and had to attend Mass at dawn. I took along my pencil and a small pocket notebook, as in my cub reporter days, although back then I had not gone about with my head uncovered around the time of the first snowfall. The stones of Matthias Church were cold; not even the Coronation could change their impassivity. But the heat emanating from beneath all the assembled ornate Hungarian costumes seemed to suggest that Hungarians had been saving up all their warmth ever since 1867 for the occasion of the next coronation.

At a time such as this it becomes apparent that everybody hides at least two personae within themselves. One of these, the person wearing slippers, stayed at home, leading the everyday life of humdrum animal vegetation comparable to shelling corn—while it was the Holy-Day Human who came up to the Royal Castle now, the one who yearned to live a life in stances similar to the ones depicted by great painters and whose soul pined for those intuited, great harmonies that resound somewhere beyond everyday life, and whose heart longed for those sublime truths that reside in the pages of the Bible and all the other great works of world literature that remain unread... I do not believe that anyone present at Matthias Church on 30 December 1916 could possibly have entertained wistful thoughts about how nice it would be to still be lolling around in bed, or having a breakfast of a small portion of pörkölt at the neighboring pub. This was Coronation Day and every soul present acquired eagle wings and soared toward unknown heights.

The journalist stood there by the church portal, near the entrance to the Loreto Chapel, where a stove had been installed to radiate some warmth on this singular morning when the weather was as doleful as the morning after the first night of widowhood. As staged by Count Bánffy, the director of the Opera House, Their Majesties would enter this Loreto Chapel; therefore a conscientious reporter would want to post himself nearby. Until then, let the gold glitter and swansdown fall from the dresses of the assembled ladies as they pass in front of the journalist. Crimson, purple, velvet and brocades hug each other in a sisterly manner. Scarlet silks and gold exchange vows lasting unto death. Rushing through the portals of Matthias Church are ermine, sable, chinchilla, and other esoteric furs whose noble origin, if not their name, is obvious to the reporter. Lobster-red moiré is allied to old Hungarian lace; strident scarlet reds flare up like fulfilled love itself and veils and gold lacework hover as if their wearers were at their wedding today—although we must confess that there were robes here that preserved the fashions of the 1867 coronation with their silver braids, trains, and lilac-purple damask silks—for at a coronation the finest apparel is usually that made in the oldest style. My eyes wandered over the slender ankles flashing forth under the robes, ankles that were not appreciably thickened by the hand-knitted silk stockings from London that only the most select ladies—surely every single one of the Austrian archduchesses—had access to in the Hungary of 1916. Outside, on Trinity Place, the beer-bellied, chubby-cheeked trumpeters from the Opera House—who wore court outfits for the occasion—blew their horns.

...Once again I saw him, this young man from Vienna, and he still looked like a bridegroom...

The bridegroom of St. Stephen's Crown! Now, too, his face at first glance betrayed the same youthful interest and fairy tale-like curiosity for every single spectacle that I had already noted in Vienna. The obedient son, who, although he knew that this dream out of the *Arabian Nights* would still go on after he woke up, nonetheless marveled at everything that surrounded him.

With tears welling in his eyes he cast a glance of ineffable gratitude at the nave of the church where such a colossal orchestra of colors played its immortal march, a harmony that the eyes would never forget... In the world of folktales, which was the first thing that came to mind, these must be the colors seen by the blessed who ascend straight to heaven from the grayness of earthly life. And this marveling young man, who thus far had not yet known apathy, fatigue, or the pallor of ennui, at this moment showed his true colors, that all-consuming curiosity toward everything, which had no doubt been acquired in childhood when he played with tin soldiers and building blocks...or sat on a foot-stool listening to his mother's tales while the autumn wind howled outside the castle. For all children are alike, whether they become kings or beggars.

And this grateful glance in front of the Loreto Chapel, provoked first of all by the splendor of the gathered ladies, the ornate Hungarian outfits of the gentlemen and their national colors swaying above the convocation, next went in search of the gaunt, beetling figure of István Tisza, whose determined aspect and dark outfit, next to the scarlet red of the king, marked the experienced elder statesman who promised to be a worthy successor to those grand palatines who had crowned our great and saintly kings of old. Tisza walked ahead, cautiously upholding the sacred crown on its crimson cushion, while Charles IV stood by with a military bearing, his eyes on Tisza's slightly forward-bending figure, waiting for his deputy, the palatine, to advance a few more steps before suddenly setting off after the crown.

He progressed down the lengthy nave of the church, among all those human forms clad in ornaments, adornments, and ancient textiles, and among the fluttering banners that symbolized Hungarian history. He passed in front of all the men who, their cheeks flushed, their eyes passionate, and their mustaches twirled to a point, or their graying manes shaggy, in those days stood for a Hungary engaged in a struggle to the death. And as he progressed down the length of the nave he was touched by a wave composed of the teary-eyed elation of the old, the determination of manhood, and the enthusiasm of the young, streaming toward him on his path so that after the tenth or fifteenth step the king's bearing had undergone a change. (Here the reporter stood on tiptoes to photograph everything accurately with his bulging eyes.)

At first all you could see was that Charles IV suddenly tossed his head back, whereas the tempo dictated by Tisza, carrying the crown, was still the same, fit for a church elder heading for Holy Communion at the Calvinist church in Geszt.

The king thrust his head and shoulders back and the youthful cavalry general of medium height who had stood back near the Loreto Chapel a while ago suddenly started to grow in front of the reporter's eyes that had become used to seeing him over the years in the springtime of youth.

Do not say that there is nothing on earth that passeth understanding. As long as kings and poets walk the face of this earth there will always be miracles. Mór Jókai, who, as a recipient of the Order of St. Stephen could have claimed the title of baron, was probably better qualified than this plain journalist to describe the wondrous metamorphosis of Charles IV. The novelist author of the "Four Georges" could also have explained the state of mind that exalts a king as he marches in the wake of his crown. The reporter can only register the plain, dry

191

fact that the king, on the way from the Loreto Chapel to the high altar of Matthias Church, had grown. You could no longer recognize in him the little general clad in field-gray who had not long ago stood by the side of Francis Joseph's casket. Nor was he recognizable any more as that carefree, youthful figure who had at times appeared by the side of the wintry old ruler as the embodiment of the Monarchy's smile, the spicy fragrance of Tyrolean forests, the sparkle of rushing mountain brooks, and the nonchalance of peacetime Vienna.

Charles IV had matured into manhood by the time he reached the high altar, even though a little earlier Lieutenant General Count Walls had conducted through the portals of the church the little boy dressed as a page, wearing a white fur hat, who had been brought here to watch the coronation of his father.

Yes, he tossed back his head, drew back his shoulders, elongated out his waist—although they say his eyes had filled with tears by the time he reached the high altar.

And it was there, in front of the high altar, in the roughly ten-minute interval between the acts of anointing and coronation, that an ominous thing happened which went respectfully unmentioned in the newspaper reports of the day. Following the rite of the Coronation Mass when the prince-archbishop anoints the king's right arm, the king descended the steps of the altar. And he lost his footing on the second step.

The royal figure tottered.

From the side, Tisza took a step toward him as if to help. The prince-archbishop paled as he stood still, his extended hand frozen in the act of blessing.

The king tottered but did not fall. The next moment he stood formally, solemnly in his appointed place.

"This morning he was still running a fever," said Bánffy, passing in front of the members of the press. But already from the sanctuary of the church there came the hoarse, wolfish, barbed voice that had issued commands for so many years throughout Hungary—the voice of István Tisza.

"Long live—the King."

The gentlemen of the press, their job done, rushed forth from Matthias Church lest they miss the deadline for the evening papers on Coronation Day.

(1 February, 1925)

If the Elder Tisza Were to Return...

The graying or brown strands were combed upward from behind and from both sides toward the top of the skull that was smooth as a billiard ball; his barber took great pains to eliminate the hairs of old age from nostril and ear; scissors and pomade trimmed and shaped his mustache to resemble a woman's lips; his necktie above the high vest was affixed by a carnelian pin, he wore a signet ring on his index finger, a swallowtail coat, a monocle slung over the shoulder, checked trousers and buttoned shoes: such was the figure of the politician in Hungary. He was recognizable from afar, and waiters, porters, and cabdrivers doffed their hats to him; "the nation's widow", this patriotic female type of yore, bestowed gracious smiles on him; at restaurants and night clubs the most experienced waiter served him at the special table; the train conductors saluted him eagerly—every step he took was stamped by authority and surrounded by respect, for in Hungary nothing was impossible for a Member of Parliament, he could get anything done, all doors opened for him; he wore the magic ring of oriental fables on his finger, which he only had to rub once to conjure up a thousand djinns ready to do his bidding.

This was indeed a happy period in Hungarian politics. The newspapers complained and created uproar, the orators of the extreme left talked themselves hoarse past midnight, a series of pushy loyalists filibustered by reading the speeches of William Pitt the Younger verbatim and using British parliamentary expressions without rhyme or reason, while on the left the writings of Kossuth were quoted as Holy Scripture. The elder Tisza sat through all of this with the composure of eternity itself. There are figures in our history who turned the country Catholic, then made it poor. Kálmán Tisza helped this country become corrupt and sinful.

Members of Parliament received a per diem of five forints, disbursed in crackling new banknotes. These banknotes with angels on them were welcome visitors indeed; even old Jókai was glad to see them although at home his wife took them away from him. Whenever a new type of banknote or cigar was issued the Minister of Finance sent samples to the members of Parliament. Even the janitor was glad to let an M.P. into the building late at night, and women vied to be seen in his company. And yet their per diem was only five forints, a miserable honorarium that Petőfi had complained about in a poem.

Elections usually cost a lot of money. One had to be a most pompous and loud stump orator to be judged indispensable enough by old Tisza for him to open the party's campaign chest. Most representatives would have pawned their eternal salvation to have sufficient constitutionally allowed expenses to keep their electioneering agents from abandoning ship. They were deep in debt yet elated when they boarded the train to Budapest where they hoped to find that "pot of gold". Perhaps there was such a pot somewhere (could old Podmaniczky know the secret of its whereabouts?)—for so many had written, talked, and clamored about it! But actually very few reached the promised land close by the side of that pot. Most representatives had to be content with misallocated funds and various petty fixes, specializing in industry and commerce, catering to bank managers until they could become bank managers themselves. There were many suspect careers of this sort in the Hungary of old, careers of such longevity that no one complained any more. People grew resigned to the fact that there were representatives who grew rich on graft, who established banks, were shareholders and died as millionaires, and maybe even had a street named after them. The more honest or less clever ones, or, let us say, those who were more modest, had the decency to retire after a brief stint—if indeed they still had a place to return to—or else concocted sinecures for which they danced attendance on the Prime Minister; or else they married and told tales of parliamentary doings for the rest of their lives. Those who kept their seats (on the far left), whose beards turned white on the benches of the palace on Sándor Street; who for decades ate their meals at Pelcner's or Szikszay's and fought their battles with the composure of warriors; who always thought of the House of Representatives with a capital H, the way it appeared in the papers; and who demanded vacations only in the summertime in order to go home for the wheat harvest or to sit in quietude under the plane trees of the Buda esplanade, were mostly men of modest means. Betrayal and loss of principles were essential in those days for success in Hungarian politics. No one went to jail for this and people continued to shake your hand. Parliamentary immunity was always claimed by those who had something on their conscience.

*

Ah, if those gendarme-faced elders were still around, they who had sprawled, blinking as if in the bliss of a steam bath, on the parliamentary benches in the vicinity of the premier of the moment! And if the brash young provincial loudmouths were to press forward again, they whose ambition ever since childhood had been to become the director of a bank or Lord Lieutenant of a county! If the elder Tisza were to return for one day to survey Hungary with his vulture eyes and see what has become of this province he had always carried on his palm as an offering to Francis Joseph! (He would most certainly give his son a good spanking for not taking better care of this country.)

The "Mamlukes", the old-time Liberals ("*mungos*", as the members of this privileged lot liked to call themselves), would now stand in their former places flabbergasted, utterly amazed. What has happened here?

What has happened?

The Jacobins, those without neckties, the rebels, the subversives, the despised, downtrodden forces of the opposition have made a comeback. And they have come brandishing their swords.

Yes, the war has produced some truly incomprehensible phenomena.

(13 June, 1917)

The Golden Age of Budapest

Were Budapest twice the size it is today, even then it could not comfortably accommodate its present population.

Even if the difficulties of earning a livelihood were to triple in the city, along with a tripled cost of living—food, clothes, housing—even so, the population would remain essentially the same.

Were the number of beggars, cripples, the down and out, and the impoverished to quadruple: even then not one heart would be touched in this metropolis.

If the cost of luxuries, women's fashions, shoes, and jewelry had to be paid in human flesh, even so they would not remain unsold.

And if there were no more decent men or women to be found in Budapest, even that should not be surprising in 1917, in this fourth year of Bravery and Infamy.

On a hot day in August Budapest smells like a menagerie. This is the smell carried by the traveling circus with its animals, the fully loaded caravans of the itinerant troupe of clowns, a smell that irritates the noses of long-time residents in this city.

Formerly no one was surprised to find that Dob and Király Streets emanated a fragrance of ripe cheese in the summer months; the dominant odors in outer Józsefváros were provided by the carters' horses and axle-grease, the worn leather interiors of hackney cabs, the redolence of rotten plums and melon rinds; when the dog days had arrived and the wind from Rákos Plain went to sleep like a slothful stable boy, the narrow back streets of the Inner City offered a bouquet composed of the scents of thread and of young seamstresses from salons and milliners' shops, mingled with the beer-barrel and sausage aromas exhaled by small taverns opening from entrance-ways. Each shop and every building, possibly every single apartment in Budapest, sent its own scent into the street, the way small children are expelled from home by negligent parents. People slept by open windows, performed their ablutions outdoors on the balconies, aired their bed linen; the kiosk's slender beauty would walk about barefoot at home; and in the narrow streets of Erzsébet-

197

város, through the open windows of the ground floor, one could glimpse all sorts of flea-hunts ordinarily carried on by women in shirtsleeves; the janitor would open the front entrance in his underwear, and occasionally a naked figure would fall from some upper floor where he had intended to spend the hot night in a flowerpot.

...I agree that the nocturnal doings of the citizens of this metropolis do not make for very appetizing reading; there is enough play-acting during the day— let them live naturally and as they please at least during the night. Oftentimes I think this city is like a cheap hotel in a back alley where the window shades are forever pulled down tight, never a loud word escapes into the night, the piano player has gone to bed long ago, the desk clerk is nodding off; but when the police raid the place they find a traveling salesman bricked into the wall, a woman choked to death by pillows, and a small child squatting in the unused summer stove.

And yet, in the summertime, Budapest asleep had a certain feminine fragrance. Perhaps these exhalations came from sewing schools, girls' boarding schools, the old telephone exchange, or the dormitories of the Sacré Coeur. I readily agreed with those painters who depicted Budapest as a female with big eyes, a Near Eastern nose, peach bloom on her neck, her feet white after her Good Friday bath; a woman who is voluptuous but hardworking, who can laugh lasciviously but who observes morality; who bestows flirtatious looks but carefully locks the front door; a woman desired by many, but rarely possessed. I nodded acquiescence to the lies of poets who claimed Budapest women were as sensible as grandmother's ivory amulet and stood by poets in their dreams; that they yearned for pure love in their reveries over the music of a dusky Gypsy violinist in the café; that noble and kind hearts were beating underneath all of their silliness, debauchery, stupidity; that they went to the Hangli café and the Danube promenade merely to take the air; that they whitened their shoes solely to look good for their husbands; that girls had no other desires than those ascribed to the Gyurkovits girls; that only provincial girls went to secret rendezvous at bachelor apartments and other meeting-places such as the premises of the seamstress, dentist, fortune-teller, manicurist, or midwife—while the most they, the Budapest ladies, ever did was to sit under the ancient plane trees at the Császár Baths by the side of old village priests and their breviaries—and that they went to Buda in carriages with the top up only in order to pick flowers for their mothers' birthdays.

Now, looking back at those long-gone prewar times, how desirable the Budapest of old appears! Budapest, the city that used to be scorned as malodorous, immoral and "too Jewish"! That old Budapest, seemingly frivolous, empty-headed, an inane imitation of Paris, tasteless in its fashions, living on borrowed money, trading in women, dying for the theater and entertainments and thriving on fleeting amorous encounters! City of tireless salesmen and poets with empty pockets! The Budapest of the so-called *gentry*, who, having gone bankrupt in the countryside, had taken refuge here to start a new life of swindles, casinos, horse-races, cards! But also the Budapest of another, respectable middle class uprooted from the soil, blown by the wind to the city, where it accepted modest employment, office or professional work, without any pretensions; the fathers wore the same overcoat all their lives, the mothers reused their old silk dresses to sew a new one every year, the daughters became teachers or post-office workers, the sons strove to complete their university studies, and only the grandchildren would again wear the signet ring with the twofold family coat of arms.

Oh, Budapest of old, where each morning the passenger train arriving at the Eastern Terminal brought young, enthusiastic hearts full of budding hopes, credos, and brains and brawn ready for action! They arrived in a waking Budapest—into the foggy metropolis, to the clanging of streetcar bells, the scent of newsprint, a thousand footfalls heading toward the city's center where waiters wore freshly ironed clothes—as heroes of romantic novels, for whom great things were awaiting behind all those apartment-building windows that were open for airing. The men, whose positions they would have to win, were being shaved by barbers, or were still lazily yawning; the women, whose lives and peace of mind would be disrupted by the stranger, were troubled by bad dreams, feeling a constriction of the heart as that future someone walked past their windows; the old men, with eyes like the hollows in ancient trees on János Hill, began their inspection of the newcomer by handing him the heaviest hammer; the quiet streets in the Inner City or Józsefváros, where today a sour remembered smell fills the rooms formerly rented by the month to students or young men with jobs, had once awaited with curiosity the approach of the stranger with the small suitcase and unlimited hopes, who came to that bygone Budapest where offices, bureaus, libraries, cheap little taverns, the love of seamstresses or girls of the street, possibly solitude in a hospital and an unmarked grave, would constitute the lot of the ambitious young man who was so eager to work and learn. The city sidewalk was still a gold-mine then, willing ears gave credence to smooth tongues, the dull-witted made way for the strong and the clever; talent and knowledge could dig themselves a passage even through granite walls like a mole with claws of steel; good fortune was awaiting to be grasped; life would challenge the champion only up to the age of forty-five at the most, after which one could relax, for by then one would certainly have attained one thing or another—a pension, or else despair... Oh, Budapest of old, when one could survive here simply on will-power!

Let someone come to Budapest nowadays and try to make a living by actually doing work! You can strain your nerves taut as a drumskin, walk your legs off, work your fingers to the bone, go mad with work, saw wood, lift the heaviest loads like so many sacks of flour—but if you are unwilling to transgress the law you will remain unsuccessful. The city smells like a menagerie not only because people are sparing in their use of water and hygiene, but also because bloodthirsty tigers and treacherous hyenas inhabit Budapest. The war has turned just about everyone into a scoundrel. Anyone who has modestly refrained from making a fortune in this era certainly deserves the Cross of the Order of King Charles. For by now indigence, hardship, and humiliation have come to be just about synonymous with middle-class virtues. The tax registers containing the records for the war years will some day provide the gaudy but true portrait of Budapest.

We look on dumbfounded at the trains overloaded with passengers bound for the capital; we stop and stare incomprehending at the crowds milling in the street and filling the theaters, the riotous, stifling gambling casinos, and the Budapest tenements from cellar to chimney: Where have all these people come from? It is as if the entire population of the city had been replaced over the past three years. The number of immigrants has taken on American proportions. The stone cast by the war has stirred up the muddy bottom of the pond. It is impossible to recognize our much-maligned and scorned, but now unforgettably dear old Budapest. They are all gone now, our old friends who used to take walks in little parks resembling Parisian woodcuts, the passersby on the tree-lined avenues of Pest and the little streets of Buda, the amiable Inner City shopkeepers, the intimate restaurants, the friendly cabdrivers, the familiar barbers, the well-known neighborly faces on charming streets, refined ladies we had fallen in love with from afar when they attended Mass at the

Franciscan Church, the noise of the children's room: all of the occasionally vulgar but never ornery or soulless daily life of Budapest. The city of the pre-war years has receded as far into the distance as the city of the mid-nineteenth century. Soon the chroniclers will be able to write touching reminiscences about the past life of Budapest, its fashions and men-about-town and maddeningly beautiful women who have since then dared to emerge only this summer, for now they can hold their old-style hats in their hands, according to the currently reigning fashion of the boulevard. A few crumbling and grizzled old dandies are still standing around on street corners, wearing white and sporting a broken monocle, in the mistaken belief that they can please women in the old manner. Gradually we must bury the old, lovable Budapest, along with the casualties of war. Budapest has died a hero's death in the world war.

(19 August, 1917)

Budapest Stark Naked

One of my readers told me about a dream of his that predicted a time when the only people in Budapest wearing frock-coats would be those respectable gentlemen one sees on barber's signs, smiling or else solemnly staring, showing off their beards and mustaches waxed to a point—for the male population will be going about stark naked. But eventually the women will also remove those colorful skirts that are so transparent in the summer and cut so short in the winter that they leave as little to the imagination as a fig-leaf. Only the wax mannequins of fashion salons will retain any trace of so-called street or evening wear, and prominent ladies will only be recognizable by their hats; former beauties will be dethroned by new belles who will triumph through the vogue of nakedness, which is approaching from the direction of Russia where the peasants in certain provinces are already going about unclothed. This is how they demonstrate their woeful poverty and also protest against the war. If the prediction comes true and the future salvation of the world is on the way from Dostoyevsky's land, then most likely the fashion for bare feet will not spare us. Although for at least the past year and a half everyone in Budapest could well have gone around unclad, the prices have been that high. But a time will come when the shopkeeper will have the same thing to say even to the wealthy and the thieves, Vili Medvegy and the profiteers, the oil dealers and the bookmakers: that he has run out of bolts of cloth, that nothing is to be had in his shop for love or money except corsets and hats; that old clothes will have to be worn until they are rags. If the war lasts another ten years, the fashion started by fanatical Russian peasants will take over in Hungary as well.

*

But our souls are already as naked as the heroes of Dostoyevsky's novels.

So many principles and so-called moral viewpoints have been turned topsy-turvy by all the pain and torment of three years of war!

Take for instance the fighting spirit which flared up in our midst at the start of the war with an ardor resembling the crusades. Citizens sang in the streets of Budapest like actors upon the stage. Civilians felt ashamed that they were not at the front, shedding their blood for the fatherland. Truly enthusiastic citizens as well as those with ulterior motives volunteered for military service. A heart-gladdening warlike tide surged above the populace, obliterating pain and confusing the emotions. People felt fortunate to be in the war: Hooray, the hussars are going to charge! The older generation incited the young, as if unaware of their real motivation: the renewed glory of their own setting sun, by the destruction of the younger generation. Both our pediatrician and Professor Zemplén went off to kill and be killed on the battlefield. The poets howled as loudly as dogs foaming at the mouth. It was one nation undivided, the same flame, Saint Anthony's fire in each soul. Women challenged men on the street to inquire why they were not at the front. Gray old men wept outside the barracks after being rejected for military service.

And today?

The war is still on, like a steam mill working night and day. But the chores get done in a sober, calm, and as it were bored, everyday manner. The fancy rags, flag-waving, drunken shouts, and military emblems have been put aside by the soldiery. The soul has emerged from hiding behind the scenes and now thrashes naked in the open. It hurts and it hurts.

Love, out of which people have built a tower as tall as Babel, has over the past three years lost as much of its stature as a fortress under siege.

We have found out that love does not last forever but is so fleeting that it is barely worth talking about. The warriors have gone away and they have been forgotten at home. The letters stopped coming, soldiers on home leave began to look forward to returning to the front, females were running loose all over town, people now denied they had ever been in love. Hedonism, fashions, intoxication, and the never-ending anxieties of everyday life have combined to shake that earliest, childhood determination of women to devote their lives to one great love. Since the start of the war only in old novels by Jókai can one read about lifelong loyalty, self-sacrificing devotion, and imperishable love. For a decade before the war women absorbed all the adultery, frivolous nonsense, and debauchery of the Budapest stage with the same fascination they devoted to the ocean snails in the aquarium at the zoo—well, now they have pillaged the aquarium and cracked open and devoured the exotic shell-fish. For women, these last three years have been one long vacation. They have been on a prolonged leave of absence, left to their own devices, put to the test, and it is best to forget the experiences of the past three years, especially since it seems they have lately been trying to make amends, to stay within themselves, and to begin to think wistfully of trading their freedom for the so-called prison of old-time morality. I happen to know of several married couples who, after frequent disagreements during the war years, have been legally divorced and who have recently remarried. There have been too many such stories in recent months for all of them to be reported; formerly, we would read about such events in novels and shake our heads in disbelief. A married couple gets parted by great distance. Comes the solitude of being far away, recollections of the past, and those forgotten sweet nothings. Most people tend to remember only the good parts of the past, the charming and enjoyable portions. There are only a few of us unfortunate enough to be unable to forget and to forgive. Most men cling to the woman for whom they have made the ultimate sacrifice in life, by marrying her. In spite of the debasement of morals, the naked parade of debauchery, the heights of coarseness and depths of baseness attained, most men, especially the far-flung soldiers, still think as chastely about love as they did before the war. They are not aware of the details of what has been going on at home while they have been away, have not witnessed poverty showing itself more and more naked day by day, nor the apathy that accompanies penury; they have not seen that only the cheaters, the jail-birds, the unscrupulous have been feasting on steak, buying expensive outfits for their women, and partying loudly and conspicuously. Those who were far away could not have seen how society had split in two, into the rich and the poor; how the shoes of decent, educated folks had become down at the heel; how a whole lifetime's hard work and learning had become devalued, along with culture and heartfelt ways; how feminine morals, fragile as butterfly wings, had become crushed; and how flat-footed finance and crude, dull trash had walked all over the city... But let us leave for future chroniclers the accurate and forthright description of these times for people of the future when grandmothers shall not suffer any recrimination worse than no wreath upon their graves. Let us now rejoice that in the fourth year of the war love seems to be making a comeback, along with forgiveness and a longing for the beauties of the old ways of life. Lovers who have grown apart come together again; those who have said their farewells and hoped never to meet again in this life are again reaching out toward each other from distant windows, their sighs and prayers meet over the rooftops;

names are uttered that had been put away, never to be uttered again; sad husbands and broken wives hold out their hands to each other, having done their penance; fathers and mothers are returning home to their children... What is this, if not a chapter from a Dostoyevsky novel, when people break away from prejudice and moral bias, their souls thrashing about in newborn nakedness, and they are able to act as humans, as they desire, instead of obeying the wishes of society? ... They throw away their glad rags, their worn-out principles; couples huddle together again, dwellers in a storm-tossed nest; the loving feeling of old once more imbues hearts that cannot find consolation in the bleak and melancholy present unless they again attach themselves to a feminine strand of hair, the moonbeam made of the perfidious gold of former times.

*

The supply of clothing materials will last for quite some time in Budapest; ladies with bandy legs or crooked waists will continue to conquer, clad in the creations of their seamstresses; gentlemen's paunches will remain hidden; and fanatic, happy Russia will have a hard time making the nakedness of her peasants a worldwide rage. However, souls have disrobed themselves all over the globe. For those of us alive in these times, taking a good look around ourselves, there will not remain many secrets about our fellow humans taken into the grave. Many things will have to change for people to believe and trust each other again—and to love each other once more.

(26 August, 1917)

A Revolutionary Conversation with a Russian Lady

Once again we are witnessing real life playing out one of Jókai's novels, just as the most fertile imagination in Central Europe had once upon a time written it; as he had conceived and pictured Russia and put it all down on paper in his minuscule handwriting. Yes, it is as if Jókai's never-glimpsed czars, grand dukes, mysterious ambassadors, and secretive political agents are once more resurfacing as Russia begins to write its own historical novel, whose introduction is a telegram arriving via mysterious channels, the enigma of which is meaningful only for great novelists and ambassadors plenipotentiary. The fanatical czar, trembling in his romantic-sounding Winter Palace in Jókai's ineffable work *Liberty Under the Snow;* the revolutionary howl rising on the banks of the Neva; the decommissioning of the cannons turned upon the mob; and the rest of the well-known décor employed by previous Russian revolutionary accounts following Jókai's stage directions, once again parade in the imaginations of the readers of newspapers: in thousand-domed Moscow the spirits distilleries are on fire, the British Embassy is protected by reliable marines, the czar escapes by sled accompanied by faithful Cherkess guards.

These events belong to the immortal canvases of the panoramas of our childhood, when the early movie theaters and fairground spectacles would show the itinerant daub depicting the anarchist throwing the bomb at Czar Alexander, with blood on the snow and with streets burning in the background; the horses are rearing and the bearded czar, clad in a red coat, lies bleeding on Nevsky Prospekt. Nowadays the old-fashioned fairground savage rattling his chains has been replaced by gentlemen clad in circus-style liveries touting at the entrance to the panorama show, but the pictures inside remain the same. Russia keeps repeating the well-rehearsed old scenes, events full of cheap, folksy effects and fireworks, worthy of Jókai's brilliant imagination—without making much of an advance, historically speaking, since the revolt of the Cossacks. Revolutions in this ancient land do not necessarily bring about historical leaps, as they do in France. The revolution comes and goes, the new czar recites a prayer, the imperial ballet corps learns a new fairy play on top of the old ones, a few students and journalists are shipped off to Siberia (since the revolution came from the direction of Asia!), and at the open fires set at street intersections it is still the same muzhik warming his hands as in centuries past. Russia, this prehistoric white mammoth is still obstinately determined to turn its shaggy brow toward Europe, its shoulder muscles as massive as the craggy Urals, its tufted tail being pulled somewhere in the region of the Yellow Sea by all sorts of clinging, fearsome creatures as it flicks aside, unscathed, the tired old flintlock bullets of revolutions and lost wars. To fell this splendid beast with a mortal blow would take a butcher possessing unheard-of power. For now, throughout this world war (which will prove indelible in the history of every warring nation), things have remained as they were in Russia; the army contractors steal, just as in peacetime; the big city mobs still starve; and, like the ace of diamonds on the wall, the monk who had become too powerful at court is shot by a grand duke; the ruling cabal puts on a revolution in Petersburg to shore up its power, while the czar supposedly abdicates due to ill-health and ennui. Have we not seen similar scenarios in peacetime? Russia, with its endless territories leaning like a giant on top of Asia, from where no news ever emerges (except for the censored postcards sent by prisoners of war), carries on the ways of past centuries in silent introversion. Is it conceivable that in the Caucasus, the Urals, or Siberia they attach any special significance to this war in which all of Europe is involved to the last breath? The fusiliers, the Cossacks, had in times past obeyed orders to march forth from their Asian garrisons; they had marched against the Turks, the Japanese, and now, as once before, against Hungary. No one in the empire considers this unusual. The Petersburg ministers (who are profoundly despised as clowns by the governors of Asian provinces) from time to time arrange a Potemkin-style revolution to entertain the naive Europeans, to mislead the ambassadors, to subdue the urban mob, to strengthen their own positions, and for any number of other reasons the comprehension of which would be beneath the dignity of a true subject of Holy Mother Russia. They just wave it off and carry on in the heartland, leading the life of the forefathers while the capital, in its Parisian-style debauchery, flips somersaults on the stage at the western edge of the land. In place of Nicholas, the new czar is Alexander. This makes not the least difference in the ancient way of life—just as the death of the pope does not disturb the continuity of the Holy Roman Church.

*

My acquaintance, a Russian lady in Budapest, waves her delicate hand, the color of pale ivory, in gentle resignation. Russians traveling abroad take it for granted that European public opinion misinterprets the events in Russia and questions the security of the empire whenever there is a revolution or military campaign within its borders. The European revolutions (when such were still imaginable, and even if politely middle class) plowed deeper beneath the topsoil of the histories of nations than the present skirmish in Russia, where cannons are aimed at barricades. One may write articles and essays about the popular upheaval, but the Russian people care more about next month's Easter celebrations than about the hullabaloo in the capital. The intellectuals note with regret that fewer of their favorite French periodicals are available than before; Parisian books, silks, cosmetics, theater plays, and perfumes have become rarer and more costly. Hungarian prisoners of war, situated deep in the war-free hinterlands, have as much insight into this state of affairs as Russian prisoners of war in the provinces of our own country. War does not change the great and profound problems of human existence; suffering, torments of the soul, sleeplessness, melancholy feelings are all part and parcel of every true Russian household, along with the icons, nor have they been evicted in our days. Russians are fundamentally different from Europeans, who are capable, in their science, politics, and possibly philosophy, of once and for all delivering themselves from the various miasmas of the soul, national melancholia, unnamable yearnings, and inchoate vaporings. Every Russian at a certain level of education is a brooding reformer who first and foremost would like to arrive at an understanding of human existence. Nowhere do people cogitate as much as in Russia, and nowhere greater the despair over ever finding the right path to one's self through philosophy. In Russia there are adherents of every European school of philosophy, but actually they sense that these are as alien to their soul as another religion would be. The true and incommunicable Russian philosophy of life was most closely approached by the writers of old, those who wrote about Oblomov and the Hamlet of the Shchigry district, who empathized with Lermontov's regrets and Gogol's misty melancholy, who studied Pushkin's sentimentality and yearned for a village house with a smoking chimney. Tolstoy's novels were formerly discussed only in Petersburg salons; real Russians grew tired of them and put these books down. Sanin's stories are read by Russians when they are university students and are soon forgotten. Gorky's works find their greatest enthusiasts among workers, Jews, and foreigners. Voltaire, Kant, Hegel, and Nietzsche, who were once upon a time received with open arms in Russia and created classes within educated society, are now the stuff of memories. The theses of Master Marx have been much discussed of late. The appearance of any innovator in Europe always gave rise to fresh hope in Russia. But eventually they were all forgotten, for a real Russian is capable of forgetting everything after sleeping on it. Thus it will be with the Petersburg revolution.

*

"So what do real Russians believe in?" I asked Nadiezhda, the former Berlin University student who is now stuck for the duration of the war in Budapest.

The young lady, who bears some resemblance to a Zichy drawing that was executed at the command of the artist's imperial friend the czar, to illustrate Pushkin's poem about a Gypsy girl, whispered with a voice that trembled like the Volga mists:

"Nothing... At most in God and the Czar."

(18 March, 1917)

István Tisza's Journey Toward Death

October, 1918 on Margit Island

"Whatever happens, we're not leaving the island. Keresztes, our innkeeper, makes sure the marrowbone baked in a pastry shell is on the menu every day; Feri, our little waiter, is just as clever as his immortal namesake at the Boar's Head; I have deposited ten thousand gold korona at the hotel director's office... That should take care of us for a while!" said I to myself one afternoon in late October. But that evening around nine, mortally wounded limbs dropped with a final crack from the centuries-old trees around our inn; there were knocks on the walls as if Death were rummaging around for someone who had chosen this place to hide—perhaps some fugitive who had refused to die in the war; the windowpane tinkled like the four-kreutzer coin we used to toss for heads or tails, and suddenly there was a hole with spidery cracks around it in the glass. Someone shouted in the corridor:

"Lights out! The hotel's under fire from the Óbuda side."

I placed Thomas Carlyle's *History of the French Revolution* on the bedside rug and turned off the lights.

In those days I went to bed early and got used to carrying on half-awake conversations with the spirits that, as a result of things heard or read during the day, felt obliged to visit the invalid on the second floor. On this evening, in the enforced darkness, while bullets from Óbuda smashed into the stucco instead of the putative revelers, the door opened without a sound and in walked the lanky figure of István Tisza.

(All my life there have been only two men who intimidated me. One of them was Dezső Szilágyi, whose eyes were like a desert lion hypnotizing its prey before leaping. The other was this man whose glance and eyes could not be seen, who always seemed to be as secretive as those hooded men with invisible faces who had governed the world in medieval times with a mere flicker of their eyelashes... But in my musings I had most often associated István Tisza with someone else, that magical and wondrous being in Asia

211

about whom we in Europe know only that he dwells among the great mountains that originated at the creation of the world. No one really knows him; referred to as the Dalai Lama whenever a London journalist thinks of writing a piece on him, he is perhaps the most powerful man in the world as we know it—although conceivably István Tisza was simply one of those tough Hungarian village sheriffs, found by the dozen in the nineteenth century.)

His shade entered and stood before me, arms folded, ice cold, seemingly without earthly passions, omniscient, as if he had returned from the beyond, having gone through all hells including the front lines, and he alone knew what would happen to Hungary in this war and afterward.

He stood there in that memorable pose, self-assured and secure, his conscience cleared by the sternest balancing of accounts, implacable, Justice and unshakable Strength personified, without any panic, holding his ground as a church tower around which the whole village is on fire. (It is not surprising such a steeple had so many bell-ringers.)

That was how I remembered him from the unforgettable parliamentary session I happened to witness from the press gallery: standing tall, craggy, arms folded, inexorable as fate itself, like a gladiator ready to take on the whole world. And I can still see Márton Lovászy, my editor at the time, outraged, his face crimson, his curly gray locks flying, in all his splendid, handsome manhood—he possessed the dashing Hungarian good looks of those men who, ever since the *kuruc* campaigns, have been gladly giving their lives for their country and whose portraits on steel engravings survive in ladies' bedrooms as ideals against which fiancés are measured—I can see Lovászy in the dim gallery, tossing his head in a gesture that evoked with perfect clarity, for this reporter looking dreamily on, every protagonist of Hungarian history from Petur *Ban* through the Zrínyis and Rákóczis to the present...

He brought his fist down on the bench with a crash heard to this day, and his voice flared up in protest, a voice originating back in the casemates of the Kufstein, Olmütz and Josefstadt prisons: "But we're still pro-Entente here!"

Two million Hungarian soldiers, bearded martyrs facing death each day, and each night by the campfire thinking with tears in their eyes of the children at home, two million Hungarian soldiers stood at that moment on all fronts in the four directions of the compass, when that fist slammed down in the Budapest House of Representatives: desperate and timely words, a last Hungarian outcry.

212

...The next instant my eyes sought out István Tisza.

He was the man on the spot at whom the challenge was flung, like the gauntlet worn by our ancestors when they went to war in defense of the home.

The man with the iron mask and invisible eyes calmly stood his ground, as if he had just at that moment attained the end of the sevenfold path reached only by the most favored sons of the Lord Buddha: the predestined peak of clarity, a strength and wisdom beyond all volition.

He stood his ground like a man who, through some miraculous dream, can see not only times past more clearly than anyone else, but can also see, impassively and unchangeably, the coming future that no amount of human power can alter any more.

This is how the condemned stand on death row at dawn, while their relatives—stammering senseless words perhaps only for their own reassurance—insist that a reprieve may yet arrive.

Only he can be this calm who has arrived at a crossroads in life, where the road bifurcates: in one direction lies the labyrinth of madness, with its dull, trance-like, otherworldly laughter and the incomprehensible gibberish of fleeing wild geese; in the other direction gentle, soft footfalls lead toward the village cemetery of Geszt.

Tisza stood still, with arms folded, and all of us, small shopkeepers, itinerant peddlers and salesmen, timid owners, trembling tenants, market-women, drovers, steaming little cups in the vast kitchen of life, mere axes in the hand of gigantic wood-choppers, orphaned sparrows out on the highway of Hungary's fate—we all believed that this man with the invisible face, whose sunshine, playful meadow, birdsong dawn, even the color of whose eyes, were hidden from everyone in Hungary, just as little known as the Dalai Lama in Asia: we felt that this man alone knew the fate of the war, its present state, its future outcome. We had to place our faith in him, as one does in the horseradish that superstitious kinsmen thrust under the nose of the dying man after the doctor has departed.

"So they're shooting in Óbuda", I said in a voice hushed by the rat-tat of bullets, in the dark, to the poor woman who had at that time undertaken the martyrdom of putting up with my insanities—"have no fear, Tisza will set things right." For Lovászy may have signed the paychecks—with eyes closed— in the editorial offices, but in the end it was up to this bespectacled sheriff to make the gendarmes and army deserters toe the line.

Possibly in confirmation of this, as at an old-time itinerant theatrical production, a Mannlicher rifle went off with a thunderous report right in front of the hotel.

The corridor instantly filled with corpulent ladies in their underwear, who forgot all about beauty parlors, cosmetics shops, and milliners. Their gentlemen dragged all types of monogrammed suitcases usually lugged by fearfully panting porters who were made to earn their pay. Feri, our speedy waiter, rushed in waving his napkin to announce in his twittery way that it was only Jani the groundskeeper who had fired a shot in the air, to let the ladies and gentlemen staying at the hotel know that the local guard was on the alert and would defend the rosebushes and the members of the gentle sex from harm.

Ah, what feverish daytimes followed for the invalid on the second floor, who only yesterday had gullibly believed he could devote his remaining time to curing his real and imagined ills!

A frightened little old gentleman lamented, under the potted palms of the hotel lobby, that recently several of his acquaintances had died in the city, although in his opinion they could have survived all their ailments had it not been for these eventful days... A lanky young man in civilian clothes, about whom it was obvious from ten paces away that he had never been near an enlistment center, claimed to be an officer, took liberties with the women, and had to be slapped in the face before he departed, uttering threats... I took photographs of policemen with rifles who, like recruits at the front, dug in near the landing dock at the upper end of the island, anticipating an attack from the direction of the Óbuda shipyards. Boats I had never seen before, gray and smokestacked, were progressing single file upriver toward Óbuda, and, having executed the required maneuvers one after another, sounded their doleful foghorns like wounded beasts. They were river gunboats and patrol boats from the lower reaches of the Danube—I wondered how the starched naval officers would pass their time after steering their gunboats into the backwaters near Óbuda... I ventured out as far as Margit Bridge, where gray trucks rattled past, transporting, as if to a wedding, soldiers wearing asters in their caps—no one could tell where to and what for... But equally heart-stopping were the trucks carrying policemen armed with rifles, their legs dangling from the back, letting the wheels do the walking. (Didn't all these men have families?) In the old days we thought a policeman was someone wearing an armband with the national colors standing at intersections, giving his mustache a twirl with his white-gloved hand when village girls asked him where to find Király Street. It was hard to imagine these men, with their grim, determined faces, who seemed to be getting ready to continue on the streets of Budapest what had been left off at the front, giving directions to anyone... From the direction of the Újpest factories' smokestacks we kept hearing the sound of sirens... I thought of throwing my pocket watch away for it did not seem to show the time when those factory horns usually sounded... I saw Mr. Kéri rush past on the sidewalk; he did not stop to talk, whereas formerly he used to like to exchange comments about the books he read when he visited my night-owlish den... I also saw Keresztes, our innkeeper, leaving the island, although only yesterday he had been bragging that he knew how to keep his cool, being an American citizen... Hansom cabs loaded with suitcases were fleeing toward the city from the direction of the hotel, and the drivers were much rougher with their horses and passengers than usual... At noon, decrepit Werndl-rifles were handed out to the guard at the bridge, although no one would dare to fire these weapons that reminded me of the shotgun old Kunfalvi toted to shooting-parties around Nyíregyháza... The groundskeepers donned all sorts of military caps; the cyclamens in the greenhouse were watered by a young man sporting a hussar's shako—the asters had all been taken in the morning...

"Ah, don't worry, Tisza will straighten out this mess, that's what he's for", I said to myself. "So why not take a walk on these autumnal paths of the island where poets once sat on the white benches to write love lyrics addressed to the lobster-red leaves, to trees twisted by unknown sorrows, to small shrubs that trembled with each breeze, and to the women whose white feet had trodden upon these leaves that still blush at the memory in late October. Go and sit on a bench near the bust of wise old János Arany. He too was a Calvinist, like Tisza, and came from the same parts. He could probably tell you what Tisza is up to..."

But by late afternoon I was on my way to Pest, carried by that mysterious anxiety that at times like these flies over the Danube more easily than a flock of crows.

On the streetcar I saw Tisza...

Which is somewhat surprising, since according to his biographers he hardly moved from the Villa Roheim during these days!

Yes, it was Tisza, seated in a corner, I realized with a shudder.

215

Let's see now, how many years have passed since those suppers given by *Magyar Figyelő* at the István Cellar for the purpose of getting Tisza acquainted with those younger writers who avoided politics and had therefore not been seen at the party club premises? Tisza showed an interest in contemporary Hungarian literature... I was among those writers this mysterious man favored with his attention, although he never let on whether he liked what he had read. (He was too much of a gentleman to give an opinion on a subject, such as literature, about which he could not speak with full authority.) How many years ago was that? It must be about fifteen, for it had to be before the war, when Tisza still paid attention to the armies of minuscule letters scribbled by writers...

On one side he was flanked by Ferenc Herczeg, on the other by Pál Farkas, the editors of *Magyar Figyelő*. Herczeg, especially in front of the half a dozen or so writers, acted in a cool and reserved manner toward the commander in chief of national politics, for, after all, writers must demonstrate through social contacts, too, that they are in no way inferior to politicians. (Dear God, back in those days we still competed about distinctions like that—not much later, everyone became identical in the uniforms worn by cannonfodder!)

Pál Farkas, on the other side, with his blazing, aggressive manner, made more of an effort to engage Tisza's attention in certain conversational topics. Károly Lovik and I were sitting across the table from Tisza. (As a gourmand with a healthy appetite at the time I made a note of the excellent pork *pörkölt*, accompanied by a fine wine.) After supper Tisza suddenly turned to Lovik and started a conversation about horses, showing such expertise that the editor of *Vadász- és Versenylap* [Hunt and Turf] was once or twice caught red-faced. Back in those days I had considered myself as knowledgeable about horses as an average horse dealer at the Debrecen Inn or as any tipster at the racetrack, having had occasion to study the calculation of handicaps under the tutelage of Miklós Szemere. Therefore I listened to the conversation with undivided attention. Tisza did not make one mistake in his statements about horses, whereas Lovik became uncertain here and there, possibly because he wanted to give only absolutely correct answers. After horses the next topic was the hunt, the approaching snipe season and the rest, gradually lending our table (which had been set apart by a folding screen) the after-dinner atmosphere of a country mansion. The air was thick with pipe-smoke, faces grew animated, flushed, as if we had spent the day amusing ourselves with the entertainment offered at a battue hunt. Little by little Tisza turned in front of my eyes into a provincial huntsman, as he seemed to grow younger, his eyes more focused behind the lenses, his beard with hardly any gray in it, the posture of his shoulders as easy as those of a cavalry officer dressed in civvies at a rural name-day celebration. (His horse is tied up in the stables; next morning he has to be back in barracks.) Then he turned to me:

"Tell me, does old Andris Kállay, back in your neck of the woods in Szabolcs, still hunt small game with a rifle?"

Well, that was back then, and now here we were riding on the streetcar, on which no one actually purchased tickets in those days—the conductor thanked his stars if he escaped without a beating from the passengers. There were people on top of the car and hanging off the sides, front and back, like swarming bees. Countless men wore field-gray uniforms, and ecstatic women and children clung to them, as if these men had just returned from beyond the grave. There was pushing and shoving, tumultuous noise and loud guffaws, swearing and drunken singing as at a provincial railroad station after the fair is over. Soldiers' usage filled the air—new words, resembling flea-bites and scabies, that had come to Budapest straight from the trenches of the front lines. Everyone acted crazed, as if this were the end of the world. Neither top hats nor Prince Albert coats carried the least authority any more; a silver-haired old gentleman was loudly dubbed "old geezer", and a dignified matron sporting a hat was lucky to get away with some light ribbing from the fellow passengers, squeezed as she was in their midst. The devil's ball was about to begin, having started early in the day; what would happen later, when darkness fell over the city? (I would be grateful if Mr. Carlyle would loan me his pen to transcribe these journal entries.)

But back to that solitary man sitting in a corner of the streetcar, wearing a black overcoat, a hard black hat, his barely inch-and-a-half-wide starched white collar over a worn necktie; his spectacles empty, devoid of eyes, his unruly beard similar to a stand of autumn acacia trees with clearings of low scrub, in places white with snow—under a grim sky where a flock of crows sound their doleful cawing. There he sits, lost in thought, impassive, not wasting a glance at anyone, showing no interest in anything, as the dead; and still as a wooden grave-post that cares not a whit whether it is a wedding procession that goes past on the highway, or a funeral cortège of weeping and lamenting folks bringing someone recently dead to be planted nearby. There he sits suddenly aged, as a squire whose estate has just been auctioned off; grim as one about to make his last will and testament, wondering whether the heirs will execute his wishes... Were he to remain so still much longer in this streetcar loaded with madmen he would start to resemble rusty old battle axes, herdsmen's dusty long whips, outdated war clubs, worn old helmets that lie neglected in some collection of armor... But suddenly he stands up.

This tall, broad-shouldered, narrow-waisted, deep-chested man's figure is seen as some ghost materialized here from above or below to frighten the mindless market-women, hussies, drunken soldiers, and civilians who are even more intoxicated than the soldiers.

At first only those among the deranged fall silent who hang and swing on the straps right beside him, as if a freezing wind were coming forth from under the coat of this man with the invisible face.

"Tisza," I hear the word from the other end of the car in rapid flight from mouth to mouth, from the throats of apprentices, the parched lips of strumpets, the unkempt mustaches of veterans, the half-crazed passengers of this streetcar—the way the chilly exhalation of death usually approaches people.

The whole menagerie pricked up their ears as if a cruel lion-tamer had entered the cage. The rough, convivial soldier, who a moment ago was beginning to resemble a guffawing medieval mercenary eyeing the females of a newly conquered town, now abruptly snaps to attention. The current of chatter, that ticklishly squealing tone of voice females have been assuming over the past few days, suddenly freezes over, as if a whiplash had landed on a wanton's shoulder. The non-paying passengers on this streetcar—the men who took off from work to plunge head first into the mad chaos of these days, the women who fled their kitchens, the children who believed themselves to be men—all stop talking for a second... Unless I am mistaken, this feeling is called sudden fear.

Tisza, impassive, without even a sideways glance, notes that people have made way for him in the crowded car. You can see that he takes this completely for granted, as he advances slowly, a head taller than the men and women around him. A soldier with a biblical beard shoves an apprentice boy, who was clinging to the steps, out of the way. Tisza leaps off as lightly as if he were dismounting from a horse.

"There goes Tisza!" says someone behind our backs in the still hushed streetcar, which, amidst mad clangor and banging and clatter—like everything else these days—careens on toward Múzeum Boulevard.

218

Tisza, his face invisible, turns into Dohány Street; for a moment I follow his lanky, flagpole figure in the thick crowd on the sidewalk. I can't say I am slow on my feet, but the hesitation, the indecision that restrains perhaps even the fastest runners' feet these days, does not permit me to take strides two feet long. As for Tisza, his strides are at least two and a half feet. Where is he hurrying? What could he have learned for him to be in such a rush? ... If anyone knows how things stand these days, it has to be him. Oh, why can't I run into a cub reporter who is not loath to rush around in the street, so I could send him in Tisza's wake! What's going to happen to us? Where is Tisza going? Is there a telephone somewhere nearby on which he can talk with the King, or with Kaiser Wilhelm? To order loyal troops to Budapest and hang everybody who obstructs law and order? No, this man who has given the orders in Hungary for so many years is not going to just let himself be stood up against the wall! ... I must talk to him!

My thoughts race wildly, but Tisza, too, races ahead on the street in the falling darkness, as if sensing that he is being followed.

I give up and stop on a street corner, as Tisza's figure vanishes for good in the Budapest street. I start walking in the direction of Margit Island. As I reach the bridge I hear the carillons of church bells playing from steeples here and there; so perhaps the situation is not so grave after all... And why should I fear anything while Tisza still goes about on a streetcar and on foot in this maddening town?

He was dead by the next evening. He lay stretched out on the floor of the vestibule of a villa near the Municipal Park. As unknowable a man as he was, I wouldn't put it past him to have gone to his death gladly.

(1925)

The New Conquest

Which minister or public commissioner is in charge of the soldiers returning home? I believe this task belongs to the entire nation; this is a colossal event, comparable to a new Conquest.

With this second Conquest a new and uncharted chapter in the history of the Hungarian nation is about to begin, just as it happened a thousand years ago at the time of the first Conquest. Between the Danube and the Tisza rivers a new world is about to be constructed, one that is for now still wrapped in mist, even for the wisest sages. We cannot as yet see the coming towers of the near future, events are so unpredictable; the face of tomorrow's Hungarian is still hidden behind the murky veil. An entirely new Hungarian history is about to begin. The last pages of the old history book have been filled up by the war.

How will our new history begin? Not with the Magic Stag or the *turul* bird, not any more. They have gone to eternal rest with the ancient Magyars. Our nation's kings, "the saintly and heroic ones", have ridden away; and the Habsburgs will haunt us for a while, the way the lugubrious ghost of Hamlet's father roamed Elsinore. All of "historical Hungary", with its gold-braided laws, insane Dual Monarchy and crypt-scented politicians, has sunk into the endless ocean along with the setting sun.

In the gray gloaming the shadowy, unknowable bands of the new conquerors are approaching.

They are returning from that hell to which the Hungary of old had consigned them.

The chroniclers open up the new volume and write on the first page: "Ragged, wasted hordes of wandering soldiers arrived from the north, south and west, and started to rebuild a Hungary in ruins."

The day has arrived about which we have talked so much and for which we have done nothing to prepare; a day that only lamenting women have been awaiting with anguished hearts, while the bloated leaders have refused to believe in its arrival: all of the soldiers are coming home. Whatever they find here, even if it were the old world they had left behind, would be new for them, for one can forget everything in the course of four years. But they will find a new country about which they cannot have the least notion. They will have to find

221

their places in this land turned topsy-turvy that longs to be a republic and yearns for liberty for all. Just as we leaped into this war four years ago with blindfolded eyes, without any agenda; just as none of those singing recruits had the least idea they were being taken from home to the slaughterhouse of Europe; just as we had believed we would triumph and win the day with our handful of strength and lion's share of courage over the pride of nations that had done us no wrong and whom we did not hate—this Hungarian army, millions strong, has now returned from its argonautic journey with the same ignorance. And they keep arriving, without the least idea of what to do here at home.

When they went off to war there were some at least who shouted at them: "Why do you want to die for Francis Ferdinand, who never had much love for you!"

Now, back home at last, they look around in their own homeland and barely recognize it.

At the joyous moment of Armistice there is no one to tell them they will never have to bear murderous arms again. That there will be no more need for killing and bayonets, because peace shall reign on earth and everyone will find his place in this land without having to resort to the use of arms. No, our finest public orators are not urging them in a loud voice to remove the dark burden of revenge and anger from their hearts and leave it at the border. That this country has regretted, and has suffered, for the mistake of sending its finest sons off to war. No, there are no persuasive, kind words awaiting them, no embracing arms or friendly handshakes to make them forget four years of their lives so they can begin new and happy lives. There is no one to tell them they must not harm anyone here at home: the poor woman broken and dazed by suffering, the neighbor who has grown rich and his private property. But let us have new legislation within the shortest time possible, to separate the heartsick soldier from his wife before he thinks of murder. Let there be new property laws at the earliest opportunity, so everyone has their own place in this land. Let every mouth shout and every pen write that we have been reborn, and let us put the dark past finally behind us. Let us all be brothers, and let all hearts, and hands, drop the knives with which they had approached each other.

Where are our public orators? Where are the writers?

There will be plenty of time to look for public office—once real order has been established in Hungary.

(10 November, 1918)

How the Revolution Broke Out

János Hock was getting ready to go home from the Hotel Astoria; it was around six-thirty in the evening and as usual the parish priest was expected for dinner at the Józsefváros parsonage.

He had just finished presiding over the afternoon-long session of the National Council. The exhaustive discussion was centered around the events of the previous day, when the Budapest policemen had volunteered their services to the Council. But during the afternoon ominous news kept arriving from Zrínyi Street. One after another, policemen who were committed to the revolutionary cause reported that the Chief of Police was trying to prevent the reorganization of the force. There was fear that the chief's practiced hand might succeed in pressuring the officers who took the oath of loyalty yesterday—vigorously enough to abate their enthusiasm...

The atmosphere of the Council's afternoon session was grim.

Károlyi had nothing cheerful to report; Archduke Joseph, the occupant of the Royal Palace, was considering himself just about installed as Palatine of Hungary (having been appointed by the king). And Hadik—although inexperienced—was obliged to take action in case there was a flare-up in the city. He was, after all, the Prime Minister, responsible for the maintenance of law and order in the country and in the capital. At least he was a patriot with his heart in the right place. Presumably he would not start hanging people if things went wrong. It was a lucky stroke of fate that the crafty Wekerle and Tisza, a man who was capable of anything, were out of the way.

But the mood remained unchanged and the afternoon session of the Council ended on a gloomy and troubled note. Hock went looking for his galoshes, while Purjesz telephoned his editorial office to say that he was on the way.

At this point two postal officials show up at the reception desk of the Astoria, looking for Mr. Hock, President of the Council.

The desk clerk happens to be bright and his heart is in the right place. He has just resumed his old job after four years of military service. He is an ardent revolutionary. He quickly directs the two postal officials to Hock and Purjesz, who are getting ready to leave.

Coming straight to the point, the postal officials inform the President of the National Council that the Budapest postal and telephone workers intend to depose the incumbent chief postmaster at a meeting to be held that same evening. Were the National Council to show some support, it would not be difficult to steer the meeting toward the new, revolutionary direction.

Hock asks Purjesz to go and motivate the postal workers to follow the lead of the policemen.

Purjesz, in turn, is of the opinion that a personal appearance by Hock would have an electrifying effect on the undecided postal workers.

"Where is the meeting?"

"Number 30 Rákóczi Avenue."

They set out on foot. Hock's supper will have to wait at the Józsefváros parsonage. (Eventually he will make do with a small portion of stew at around midnight from the kitchen of the Hotel Astoria.) Nor will Purjesz's colleagues find him at his editorial desk on this day. It is the 30th of October. Dark clouds hang over Rákóczi Avenue. The gas light of street lamps falls on the exhausted faces of pedestrians who trudge past listlessly. This is a city where nerves have been stretched to breaking point until they simply fail to respond. These are tormented, embittered people, whose smile turns vinegary when they hear talk about the revolution. Who would have energy for a revolution here? They wave off the very thought of it and walk on. The Budapest citizen trudges on impassively in shoes that took a government coupon and much cunning to obtain from the snarling shoemaker. Behind the windows of tenements the domestic lamps are lit; their glimmering, dim glow seems to confront emaciated families with the question: Is life still worth living? In a few shop windows one can see droll Santa Claus figurines, white-bearded elves, devils clad in red. Funny, how people always remember the day when gifts are to be purchased... An old woman in rags, helped by her equally ragged offspring, is hawking the evening newspaper. Passengers clamber aboard streetcars with an air of humanity seeking refuge from the Flood on Mt. Ararat. Women wearing white skirts head for the theater, having spent all afternoon brushing their hair, putting on fresh underwear, washing their hands, and spraying perfume on their clothes. Life goes on, and it is the same old life, miserable, dazed, beggared, with a face made up for the night, like an aging

224

actress who still entertains hopes... Who knows, perhaps the flutes and violins of yesteryear will strike up once more. The skinny shop-girl from the Inner City diligently slogs along and her eyes make no effort to avoid the speculative glances of the self-assured horse dealer. Gypsy musicians, pomade in their hair and dressed to kill, are tuning up their instruments behind the plate glass windows of coffeehouses. A dazed provincial in a leather jacket gawks at the female apparition that turns the corner at Síp Street. Each passerby carries his personal portion of care under his hat. You'll find there the faded snapshots of poverty and boredom, the bleating billy-goats of hedonism, the lamb-like clouds of distant hopes and the flower bouquets of the day's successes. None of them give any thought to the revolution that is about to break out in a few hours—save for an occasional starveling who reaches for his knife at the sight of the carefree, well-heeled loafers.

*

It was on this night that, at the general meeting of postal and telephone workers, the parish priest from Józsefváros had all those attending take the oath to uphold the National Council.

János Hock told me that the idea of the oath-taking came to him at the meeting. Originally he had simply intended to say a few words to inform and encourage the disgruntled postal workers. But once he began to speak, his customary gestures and musical voice took over.

"I was seized by a kind of inspiration... An ineffable feeling took hold of me when I decided to have the entire audience take the oath of loyalty to the National Council. Why not give it a try?"

The telephone operators and postal employees, mostly women, could barely restrain their exultant squeals when called upon by the clergyman to take the oath. Hands high in the air, their voices resounding and eyes gleaming, they repeated, as if in a trance, the oath of loyalty that János Hock read out from a sheet of paper. The entire gathering was aflame, roaring and screaming. This oath, sounding their hopes for the future, was like a rebirth—a moment that would mark the end of their wretched former existence and its withering tribulations, bitterness and remorse, slavery and heart-wrenching misfortunes. They took the oath, like survivors of a shipwreck, hoping that their lives would acquire a new meaning from here on. They took the oath as a means of escaping the gates of hell. They took the oath with a shout that

225

had all the desperation of the scaffold and annihilation in it—these poor, gray-skirted, dissatisfied postal workers who now pledged their loyalty to the all-redeeming Council.

Hock, that most accomplished of orators, looked around in astonishment at the assembly of flushed faces surrounding him. He was confronted by eyes that were incendiary, voices that were firebrands, and faces transfused by an otherworldly passion... This was the moment of his greatest success as an orator.

A tempest raged and whirled around him; high above it all rose the *Arabian Nights* genie freed by the fisherman from the imprisoning bottle. The József-város parish priest even forgot to resort to his usual snuff on this occasion. He could only stand in awe, as if the seas had parted before him.

The seas of revolution.

His visionary eyes could already foresee the sky-high waves that were about to inundate the Hungary of old. It was as if on this night Budapest had been at last touched by that vast and unstoppable current that is mightier than the Gulf Stream—the wind of revolution, originating we know not where on this globe, about which Mirabeau, over a hundred years ago, had observed that it would "travel around the world". Where did it come from, this wind, to suddenly stir up, seize, transform, and transmogrify these wretched office workers who had endured, neglected and impoverished, the four wartime years until their once dashing gold-braided postal uniforms hung on them in tatters? Where did it come from, this rain of fire that flooded Budapest on a melancholy, late-October evening, to set fire by the following morning to all hearts and minds just as it did the postal workers and telephone operators, who certainly could not have imagined earlier that on this night, instead of going home to make supper, they would be starting a revolution, that they would neglect to bring home the medicine for their sick children, that their beds in the cold little flats would remain empty, and their dreams, like birds on the wing, would look for them in vain: for they would return to the central post office and work through the night receiving telegrams and telephone messages, accomplishing the first fact of the revolution—the takeover of the Budapest post offices... And in the midst of this raging deluge none seemed to be aware that they were risking their lives, that the authorities, if the coup did not succeed, could send them to the gallows. Having been sworn in, delirious to act as messengers of a new world order, they ran out into the night, in their humble apparel that was like the robes of the apostles.

For at the time very few people in Budapest were aware that the armies along the River Po had already set out for home, and that in the city of Kecskemét a young lawyer named Szigethy, hoisting himself up onto the statue of Kossuth, had proclaimed the Republic.

Budapest was getting ready to go to sleep.

Over the city, church bells were tolling 8 p.m. This was the hour indicated on the large electric clock at the central post office, which from this moment on was under the authority of the National Council.

(22 December, 1918)

227

Land Distribution at Kápolna

On 23 February 1919, a rainy Sunday, automobiles were speeding on the empty streets in the direction of the Eastern Terminal. We had gotten to know these contraptions during the war. In the dark green one, gliding on noiseless tires, Queen Zita used to sit on the rare occasions when she was seen in Budapest. Today sleepy, red-eyed editors and journalists occupy the splendid French-made vehicle. The other automobiles, equipped with the red, white and green license plates of the Republic, also used to carry passengers of another sort. Austrian generals, deposed and forgotten ministers, central directors, and wartime entrepreneurs had sprawled on their seats, casting bored, haughty "automobile glances" at Budapest the accursed, the city bent double under the curse of the never-ending war. Today it is the leaders of the Republic who scan the weather from these cars. The sky is leaking. The water is ankle-deep on the sidewalk. We shall have to get out of this comfortable car, and, later, also get off the special train (heated) that we know is waiting for us... What will it be like in the Alföld, where we are headed to distribute land? Those who know the Alföld are betting on the mud being at least knee deep.

The car arrives at the train terminal. [...]

We enter the ministerial waiting room. Persian carpets, fine furnishings. How often have the shaky, decrepit ministerial feet of former times carried the bearers of briefcases through here on the way to Vienna, to sell out Hungary one more time! We now stand here with our hats on, it is cold; only the bald old porter holds his cap in hand, the way he learned in the days of Wekerle perhaps.

In a minute the special train is scheduled to leave.

This "special train"—the first in the era of the People's Republic—is a train just like every train used to be in peacetime (long ago), that anyone who had bought a ticket could take. It has a few first-class carriages that happened to survive the German locust hordes. It has windows that have not been broken by refugees. Dining cars, that still have white tablecloths, and waiters with prewar tailcoats. The tableware, plates, glasses, salt shakers must have been

229

well hidden away somewhere to have survived the four-year-long age of migrations. The floor is clean and the copper rivet heads gleam on the leather seat-backs. Peacetime. The comfort and pleasure of those former peacetime train journeys, which nowadays still only ministers and their guests can enjoy, although soon M.Á.V. will re-establish its former reputation when the express train had the best cuisine in the country.

[...]A merry breakfast is served. The good-natured Italian reporter Fraccaroli is being entertained by ministerial aides... It seems the old-time editors seemed to have stayed at home—perhaps fearing the counter-revolutionaries who were rumored to have been planning to blow up our train. Indeed there is no test-train carrying security guards ahead of us, as back in the days when old Francis Joseph traveled across Hungary during his final years. But we have faith in our railroadmen. They will take at least as good care of the special train of the President of the Republic as they did of the emperor's. I catch a distant glimpse of our Pacific locomotive at the head of the train, and the next morning I search the papers in vain to find that the train was driven by engineers X and Y, as reportorial practice had it in the case of special trains in former times. And yet the departure of this train is perhaps laden with more significance than any imperial visit in the old days. For it carries the President of the Republic, who is going to distribute his land among the people—whereas the kings of former times never brought any gifts other than a few ridiculous medals. In return they took with them our gold and our blood, and flippantly returned the salutes of ramrod-stiff chiefs of police and lord mayors. My God, to think that never again shall I see a guard at the Viennese Burg, with the white horsetail decorating his headdress, and his silver breastplate! The presidential bodyguards on this train are all baldheaded, courteous former non-commissioned officers. They are neither intimidating nor slovenly. They are mild-mannered shepherds who tread on tiptoes around the white lamb of the Republic.

The Commander of the Republican Guard is a youngish man with gray hair who wears a red hussar shako as his only decoration.

[...]The train is slowing down. We are in Hatvan.

[...]The four war years have certainly left their mark on the famous Hatvan train station where the lines branch out and where, once upon a time, travelers from three or four counties could be seen mingling. Everyone used to stop at Hatvan for a glass of beer or a cup of coffee. All those merry travelers have been swept away by the war. The station had been occupied by German troops. Hardly an intact window remains. Broken doors, trampled handrails, toppled advertisement hoardings (on which the quondam passenger could see all the famous spas of Austria and Hungary). And this place had not even been bombed. So much will have to be rebuilt in this country!

A red flag is planted between the rails.

Around it throng poor people, shabby workingmen and field workers in rags. Where are the frock-coated deputations of the former dispensation who would send in gendarmes to shove these people away from the reception? Where are those medal-wearing, baldheaded mayors, spic-and-span commanders of local outposts, excited toadies, beribboned organizers and the Mayor's rosy little daughter to hand her bouquet to Archduke, Archbishop, Lord High Lieutenant, whoever happened to be passing through! The gendarmes would usually beat up some people, the Mayor would receive another decoration on his dress coat, and the train would speed on with its load of notables.

In Hatvan it is only the people that awaited the train carrying the President of the Republic. Nowhere a tailcoat or a bow tie; as if all those folks who used to stand in the front row at receptions had passed away. It is the people who now stand in the front row in their impoverished peasant togs, work-clothes, proletarian rags. As the train comes to a halt the red flag is dipped, and a worker with short-cropped gray hair shouts out at the top of his voice:

"Long live the world-redeeming international social democratic movement!"

Once upon a time this old worker would have received his share of slaps and kicks from the gendarmerie, and imprisonment to boot! Now the day has arrived when he is free to shout the forbidden slogan. We still remember police captains who would see red on hearing these words. The apprentices who, as boys, first screamed the social democratic slogan and ran fleeing from police boots, are all old men today.

Károlyi gets down from the train.

He stands among the people, shakes hands, his felt hat and brown mackinaw pelted by the rain.

"Please put your hats back on!" he entreats the men around him, an entreaty that would be repeated many times in the course of the day, whenever people greet him with uncovered head.

He has the habit of looking at the chest, at the heart of the speaker addressing him, as if he wanted to see through the coat to decide how much truth resided in the words leaving the speaker's lips. Then he takes a step backward. He looks the speaker up and down from top to toe, as if etching into his memory the person who has spoken. Since he has become head of state he has had to rely more and more on his knowledge of character. His piercing glance sees through the words that are said. This could confuse someone who spoke untruths. But in Hatvan there is no fear of that, people here address the President of the Republic with a pure heart. The Social Democrats are the first to speak. The bright-eyed, dignified worker, speaking his well-considered words and now greeting Károlyi, is one of the hundreds of thousands who are ready to defend this man who brought them high hopes along with a revolution that swept away the war; at whose appearance, as if by magic, the former Hungary, its heart grown old and rotten, all its chain-rattling ghosts, bayonet-fixing horrors, and red-coated vampires have at last subsided. This man has brought us peace. All the more reason for these workers, forced into idleness or slave labor during the war, to be ready to go through fire for him.

After the solemn worker the local leader of the Independence Party and a citizen representing the town are the next to welcome Károlyi.

It is drizzling, the passengers of the special train keep anxiously consulting their watches, the engineer looks askance from the locomotive, but the speakers do not pause. After four years of enforced silence they are here to bare their hearts and souls; free to speak now, their thoughts can take wing, the new world we have dreamed of is here at last. How could they be brief, after so much suffering! For we have all been released from prison together... The special train will eventually get to Kápolna, but right now we are at the Hatvan train station that not long ago was still occupied by German troops.

Károlyi shakes hands with the orators and begins to speak. At first his voice sounds tired, but after a while it rises, like mercury in a thermometer. All could hear him now, even that dark-eyed young woman who had been eyeing the visiting authors, possibly wondering if she could get an autograph from Zsigmond Móricz, who is leaning on the window-ledge of the ministerial Pullman coach...

Károlyi's voice rings out:

"We are here to deliver on the promises we have made. I am proud that the distribution of land will start on my property. By distributing the land we are carrying the ideals of Lajos Kossuth one step further. Kossuth freed the serfs; we are freeing the cotters and agricultural laborers. To the poet's words, 'here you must live and die', we add: and here you must work."

The crowd cheers.

I have heard a lot of cheering in Hungary in my day, for electioneering was always full of the cheers of paid election agents, it was their livelihood. But this crowd was an army of the poor. They had perhaps never cheered before, because there had been no reason for it and no benefit. Orators had never said to them what Károlyi did on this day. Not even the most calculating stump orator would have dared to promise them what Károlyi was delivering today. The cheers at the Hatvan station were not set off by cues from an electioneering agent. They came straight from the heart, exploded from so many throats, and flooded the eyes with tears. It was the first sincere cheering in Hungary in a long time. (In the remaining part of our journey we were to hear much more.)

[...]The train station at Kál-Kápolna, where the distribution of land is to begin, stands in a flat landscape punctuated by well-sweeps, sunflowers, birches, and acacia trees. Till now its sole claim to fame had been that it stood on the train line leading toward Szerencs, Miskolc, and Nyíregyháza. [...]

The rain is still pouring indefatigably.

The endless flatlands are wrapped in fog and spring mist, and a veil of water droplets. The Mátra mountains loom blue in the distance, as if at the edge of the world. A rolling river of humanity surrounds the train as it pulls into the station. [...] Károlyi had left the Pullman, and now steps from a second-class carriage onto the soil of Kápolna, where the land all around as far as the eye can see belongs to him. The fields of black soil steam as if with an inner heat, the wet fallows where only hares abound, the fat meadows where usually cattle bells resonate; the endless plains, guarded by solitary well-sweeps, the grasslands visited by crows, the bulging furrows; fields with their coats of retreating snow worn away and faded; unpeopled paths where only a komondor runs following a scent, distant village spires obscured by the rain, and manor houses barely glinting forth amidst the earth tones; a hilltop tavern with a fresh hat of thatch—everywhere this early springtime had been silent and expectant, like a bride on the morning of her wedding. Here is the time for this land to recall its sad orphaned fate, its early sorrows, childhood servitude—even though it had belonged to the best landowner in the country, Mihály Károlyi. Nonetheless, this land was a mere cotter to its lord during the former dispensation. Now he will marry off this beauteous cotter's daughter to the honest man who has earned her: the people of Kápolna. Here comes the best man, the all-powerful lord of these lands, on a rattling peasant cart,

233

instead of using his fancy carriage which had been sent to receive him at the station.

A long procession of horse-drawn carts advances on the Kápolna highway. The small peasant carts, with their ancient stake-braces, wickerwork bodies, and seats of straw lurch along carrying pampered Budapest editors and ministers with many a jolt on the road where the mud reaches halfway up the wheels. No ordinary Budapest footwear could slog through this mud. Only a few among the guests had enough foresight to wear boots. Most of them came on this Kápolna outing as if they were going for a stroll on Váci Street. But everyone is in fine mettle. A famous bride will be given away today. In her honor the maidens of Kápolna, dressed in white and wearing wreaths Károlyi, the best man at the train station. [...]

There stands Károlyi now on the Kápolna plain, on a platform raised around the battle monument. [...]

We are witnessing a history-making prodigy. I would like to save and record for posterity each and every face. Even those politicking gentleman who busy themselves around Károlyi's person, although they change their facial expressions at will. But down below, where Károlyi's voice resounds with an echo, stand the people of Hungary. This is not the folk we have come to know from old comedies and almanacs, not the folk of the theatrical and romanticizing nineteenth century. The people standing on this plain have arisen from the sufferings and devastation of a lost war. During Károlyi's speech the sun comes out from behind the clouds. It is the eyes, faces, and figures of these people who have found themselves and placed their trust in tomorrow that I would like to etch into my memory so that never again will I lose faith in my nation's future.

They stand, innumerable, in a semicircle in front of the platform. My eyes cannot have enough, trying to take them in.

That man down there, dressed in black, wearing his Sunday best, why is he hanging his head and thick mustache so downheartedly? He has seen the war and has not yet been able to forget the horrors he has witnessed in his four years of Calvary.

But he begins to lift his head as Károlyi addresses him and the others. His worn and tired face turns with more and more attention toward the speaker. As if those deep creases were already somewhat smoother on his visage! As if some new flame were flickering in his eyes. As if the small hut of that soul were becoming tenable again, after its door was blocked by the collapsed ruins. Out of his discouragement he may yet become a man again, a working, productive man of wealth. As yet he is incapable of comprehending the trance that the May rainfall of the speaker's message is casting over his soul; but he will go home and reflect about what he has heard. If he has a shred of unconquered Hungarian soul left in him, he will realize that Károlyi intends to lead him out of a world of suffering and misery into the land of promise and salvation. That will be a beautiful morning and a triumphant springtime indeed, when this sad and despairing Hungarian recovers from the wretched stupor of his poverty to realize he possesses his own land. That will be the day of paradise achieved, when he finds his hands are holding his own tools. That his is the meadowlark in the furrows, the cloud over his head; his is the sweat of his labor as well as the golden results of that work.

[...]

And that sad man keeps his eyes on Károlyi from now on. There is no power that could sway him from the side of one who renounced his ownership of the land, to be lord of the whole country, of every heart in the land.

As for that woman with those cried-out red eyes and the black kerchief on her head, the sadness of cemeteries in her face, her forehead bearing the inscription of a village graveyard cross (inscribed with the name of her husband or son), why does she start smiling after all these years at the same time that the sun comes out from behind the clouds?

[...]

Today it is Károlyi's heartening words that fly over these fields where tomorrow the greatest blessing, human labor, will take its own course: the first stroke of the hoe in liberated soil.

This is what Károlyi said to the people:

"We are here to right the wrongs of many centuries. We set the foundation of a democratic land reform, prepared for the people by a government of the people's will. This day, from now on, will be a day of celebration in our country for we are burying the last remnants of feudal Hungary. In the new, independent, democratic Hungary full of social institutions the land will belong to those who cultivate it. We have fought for a working Hungary, and today is the first triumphant unfurling of our revolution's flag.

"We have accomplished the reform of landed property. But this is only the first part of our task. To make our accomplishment lasting we now need the efforts of the working people. If you, the people, do not set to work, our accomplishment will lie in ruins, and under those ruins will lie an entire nation. If you allow the forces of reaction to wrest from your hands this flag that is about to triumph, you will be forced to pull the yoke again. If you truly wish to help out the Republic, if you truly want the land to belong to the people, then help the government in this difficult task. The greatest help is to take up the spade and the hoe and grab the plow handle and strive to produce more than before. It is vital that small farmers cultivate as intensively as the large landholders did before, and that they produce a surplus. You must not wait for the state to do everything for you. The state can help with some of the initial difficulties, but government support never has the vital force of the assistance people are able to give each other. The success of a surplus depends on cooperation, and therefore I call upon the small landowners of this country to unite into cooperatives. You will have to form cooperatives for production, supplies, and marketing.

"When they hear in the Transylvanian mountains and the Slovakian valleys about how everything has changed here, that here the landless have been given their own land, that honest work receives its just rewards, then our brothers in those lands will not desire to give their allegiance to Bucharest and Prague, where they are being recruited only to increase the profits of big landowners and capitalists. Instead, they will reject the servitude offered by Romanian, Czech, and Serbian imperialists and capitalists.

"We, too, are setting out on a conquest today. We intend to establish the empire of work and freedom. Our flag is white and our weapons are not guns and grenades but shovels and hoes and the plow. As temporary president of the Republic I call upon the people of this country and ask you to give your work and the sweat of your brow."

The crowd of simple agricultural workers shouted with one voice:

"We give our work!"

By now the sun was shining above the Kápolna fields as if there had never been a winter.

[...]The assembled crowd would have stayed in the field all day to hear the speakers, who, for the first time in Hungarian history, came here not with empty promises but bringing something with them to give to the people. They brought fine ideals and they brought Károlyi, and had begun to divide up his lands on the spot.

The significance of this was enormous. The kings of old, after victorious campaigns, presented their generals and soldiers with lands from the conquered provinces. But now Hungary had lost the war and chased away her king. And lo, everyone was receiving some land. And the first to do so would be a crippled soldier, János Antal by name, a destitute local man. Antal would be the first man in Hungary to receive redistributed land.

The limping soldier was led amidst embraces up to the platform, everyone tried to pass a caressing hand over him on the way.

"János Antal, how many children do you have?" asked the president.

"I have five children and a sick wife."

"And how much land?"

"None."

Károlyi shook hands with the man.

"From now on you will have land of your own. You have children. Your wife will get well. You are going to be a hardworking, satisfied man, my son."

"I promise I will work hard," replied the veteran, in the deep silence, as if taking an oath of loyalty. An oath sworn not to the emperor but in front of the people of Kápolna, who heard him with bated breath. If there is a shred of honor left in this land, he will keep his oath—the oath he swore in front of his people. After all, he is merely a dispossessed soldier. In Hungary it was usually the kings who went back on their word.

The President of the Republic picked up the pen and wrote the name of János Antal into that great register that he would soon fill with the names of every impoverished person in this country. It is a huge book, room enough in it for many a poor man's name. And there are more where that came from, in case it fills up with names.

The president once more shook hands with the soldier.

The gathered gentlemen started descending from the platform and the sea of people on the Kápolna plain also set in motion.

The president led everyone to the spot where his lands meet the properties of the Bishop of Eger. Here the procession halted. The president picked up a shovel and tossed a shovelful of land over onto the Bishop's property. Let the Bishop of Eger also distribute his lands the way Károlyi had his own.

After him others grabbed the shovel. With each shovelful the mound grew taller.

Until now, the people had only known coronation mounds, on which the newly crowned king would ride the prancing steed when St. Stephen's crown was placed upon his head.

From now on there would be land distribution mounds as well.

After the First Conquest the seven chieftains were buried under mounds. Those were the mounds of the Age of Conquest. Archeologists point them out to this day in Szabolcs county.

The mound of the second Hungarian Conquest now rises in Heves county.

An airplane flew across the spring sky, dropping white sheets of paper from the heights. These messages would spread the news of the Second Conquest to other villages and towns.

A lovely, blue-eyed lady awaited the returning train at the Eastern Terminal.

Her eyes shone through her tears. She was the wealthiest and proudest wife this evening in all of Hungary—her husband had just given away his lands to the Hungarian people.

(February 1919)

Károlyi's Strange Career

In writing these notes I am supposed to avoid politics of the sort that still in-spires violent passions, but I cannot omit Mihály Károlyi, regardless of the storm of justified and unjustified controversy around this figure... Whether he has merited it or not, he has become the scapegoat for an era, in much the same way as Artúr Görgey did after 1849, whose Visegrád residence became an object of dread for the following generation or two. Similarly, Hungarians for some time to come will pass the historical Károlyi Palace on Egyetem Street with a shudder of dismay, or else with ardent heart and mind, for the residents of this building have played a major role in the history of the past hundred years.

What follow are personal remembrances.

I, for one, would never have believed that Mihály Károlyi could, some day, play such a fateful role in Hungarian history.

He had returned from Paris back in the days when summers in Budapest were still somnolent and empty, the newspapers served up peacetime ca-nards for the dog days; the summer wind whistled its ennui in the streets and squares, and anyone who could afford it fled the city. And the eccentric Mi-hály Károlyi chose precisely this time to stroll across Franciscans' Place, on a day when even the asphalt on the sidewalk was beginning to melt. Stifling sewer smells waft from the direction of the courtyards of old Inner City buildings; the wilting female corset-makers air out their shops while all week long they think of Sunday when they can escape from the city; at noontime the promenades are filled by those somewhat suspect ladies who dare to show up only when the fine folk are away for the summer; the stylish gentle-men, who, in the Budapest of old, were easily known by name, have all flown off except for Frigyes Podmaniczky and Mihály Károlyi, who have stayed in the deserted town. About old Podmaniczky it was common knowledge that he never stirred from home: wild horses couldn't have dragged him from his beloved Pest even in midsummer when Váci Street was littered with fruit cores and melon-rinds; but what was Mihály Károlyi doing in Budapest, he who had spent so much of his life in Paris?

...He wore his beard long, like a French count!

A monocle flashed over his eye (which showed signs of this even later when, as head of state, he no longer flaunted the jaunty monocle) as he surveyed the scene, solitary, superior, and scornful—for in those days the younger aristocrats indeed resembled the caricatures that Bors Csicseri had Faragó or Homicskó, the artists of his humor magazine, draw of them.

A Hungarian count on the Budapest street is recognizable at a hundred paces. (It would be fascinating to track down, in some history of human behavior, the Hungarian aristocrat who was the originator of this incomprehensible and not very savory type, with his appearance, cut of clothes, manner of speech, cockiness, and arrogance. For the ancestors who stand fierce and dignified in the picture galleries of their castles and palaces seem to have very little in common with the exteriors of their nineteenth-century descendants, the young magnates who vied with each other in arrogance and were so many homegrown varieties of characters in *Vanity Fair*. The *filles d'amour* could testify to their legendary binges. Waiters and servants could tell tales of their thirsts and appetites. Proud of their blue blood, they were not too well versed in spelling, perhaps a skill they had little use for. Legend has it that even István Széchenyi was like that in his youth. And in his days as a gilded youth Mihály Károlyi, too, had worn this mask.)

...Mihály Károlyi, when I first glimpsed him on the streets of Pest wearing his broad-brimmed, flat, arty hat—you had to be a count to get away with sporting such a white hair—had still looked very much like the type of young magnate the ordinary Budapest mortal might sight at the racetrack or behind the fence of the Park Club. It was not difficult to imagine him sunk into one of the easy chairs at the National Casino where it would never occur to the yawning, infinitely bored lounger to get up and stroll over to the library. One could picture him at the gaming table, losing sums that are phenomenal in the history of Hungarian gambling—if we give credence to the gossip of old neighbors in the vicinity of the Károlyi Park who never saw the young count taking a walk in his garden... Likewise, we may picture him at golf, tennis, or yachting—in any way except in the very position that the mysterious hand of fate was to mete out for him. Surely he would have laughed out in disbelief had some fortune-teller told him that some day his hands would be kissed by weeping peasants at Kál-Kápolna... When I first saw him he was a happy-go-lucky young count who was the first to wear cream-colored pants with a light gray jacket on Franciscans' Place in the summer. His laugh was loud when he saw the Rip van Winkle-like figure of Frigyes Podmaniczky approaching him on the street. The two of them were the only ones still in town, among the gentlemen worth mentioning.

And in the neighborhood of Károlyi Park new rumors were being spun about why Count Mihály had to leave Paris. It was said that the sums he spent had exceeded the credit at the First Domestic and even the capabilities of the Károlyi estates.

Unforeseeable are the workings of fate.

There surely must have been some sign on this man with the asymmetric, equine face—some sign that marked him for the future he had in store, a sign that had remained hidden from us for a while. But some future author of historical novels, who will select, from his cool-headed distant perspective, the extraordinary life of Mihály Károlyi as his subject, will be able to see this fated figure with greater clarity than we who knew him personally. It is said that nothing happens by accident, but an examination of Mihály Károlyi's incalculable career must shatter all our beliefs in notions of purposefulness, calculated careers, and conscious planning. Instead, we are reminded of the unknown forces that create tremors deep underground or turbulence in the stratosphere. For it must have been from deep underground or high up in the air that the spirit emerged to guide the affairs of this bearded young man who sauntered by on the Budapest street, this impassive and nonchalant dandy, whose only worry seemed to be deciding what to do on this boring, endless summer day...

The next time I saw him was in the Prime Minister's office, in a palace as ancient and noble as Jókai's historical novels.

The occasion was a soirée for the gentlemen of the Budapest press. Down below, across the river on the Pest side, all the lights were shining as if everything were in order in the city. (It was November and the soldiers' pockets no longer bulged with bullets, which they had used so unsparingly during the first days after their return from the front.) Little by little even those residents of Budapest who had been staying up nights could begin to catch up on their sleep. The eyes that had seen so many miracles of late are now closed in sleep, and the old burgher who had not dared to stir from his residence in the Inner City now musters the courage to shamble forth to discuss events with some similarly decrepit old gentleman... By now, possibly even those who had

241

sustained irreparable losses to their shops or businesses have ceased to wonder at the extraordinary events of the Fall of 1918.

(Meanwhile countless loyalty oaths were sworn in the presence of the very reverend János Hock, to allay the anxieties of the oath-takers; however, the Reverend Hock, fated to be a prophet, once took the writer of these lines by the arm for a walk, and, just as during the war years, on the basis of biblical prophecies, he had predicted the end of the war to the day, now he predicted the fall of the National Council and of the Hungary of those days. It is incredible that this priest remained in place when he had, on two occasions, been able to see the future.)

But this is not the time to think of the Lenten preacher, who, over the past decade, has inspired the ladies and gentlemen of Budapest to such religious fervor. This evening we are at a soirée, so forget about the grim priest sleeplessly pacing the halls of Parliament... We are at a soirée, having mounted the stairs covered with red carpets. In the lobby, diplomat-type secretaries of the Prime Minister's office receive the journalists with effusive courtesy; the tea tables are being set up amidst the jingling of the spurs of the uniformed attendants; everyone goes out of their way to be amiable, for these are the days when an invitation from Károlyi still counts as a true distinction... Let's see now, how many of us Budapest editors and journalists are there whose goodwill is sought in this manner by the head of state? There are about forty of us, both old respected editors, established for decades in positions of power and popularity, as well as the younger generation of journalists, who are now making their mark. The staff of A Nap, who have recently introduced a uniquely lively, noisy note to the daily press of Budapest. Oszkár Gellért, former writer of editorials for Pesti Hírlap, now stands flashing the all-knowing smile of the press secretary by the side of Károlyi. József Vészi, the most respected editor, settles into an easy chair up front. Ferenc Göndör makes his way from the back to confront him, and, rolling up his sleeves, almost gets into fisticuffs with the old editor in front of Károlyi. Vészi is apparently not radical enough for Göndör.

...So there we are, enjoying the splendidly pleasant ambiance of those halls, when Károlyi begins to speak, making repeated mention of Wilson, pronouncing the name in a strange manner so that some of us are beginning to form a bad opinion of this foreigner with the weird name who will have Hungary's fate in his hands.

"Wilson, Oo-ilson..."

242

And again:

"Wilson, Oo-ilson…"

This name has a sound of wonder-working faith, full of hopes and an almost magic belief as it is pronounced for the benefit of the Hungarian editors, who, in the course of the war, had numerous occasions for disappointment in names mentioned daily, only to be forgotten.

"Oo-ilson", Károlyi keeps repeating.

Vészi, still agitated about his verbal sparring with Göndör, wags his head indignantly, as if he were angry with Wilson. This gritty individual, according to legends in the journalistic world, did not refrain from occasionally physically chastising his younger colleagues, as if they were schoolchildren. Bihari, of the Budapesti Hírlap, keeps taking notes. Lenkey stands mutely near a bay window. Sándor Bródy is testing out his new formal suit; his play will soon be opening at the Vígszinház. Mr. Hatvany is thinking about the doings of Károly Mária Kertbeny and also planning for the Christmas issue of Esztendő. Meanwhile, Károlyi keeps repeating Wilson's name in his idiosyncratic manner.

The eyes of the assembled editors, journalists, and reporters are wandering in the direction of the windows of the Prime Minister's Palace; by now just about all of them have an idea of what to say in tomorrow's article… I do not have to write an article for I am ignorant of politics, so I have time to observe all these bright people, each of whom, through their occupation, experience, and education, knows as much as the count with the cleft palate; and I wonder: Do they really believe in our never-before-glimpsed collaborator, the omnipotent Mr. Wilson? In my opinion they gave their credence grudgingly, because they had to, for there was no other hope on the horizon.

The small teacups have been emptied; by now even those journalists who had not bothered to don formal attire are beginning to feel at home in this rarefied atmosphere. In the other room Berinkey, the Prime Minister, is wooing those writers who are known to be apolitical. He talks about his reading, which is indeed remarkable for a matter-of-fact man of the law. He inquires from Mr. Hatvany about Ady, who had been invited but who could not come because of illness. In the adjacent room the head of state has concluded his speech and a general discussion is in progress; hard to believe that these bright chief editors could ask such naive questions…

"Oo-ilson", is the name reverberating everywhere, except for a few refractory individuals who pronounce the W as a V.

Around about midnight the stairways of the palace again resound with the bunioned footfalls of old editors and the coltish stride of younger reporters. The lit-up windows of editorial offices await their fertilized brains to produce tomorrow's editorials. A chauffeured automobile transports Mr. Hatvany and his associates. The late lights of Pest are being turned off.

"What will happen tomorrow?" I wonder, tired.

But there would be one more lovely, spring-like day, when the snow was melting in the fields and when Károlyi decided that, in order to take action against the torpor, he would start to give away his land holdings at Kál-Kápolna.

The special train is greeted by delegations at the stations: county officials, squires, and peasants attend with priests, banners, welcoming speeches, hurrahs, flowers, and maidens dressed in white. No one saw any sign that the Károlyi-regime would soon be over. All over the countryside were cheering, enthusiastic, happy faces—and to this day I am not sure what they were so ecstatically happy about. One thing is certain: anyone who had witnessed the Hungary of those Károlyi days could not have the least idea of the surprising things that historians would note down about the times soon to come.

We know that the country squire whose face is so red from name-day festivities, weddings, and electioneering, and who now jostles to shake hands with Mihály Károlyi, will switch his political allegiance after each election. And the sly lease-holder, the frowning, kowtowing storekeeper, the bureaucrat looking forward to his pension, the village politician, notary, and priest will surely cheer someone else tomorrow—but what will the simple son of the sod do, the peasants whose landlord is now in their midst to give away his holdings? Will they, too, forget the landlord and the bailiff so easily in favor of a new landlord and a new bailiff?

...If Mihály Károlyi was capable of being moved to the very depths of his soul, then this was the day when it manifested. The passengers thronging the special train were awaited at the Kápolna station by peasants driving carts. Barna Buza, the Minister of Agriculture who would distribute the land, finds a place on top of the hay in the back of a cart; János Mayer clambers up behind him. Leading the procession, also in a peasant cart, Károlyi himself. The gentlemen of the Budapest press crowd bounce and clamor on other carts. There is a festival air to the event, without overtones of pomposity and authoritarianism: yet order rules, for the people behave in an orderly manner in honor of the lord of this land.

Scraggly acacia trees and fields white with snow in the distance; crows wheel over the knee-deep mud in the road. This is Hungary, with her sad landscapes where now a wedding procession is advancing. Sheepfolds, barns, hamlets... The noontime church bell sounds in Kál. I wish I knew what the voice of the bells is trying to say. Perhaps this: "There's not enough bread in Kál!" And the bells of Kápolna respond: "Here neither, here neither!" In those times that was the language spoken by bells in Hungary.

In the middle of a broad field there is a platform built of wood, surrounded by several thousand people who have been standing there since morning. Bailiffs, herdsmen, estate workers hurry to receive the arrivals, and the cheering starts at a signal given by a Presbyterian clergyman. Mihály Károlyi stands on the platform, his uplifted arms point out the fields in the four directions of the compass.

"All this was mine until now. From this day on it belongs to you!"

...A finer speech was never heard in these parts; long live Count Mihály, he knows how to treat poor folk well. Well, this too was over, like everything else in the world. Dinner was served in a barn smelling of sheep, served up by such good-looking young women and girls that I felt like staying on as a shepherd. That was the last time the Károlyi estate outdid itself in the area of hospitality. There may have been as many as two hundred guests and everyone ate his fill and enthused over the events witnessed—local men and women with tears in their eyes, children reciting poetry, and ministers making speeches... Only the landlord appeared impassive. Not once did he mention the name of Wilson in front of the gathered peasants and journalists. He sat silent, withdrawn into himself, as if he had gone through a severe illness since we had last seen him. Behind him stood a tipsy peasant who was weeping loudly and who kept planting kisses on his shoulder, the way it is customary for mourners to kiss the dear departed. Károlyi did not bat an eyelash. Impassive, he checked his wristwatch to see how much time he had left.

(22 February, 1925)

"The Bolshie"

[...] On a day in early spring [1919] I went to visit the Very Reverend János Hock, President of the National Council, in that splendid, great edifice out of some Germanic fairy-tale that is still admired by out-of-towners, the House of Parliament. (Every one of our architects worth his salt was of German origin; it would seem that Hungarian building skills went only as far as tent making.)

I began by mentioning his Lenten sermons that I had so often listened to in those happy peacetime years, when I went to hear the preaching of the "priest with the golden mouth" at the church on Szervita Place or at the Franciscans' Church, always in the presence of refined Inner City ladies who resembled hothouse hyacinths.

The man at the helm, who at the time held in his hands the loyalty oaths of so many members of the Hungarian high aristocracy and nobility, replied that he believed the Buddha—who was otherwise the Antichrist—was correct insofar as all of us had to traverse a sevenfold path of suffering.

Next we recalled the evening during the previous year when, in the course of a long walk, this notable Hungarian political leader had expounded his views on why we should not place our trust in Tisza or Károlyi but pay heed instead to the prophet Daniel, who had (and he cited chapter and verse) prophesied the end of the Great War. (I had written about this in one of my Letters from Pest, but in those days people placed more credence in fortune-telling by means of tea leaves on the bottom of the cup.)

"So, Mr. President, what will happen now?" I asked. "There are no longer any believers who ask for János Hock's prayer book at the Athenaeum bookstore...and the prophet Daniel has done his share. What now?"

"We stay put until they chase us away."

"Who? Mackensen? Lukachich? King Charles?"

"No. Béla Kun," he replied.

*

János Hock was wearing a cassock that day in early spring when he said this. Because of my upbringing, all my life I have respected the clerical robe and so I suppressed my laughter.

"Who is this Béla Kun?"

"Well, Hungarian history has already had one baleful personage by the name of Kun, and even though our man has nothing to do with King László IV who was called 'the Kun', yet he will have his say in Hungarian history. And ultimately it matters little what the man who will take the next turn at the helm in Hungary is called. We are heading left, and we will head that way for some time to come. As for us, we lack the power to steer that course; our resources have been exhausted; we need new windmills that will be able to adjust to the storm raging over Europe..."

The dark-cassocked priest stood in the chamber filled with green baize-covered council tables. But outside it was no longer as gloomy as it had been when he uttered his prophecy of last year. Spring was approaching now and the seagulls had flown north from the Danube. I was unable to give credence to his words...

"So take care, make sure you hear the morning church bells—before all the bell-ringers become Béla Kun's followers."

*

On my way I crossed Berlin Place. In the middle, around the gas lamps, I saw a gathering of about two dozen men and women. Ragged soldier types, out of work janitors, good-for-nothing idlers, trollops in patched skirts, I seemed to have encountered them somewhere before. (On the pages of Carlyle's *History of the French Revolution*.) If the armed guard were to yell at them they would probably disperse. But he had better things to do than minding such idle riffraff. And anyway, this is a free country, anyone has the right to assemble wherever they want.

Actually this gathering on Berlin Place was not the sort that would disturb the appetite of a hardworking Budapest citizen on his way to lunch, or upset his well-earned post-prandial siesta. Perhaps only a military tailor would have noted that there were uniformed men in this little group, whose clothes were of a different cut than the kind delivered by the suppliers of the Austro-Hungarian army. Three or four members of the assembly were dressed in better materials. A passerby with expert eyes might conclude they came from a German source. But I gave no second thought to them, for I had gotten used, living out on Margit Island, to workers at the hot springs or members of the grounds crew being summoned to meetings where some never-before-seen ringleader gave a speech larded with all kinds of Russian-sounding names that no one gave a hoot about. Unimpressed, the workers returned to their tasks; it would have been foolhardy to abandon the emerald-green waters of the hot springs named after eternal life, or the gardens where splendid little flowers were pushing up all over like so many stars in the carpet of the firmament.

Yes, in those days there were meetings everywhere in Budapest, in every shoemaker's shop and school gym; on street corners; in the outlying districts and up on the dignified Castle Hill; in front of the Ministry of Defense; in the smallest of cafés as well as under the marble arcades of the New York coffee-house... People would "run into each other", as they say. Not necessarily be-cause someone dropped dead of starvation on the street, but just to be to-gether, to discuss things and to sound off on issues—after the long, grim war years, liberty was on tap at last and everyone wanted a taste.[...]

*

In those days Jenő Heltai lived in Baron Kohner's villa on Damjanich Street, occupying two rooms and a pantry on the ground floor. We were asked to come to the otherwise unoccupied villa, where Béla Kun, Hungary's dictator at the time, wished to meet with a few selected writers.

Who were the writers thus honored? As for my humble self, I could boast of far greater honors—such as the time when I was militating, alongside the Most Reverend Bishop Prohászka of Székesférvár, against the clericalization of the Pázmány Society. Yet I cannot leave myself last when in these notes I would deliver certain personages—and very precious ones at that—to the mercies of a public opinion that looks askance at anyone who was not a henchman under Fejérváry, a policeman under Tisza, a government commis-sioner under Károlyi, and at least an under-commissar during the Béla Kun regime... "What was the rascal up to?" they ask with understandable suspicion, all these good folks who had taken the oath of loyalty at the right time in front of the Reverend Hock, then did their stint in the Red Army, after which they crawled on their knees to the opposite camp in Siófok. What was the rascal up to indeed—at a time when everyone was trying to find a niche for himself under the auspices of various successive governments.

Well, the persons mentioned below were at no time—before or since—anything other than what they always were: writers.

*

It was dark in the Baron's garden; I stumbled to open the gate then groped my way down the unfamiliar gravel path; not a single light to signal that the "head of state" was expected here tonight. Only the sleeping lilac bushes, down at the far end of the garden, exhaled their redolence. After fumbling for the doorbell I was admitted by a white-gloved manservant whose soldier-like physiognomy was familiar to me from earlier occasions when the Kohners still resided in Pest, on Országház Place. Who knows where they are staying these days? Inside, I saw Jenő Heltai.

Those who know Jenő Heltai are aware that he usually has the anxious look of a boy who has just played some prank. On this evening he seemed to be truly worried.

"Did you come alone? But where are Ambrus, Kóbor, and the others?"

We browsed in the library while waiting for the others who had been ordered here. The splendid volumes—novels, poetry, sciences—contained all of the mined gold and spent fireworks of a happy nineteenth century. First editions of Flaubert, and Dickens in the paperbound installments as originally sold in London. The bell rang; Tamás Kóbor arrived. Impassive, smoking a cigar, he looked for an evening paper to read, as if he had just come from the editorial offices of Az Újság, which was long defunct by then.

"Today I really made the old man pay", he said, referring to his regular afternoon card game with the editor Miksa Bakonyi.

The next to arrive was Osváth, editor of the suppressed Nyugat, carrying a square portfolio as if he were on his way to the gallery of the New York coffeehouse to correct the proofs of the forthcoming issue.

And there were also others for whom it might be awkward if I mentioned their names here, lest the reader misunderstand their motives. It was a bleak and impecunious time for most writers since the publication of books and periodicals had been almost totally suspended. Amazingly enough I cannot think of a single writer who joined the Red Army even in the midst of the greatest hardships (and good old Dr. Gara helped out by declaring, one after another, about five hundred writers and journalists unfit for military service at the compulsory draft physicals at the Otthon Club). In the end the writers merely laughed at the dreadful vegetable concoctions served at the Club's kitchen (even Ferenc Herczeg lived on this fare), while those gentlemen who stayed in office under the Red government and who would later be the loudest persecutors of the "Jewish journalists", took advantage of their official privileges, which they have enjoyed ever since.

So here were the writers, incapable of earning their daily bread, sitting in wordless silence in Jenő Heltai's apartment, the seven of us feeling like the damned, wondering if the fierce commissar had ordered us here because he was thirsting after our blood.

No, he was not after our lives, he merely wanted our work.

*

Suddenly the door was flung open, as if a latecomer had arrived who wanted to be on time, with a Francis Joseph-like punctuality. It was an inconsequential-looking young man wearing a tan suit with baggy pants, fraying collar, rumpled necktie, worn shoes—just like a provincial journalist. He stopped in front of me.

"*Mister* Krúdy, I believe we have already met."

"I don't recall," I replied unthinkingly, with the superciliousness I have come to hate in myself and which had accumulated as many enemies for me as was possible in the happy prewar years.

I was obviously under the impression that some writer from the provinces had also been invited to the meeting. Or else this was some not very memorable figure connected with the periodicals and books of those days.

But some among those present already knew who this "provincial journalist" in fact was. It was Béla Kun "in person", as the local wits would have said. He bounced into the room like a rubber ball, like some reporter from Kolozsvár, who is considered is invaluable because he has around-the-clock access to the Lord High Lieutenant.

...I do not recall what he spoke about exactly. The leadership in those days employed such arcane language—a jargon composed of foreign, never-before-heard words, sweaty scientific expressions extracted from textbooks, and black-shirted adjectives—that we never really knew what they were trying to say. I do remember that he addressed me not as "Comrade" but as "Mister". As he spoke to us from the depths of an easy chair that had no doubt been intended for the idle meditations of some portly, retired gentleman and not for this insignificant-looking young man, I tried, without any success, to discover on his face any traces of the terrible beating he was supposed to have received in police detention just before he came to power. But I saw no sign of the rifle butt and the flat of the sword. He looked normal enough to pass for the bridegroom at a village wedding. He might even look appealing to some not overly particular woman susceptible to the kind of man who "talks her to death". I could hear his voice:

"Lunacharsky... The Soviet...centralization of literature...books from now on will be published by the Soviet, and the writers' livelihood will be assured... You should not have any worries on that account... You, Mr. Krúdy (as if he were trying to appease me), and your colleagues, please visit the council house tomorrow if you want, to pick up the advance on your next work... One book per year would be sufficient... You are not obligated to defend the Soviet ideas, nor should you agitate against them... At last the times have arrived when writers can exist by themselves, without the interference of hypercritical editors and stone-hearted publishers..."

...Listening to him I tried to catch that charismatic note that was supposed to make him an irresistible public speaker. Instead, I found his voice pale, monotonous, unmodulated—not quite as dry as a professor's but not as persuasive as a horse trader's. He sounded far fewer lyrical overtones than any of the poetasters who insisted on forcing their compositions on me during my days as an editor. Nonetheless, this young man's voice was undeniably resolute, well versed, competent in debate... If only Kóbor would refrain from interjecting, in that peculiar Palóc accent of his:

"In my childhood I did a stint as a tinsmith's apprentice, but still I don't quite understand how we can 'socialize' a piece of work that has not been written, that the writer hasn't even conceived... Something that will pop out of his brain only sometime later, the way a vest-button pops off..."

*

Béla Kun spoke until midnight, and I listened cheerfully (thanks to our libations) to anecdotes about the socialization of writers, communal labor, the Soviets, and Lunacharsky's literary train. The fun was interrupted only by the arrival of Comrade Szamuely, who suddenly appeared accompanied by men in leather coats carrying machine guns and hand-grenades to check on his commissar, to see if he was really meeting with writers and not conspiring behind his back (they had already had their differences back in Moscow). The intimidated writers retired to the shelter of the pantry, where the window opening on the garden was barred, so we could not jump out... There was an agitated exchange of words between Kun and Szamuely in the other room. At last Szamuely sped off with his rattling, clattering, iron-clad henchmen and the bloodcurdling howl of his automobiles. Commissar Kun opened the door behind which we, the poor, trembling bourgeois, were huddled...

"We can continue our discussion."

And he went on with his monologue.

*

It was past midnight.

I was given a ride home in Béla Kun's automobile, to Ferenc Boulevard, for we had moved from Margit Island where everyone had been arrested. It was long past midnight when the large military vehicle, complete with machine gun and two leather-coated, bayonet-wielding men in the back, finally stopped on Ferenc Boulevard, at the wrong building (for I did not want them to know my address). Tamás Kóbor, who sat next to me, was worried.

"I've got a long way home yet, what will they do to me?"

Then he had a sudden notion.

"Listen, when you get off, try and see if these people will accept a *tip*... If they take it, they can't be assassins."

I pressed a twenty-five korona note into the hand of Béla Kun's chauffeur. He thanked me, just like any cabdriver on Gizella Square. Kóbor nodded goodbye to me with a sly smile.

...Well, the time had come for me to retire to the Bakony Mountains. To the best of my knowledge no one among those present that night ever bothered to visit the House of Soviets to pick up the advance for socialized literature.

(1 March, 1925)

Hungarian Gentry

A comment on Zsolt Harsányi's Christmas article

Dear Zsolt,

Christmas 1926 was made memorable by your open letter to Prime Minister István Bethlen in the special issue of the *Pesti Napló*, the newspaper of Zsigmond Kemény, Ferenc Deák, and Kornél Ábrányi, Jr.—the paper of the so-called Hungarian middle class as far back as I can remember, and also of the "gentry", insofar as they were included among its legion of subscribers. Your open letter was addressed to the Prime Minister, who, in one of his campaign speeches, had sent off the members of the Hungarian "gentry" to go fly a kite. Once upon a time, on these same pages, Ferenc Deák had written that *Easter article* of his, which historians long ago designated as a landmark of the modern era—scholars always need landmarks so they won't get lost in the jungles of history. Well, to that famous "Easter article" the editors of the *Pesti Napló* have now added your "Christmas article", which will long serve as a topic of conversation for those of us who are not the least bit inclined to go fly a kite.

When I read your article about the condemnation of the Hungarian "gentry" I was in the countryside and had more time to reflect on it than I would have in the course of my city existence.

Only in hamlets and villages do people still read the newspapers with true thoroughness and enjoyment, as they did back in the nineteenth century. Granted, coats of Londonderry, Burberry, and Scottish tweed are no longer fashionable in daily wear, having formely been a fashion that more or less revealed the political convictions of the wearer and even the very newspaper he read to imbibe the wisdom he would spout for the benefit of womenfolk and children on rainy days. Nowadays only elderly gentlemen sport the products of the Graz hat maker (Havigner)—Kaiser-hats and chamois-hunter's hats typical of subscribers to *Nemzet*, the government-party's paper, issues of which they would sometimes keep around the house for years. But somehow it is still apparent that these country folk, the latter-day descendants of the Hungarian "gentry", indeed read the papers, although maybe only at the National Casino on empty days between a bowling match or greyhound show. Or else they might be found reading the paper on a local train between the Western terminal and Kunszentmiklós, jolting disconsolately past stations where the only noteworthy item is the autumn train schedule recently nailed on the yellow stucco wall. And there are subscribers whose only motivation may be the excuse this gives them to amble over to the post office each day—a splendid pastime that is inconceivable for a metropolitan subscriber.

Thus I can report to you, dear Zsolt, that your open letter to Bethlen received far more attention in these parts than any other news item, for a letter addressed to the Prime Minister never fails to arouse a certain excitement in the readers. What could be in the letter? Flattery or abuse? Perhaps a complaint that involves our region as well? Is it about taxes, appointments, tobacco prices, or some mishandling of justice? Or about the local stationmaster that both Jews and Christians agree has got to go? An open letter to the Prime Minister does not remain unread, my dear Zsolt, no matter how much you generalize about this "gentry issue", which actually first surfaced in the days of Kálmán Tisza and has been periodically resurrected ever since, just like any other national legend such as the fabulous inheritance left by some childless old lady, for which the ancestors fought in court until they ran out of money: although generations of lawyers have come and gone all the legal papers are still extant unless the mice have eaten them. Such litigation, in our days, rages over the estate of Miklós Szemere and is guaranteed to keep future Szemeres busy for generations to come.

A Hungarian legend, my dear Zsolt, the legend of the Hungarian gentry.

For this very reason it is manna for most readers, since it has such a sweet savor, a taste we have almost forgotten. You, who are referred to as "Mikszáth's heir" by those in the village who had a chance to see your play Noszty Boy at the Vígszinház on their last jaunt to the capital, you of all people are justified in addressing this issue, since you obviously had a chance to notice that your play-going audiences are still fascinated by this legendary world of "Hungarian gentry".

Well, all I can say to you, as "Mikszáth's heir", is that you have dropped a great big stone into the well. May you have the strength to retrieve it from there.

Truth is, those Derby-coats have not been worn in these parts for quite some time, and not even if you showed up wearing one would you be called a true member of the "gentry" nowadays, for the era is long past when a country gallant strove to represent a social class by means of extravagant clothes. That sort of thing still passed in the eighties and nineties, when it seemed certain that as a result of Kálmán Tisza's resolute policies the old-time Hungarian noble class would make a comeback. According to the popular understanding, "gentry" (if this word can be said to have as much meaning as in England) designates folks possessing a certain modest competency on which they can get by. Freeloading, carousing, and gambling are no longer acceptable qualifications. Folks with sufficient wherewithal are still counted among the "gentry" even if they are not listed in Iván Nagy's compendium of nobility, as long as they have been in the area for a generation or two. And if the individual has a diploma of some sort, some degree he can rely on in case of crop failure or ice damage to the wine harvest, then he is all the more a member of the "gentry"—far more truly than the bibulous road-inspector who still insists on dragging his *vizslas* along on an outing to inspect the county roads. *Horribile dictu*: not even the ever-present traveling encyclopedia salesmen and insurance agents go about the villages dressed in "Berci Mokány" outfits any longer—that was before the war; nowadays they wear a thin overcoat and business suit, briefcase and eyeglasses.

The "gentry" as a concept that could be lampooned in humor magazines or taken as the subject of a serious study, has passed in Hungary, although it is not dead and gone. It is just that time has eroded all its former romanticism. These are frightfully sober times for that rural class of people who still called themselves "gentry" in their dreams because that's what their fathers had called themselves. My dear Zsolt, no one cares a whit about romanticism any longer, not in Kisörs by Lake Balaton or Alsó-Dabas in the Lowlands, and not even in what remains of the Nyírség region. "Money talks and the dog barks" would be an apt contemporary inscription for the coat of arms carved in stone, if they were still building those old-time noble residences that were, let's face it, rather uncomfortable compared with a villa. The gentry has lost all its romanticism; for this reason there is no need for Prime Minister Bethlen to put it out of the way. This gentry is no longer inclined to rise, phoenix-like, upon some heavenly sign such as the coronation of a Francis Joseph, the appearance of a Kálmán Tisza, the foundation of the Gentry Casino, or, most recently, Mihály Károlyi's revolution.

In England, a little edict of old Queen Victoria's succeeded in restraining, on the streets of London, those countrified, rambunctious members of the gentry (who behaved in a similar way to ours). In the eighties the Queen had signed an ordnance stating that no one would be allowed to attend Her Majesty's theaters wearing riding boots, red or green vests, and whips equipped with whistles; evening wear would be compulsory for all. The gentry, desirous of showing off their colorful vests in London, was put in its place.

In Hungary the demise of the "gentry" is datable to about forty years ago when the old "Golden Eagle" hotel was demolished on Újvilág Street, leaving those country squires who came to Budapest to raise Cain without a roof over their heads.

On the other hand there still remains a "gentry" in today's Hungary, invisible like gold hiding underground, ungraspable by human hands, including the Prime Minister's. Instead of sporting Londonderry coats, the members of the new "Hungarian gentry" recognize each other by means of other, intangible signs.

Otherwise, thank you, Zsolt, for addressing this rarely discussed topic.

(30 December, 1926)

Forefathers and Descendants

In the old days the folks in Nyíregyháza would just saunter away.

They would saunter away to one of the local graveyards: it made no difference which one, there was a tavern at the entrance of each cemetery where mourners could stop and rest. And there would always be an heir to inherit the estate: a cluster of hamlets, some thatched huts, a horse raised by hand, outlaw-styled hats, second-hand boots (old-fashioned but still usable), along with a hardworking widow and some squalling children. The families that migrated here over a hundred years ago—the Tresztyánszkys, Pivnyiks, Csengerys; and among the Jews the Burgers, Hartsteins, Flegmans, Garas, Baruchs—were all considered to belong to one big family.

Yes, even yours truly once inherited something—an evil-smelling pipe—from my godfather, who died intestate.

Ah, to be a *legal heir*!

Why, that meant a certain status in old Nyíregyháza (and perhaps does even today), equivalent to a small bishopric. For the forefathers had busied themselves with cultivating the land and other such gainful activities, amassing great wealth. And, after a certain amount of lingering, sooner or later they all sauntered off to one of those serene spots where, on the mayor's orders, the cemetery groundskeepers plant acacia trees to bind the sand. A place where the wild doves cooed and the blackbirds warbled, and one could hear the booming contrabass from the nearby tavern when the appropriate name-days came up.

And then the legal heirs could come into their inheritance!

I cannot recall a single Nyíregyháza native ever irresponsibly squandering away his inheritance. That was for country squires, who would gamble away their fathers' last pair of riding breeches as well as the prize greyhound at the "Jewish Casino"—as the Farmers' and Merchants' Club was referred to in Nyíregyháza—or else at the Korona Inn, which became especially popular after the 14th Hussars (with the cornflower-blue uniforms) were transferred here from Galicia. The Korona was where the county officials and the military officers liked to carouse—but no true-born *Tirpák* of Nyíregyháza had ever cut down a single oak from his forest to stuff the revenues from it into the band-leader Gyula Benczi's violin. (He had a large Italian violin, with lots of room for banknotes.)

For a long time people respected and preserved intact these last wills and testaments that were as often as not dictated to one of the local notaries by one about to depart from our town, lying propped up on quilts and pillows in the cart that had brought him in from outlying farms and hamlets.

Each Nyíregyháza townhouse, usually known by the builder's or owner's name (instead of the house number) sheltered some "legal heir"; only officials who had been transferred here rented apartments and they too would buy a house sooner or later. Even András Kállay, the former Lord Lieutenant, has-tened to buy himself a townhouse, although he was given a beautiful official residence in the County Building. As soon as the opportunity arose he pur-chased the townhouse formerly belonging to Heumann, the famous defense attorney in the Tiszaeszlár trial. As for the townhouse that had once belonged to Krúdy Jr., after his decease the competition for it was so keen that a consor-tium was formed to purchase the property and convert it into a sanitarium.

Yes, it was always a great event in Nyíregyháza whenever a house, a lot, or a farm was sold.

Although back in those days the good old Hungarian korona was a sound currency, nonetheless the Nyíregyháza folks preferred *buying* to selling off. Udvarhelyi, the one-eyed real estate agent, also ran a domestic servant agency in order to support his large family. The only full-time agent making a livelihood in town sold insurance. After nailing a tin plaque on the insured house he would make sure some member of the household became a volun-teer fireman, so that next to the Generali or First Hungarian plaque he could affix another one that had "Fireman" on it surrounded by a red border. (This second sign would protect the insurance companies from large losses.)

So the people of our town, Gentile and Jew alike, preferred to hang on to their savings, townhouses, and lands.

The local *Tirpáks*, who acquired land acre by acre, had a hard time compet-ing against each other in the environs of Nyíregyháza. Most of their proper-ties were small, around twenty to thirty acres, earned with the sweat of the brow. The *Tirpáks* of Nyíregyháza had to look as far as Apagy, Vencsellő, and Kemecse, although they preferred nearby Oros, in their quest for land for sale in a region where most of the land was owned by the Prebend of Eger or the Máramarossziget College. Count Dessewffy's property alone was about fifteen thousand acres, and the Kállay family also possessed considerable holdings that dated back to the Conquest. So a *Tirpák* had to trudge a long way to secure a foothold in the sandy soil of Szabolcs county, which, according to popular belief, was hospitable only to potatoes; actually wheat and rye also grew there. But corn, too, thrives in this soil, and even the vintners need no longer be ashamed of the quality of our local wines, which formerly had a sour reputation.

Once upon a time in the village of Gesztely in Zemplén county a burly Jewish man by the name of Jeremiás Burger bundled up his worldly goods upon a cart and set off for Szabolcs county.

This was in the first decades of the nineteenth century; Burger still signed his name with Hebrew letters. He would soon become known around Nyíregyháza and throughout the county as *Uncle Jéri*—a man of great physical strength who did not back down when confronted by a troop of outlaws who still abounded in the woods and marshland reed-beds of the region, lying in wait for the creaking of an approaching cart or wagon.

Uncle Jéri traded in just about everything. Rings, horse skins, rabbit fur—back in Zemplén he had also worked as a cattle drover—until at last he had enough to acquire a farming lease and establish a foothold. By then he was fairly prosperous, and a good thing too for there were eight children to feed. His lease holdings grew year by year and included properties at Tiszadob, Tiszadada, and Pazony. By now Uncle Jéri needed the services of an attorney, and found a sharp and crafty practitioner, Gyula Somogyi of Nyíregyháza.

"Uncle Jéri," his lawyer once asked him, "would you tell me how you manage to end up with more money each year?"

"That's easy," replied Jeremiás Burger. "Even when my income was only a hundred forints a year, I managed to save half of it. I still do the same. Anyone can follow my example."

Far from it! The gentlefolk in Szabolcs had better things to do than follow Jéri Burger's example. In fact, as soon as word got out about his frugality, one after another the country squires came to borrow money from him. It made sense: the spendthrift turns to the frugal neighbor for loans.

For example, the men of the well-known Elek family of Pazony frequently experienced financial difficulties brought on by their bizarre indulgences. In

261

Uncle Jéri's days Mr. Elek married the beautiful Ilka Lánczy from Borsova. They owned in Pazony a large castle as well as a small castle. The lady lived in one, the gentleman in the other—and their marriage still produced seven children. These siblings—Guszti Elek, Colonel of the hussars and hero of many a duel (his bullet laid low Szevér Reviczky), Lieutenant Colonel Mihály Elek, the constant escort of operatic prima donnas in old Budapest, as well as László, Emil, Dezső, and Valéria Elek—all liked to indulge in strange whims that could not be accommodated in the two Pazony residences, and they came home mostly to borrow money.

Nor were members of the family who stayed home free of exotic attachments.[...]

No wonder all these passionate, amorous Eleks were unable to hold on to the purse strings! They were often in financially embarrassing circumstances and needed an infusion of cash, even in Pazony. Gábor Elek Jr., owner of the estate at Szarvas, was the first in the family to seek a loan from the Jewish lease holder.

"You can have it," said Uncle Jéri, "and I won't ask you to put up your house or land as security. The interest will be double the going rate—and I insist you pay me on time, for I don't like to go to court."

Word got around about Jéri's unusual conditions. A week later Count Gusztáv Dégenfeld, lord of the Téglás estate, came to ask for a loan, and soon enough the Lord Lieutenant himself, Barnabás Bónis of Tolcsva—whose portrait hangs to this day in the assembly hall of Szabolcs county—took the long carriage-ride to seek out "crazy Jéri".

"Jéri, are you out of your mind?" exclaimed his lawyer, Gyula Somogyi, tearing his hair. "How can you give loans without a mortgage?"

"Just leave it to me, your Excellency," replied Jeremiás Burger, who till the day of his death used no other honorific than *your Excellency*.

But even the lender could be in a financial squeeze at times: even Uncle Jéri's exchequer became depleted occasionally. Then he would turn to a neighbor, a wealthy Jew in Szabolcs county. One time he asked for ten thousand pengős, but the neighbor wanted an exorbitant interest rate. Jéri decided to take his revenge. His neighbor traveled to the fair in Debrecen, but no sooner did he arrive there when a Jew from back home pulled up posthaste.

"Have you heard the news? Jéri's gone bankrupt!"

The usurer almost had a stroke. He left the fair and rushed home in panic, where a laughing Jéri Burger awaited him at the door.

"I just had to get my money's worth for that high interest you made me pay!" he said.

While we are on the subject of old Jéri, let us not omit the story of how he became known all over the land for his boots. Locally it was common knowledge that Jéri Burger carried all the banknotes needed for his transactions in his boot-tops. But a visiting gentleman from Sáros county was unaware of this circumstance. At the house of Péter Krasznay, the magistrate of Kemecse, this man talked nonstop about the wonders of his Highlands. After a while the Szabolcs magistrate decided he had had about enough of this boasting.

"I'll bet you a hundred forints there's no one in your neck of the woods like our Jéri Burger, with enough money in one of his boots to buy up the whole county of Sáros!"

The man from Sáros took him up on the bet.

So the magistrate sent his footman to fetch Jeremiás Burger. But no matter how hard the magistrate tried to explain to the old man that the honor of Szabolcs was at stake, old Jéri kept insisting that there was nothing in his boots except for his feet.

"All right, I won the bet, let me have that hundred forints!" the visitor from Sáros exclaimed triumphantly.

The Kemecse magistrate was about to hand over the money when Uncle Jéri finally got the point and hastened to intervene:

"Hold your horses, Excellency! The question is, which boot do you want to see? The left one or the right one?"

"Let's see the left one," snapped the impatient visitor from Sáros.

"C'm 'ere János," the magistrate called out to his footman, "help Uncle Jéri with his boot."

Truth to tell, the left boot contained the smaller savings account. Only about a hundred thousand forints.

To the end of his life the strapping, bull-necked Jeremiás Burger, with his thick mustache and traditional Hungarian clothes, never learned to write—not even when he was already a millionaire. Therefore he frequently needed the services of his attorney Gyula Somogyi. He would spend many an hour in the anteroom of the lawyer's office where he kept ordering the lawyer's clerks about, usually exhorting them with:

"You're not getting paid to pick your nose!"

The clerks were intimidated by the Herculean client, especially when he bumped his head on the lintel. But not so the lawyer, who once took his best client to court for failure to pay eight hundred forints in legal fees. Uncle Jéri was summoned in front of the district judge.

"Why can't a wealthy man like you pay up?"

"I need the money for something else right now. I've just bought a thousand acres in Oros. That takes priority over the lawyer."

"Well, let's see how soon you pay up," said the annoyed attorney.

Within two weeks Jeremiás was knocking on the lawyer's front door but refused to step inside.

"I just want to say that I've paid the last installment on that land. It's time to pay the lawyer now."

"Well, come in, step right up," urged Gyula Somogyi, who was seated at his desk.

"No sir," said Uncle Jéri, holding out the money from the doorstep. "The moment I set foot in here, Mr. Somogyi, you will bill me five forints for 'consulting with the client'."

But he stayed with the attorney to the end of his life and had him draw up his last will and testament.

Ah, Jeremiás Burger's will!

That document took some doing: it was drawn up over the course of ten years.

The task was to divide, in an equitable manner among the eight children, an estate of thousands of acres, townhouses in Nyíregyháza and in Budapest, as well as other valuables that had been, in the words of the will, "acquired through tireless industry and self-denial coupled with the greatest frugality in making a livelihood that never transgressed the letter or the spirit of the law".

The drafts for the will were drawn up at the Nyíregyháza lawyer's office, but old Jéri, even when he was well past seventy, was not beyond traveling to Budapest to consult the prominent lawyers of the capital.

In the course of these proceedings word got out among Jeremiás Burger's debtors that burglars had broken into his Nyíregyháza residence and made off with the entire contents of his desk—including all the promissory notes Uncle Jéri had received from his debtors. There was a great to-do about this. But after the excitement subsided the debtors began to pay up. It was evidence of Jeremiás Burger's understanding of human character that among all

264

his debtors only one tried to benefit from the disappearance of the promissory notes by refusing to pay. But fate, which for some inscrutable reason had always favored Jeremiás, intervened, and it was found that the burglars had left behind a single promissory note that had slipped behind the furniture. It was the one signed by the man who had tried to shirk his debt.

But all this excitement had worn out old Uncle Jéri and he decided to retire once and for all—even though at the age of seventy-seven he still retained his gusto for life, eating bacon for breakfast and, whenever possible, stuffed cabbage for lunch. (They say it was a platter of stuffed cabbage, brought to the train station at midnight by his son Joseph who lived in Miskolc and wanted to treat his father who was traveling through, which prompted old Jéri to transfer one of his Budapest houses to this son. A royal price indeed, for a plate of stuffed cabbage.)

Now that the old man began to attend the synagogue more frequently he came up with the idea of leaving his entire fortune to found a hospital.

"My sons are becoming too extravagant. They all smoke the finest Londress cigarillos. This way at least they'd have a place to die in," he said to his lawyer.

"All right, we'll draw up a deed of endowment," Gyula Somogyi replied.

Instead, Somogyi drew up a paper transferring fifteen hundred acres of Uncle Jéri's holdings to Móric Burger—a property that is still intact, somewhere between Nyíregyháza and Oros and still worked by Uncle Jéri's grandchildren and great-grandchildren.

"Well, what about the hospital?" asked a surprised Uncle Jéri when the lawyer showed him the document.

"It's all right here. The fifteen hundred acres should be able to provide for a hospital, if need be."

After giving it some thought, Jeremiás Burger placed his signature on the deed. He took a snort of snuff and said to his lawyer:

"Mr. Somogyi, I have given away my Budapest house and my lands near Oros in my lifetime. I have felt young enough to do this. Now please do me the favor of accompanying me and helping me find a new piece of land to replace the one I have just transferred."

Jeremiás Burger was seventy-five years old at the time, but he proceeded to comb the county by train and cart for two full months until he found the property he was looking for, when one of the old Elek estates came up for auction at Igal. The bid called out by Jeremiás at the auction astounded the other bidders.

"Uncle Jéri must have lost his marbles!"

But old Jéri, after taking another snort of snuff, quietly said:

"I can't take my boots with me."

Although he did not leave anything for the hospital or other charities, forty years later one of his grandsons would do that in full measure, leaving his entire fortune for that purpose. Jeremiás Burger's wealth was destined to serve a philanthropic end, as he had once intended.

He divided up his fortune among his sons and daughters according to a bizarre scheme that only he understood. The finest portion, two thousand acres at Oros, Pazony, and Tura, was left to his favorite son Mihály. He also left an abundant share for the next oldest son, Ignác, and the other children received settlements during his lifetime. Sári, Róza, and Tercsi, his three married daughters in Berettyóújfalu and Munkács, all received their due shares.

But the old man had one son, Ede, with whom he was not satisfied. The will limited Ede to his legal minimum, in other words, he was practically disowned—even though among all the sons he was the one who looked most like the father.

Why was Ede disowned? Perhaps not even Gyula Somogyi, the executor of the famous will, would be able to tell us. One thing was sure, Ede did not prove to be a thrifty manager and eventually ended up as perhaps the first impoverished Burger in the Nyíregyháza region.

For even his legal minimum amounted to a considerable sum: seventy thousand forints in 1887 would buy you a palace on Andrássy Avenue. But for a long while Ede did nothing else but pass the time in the Nyíregyháza coffeehouses, preferably near the cash-register ladies ensconced on their mirrored thrones. He would stand around at the Betyár or the Kiskorona, a huge man with a bull's neck, freckled and pockmarked, paying court to the cashier ladies "like there was no tomorrow". But the family did not put up for long with cousin Ede's devotion to these ladies of questionable repute. They found a small farming lease for him at Szögliget, in Abaúj county—a long way from home. But the leased farm did not prosper. People were puzzled. How could Burger, that "golden Jew", have a son who was such a loser?

"It's because Ede always rides a gray mare," said the superstitious.

True enough, Ede had a penchant for unusual mares, just as among women he preferred the coffeehouse exotics.

Eventually he abandoned the leased farm in Abaúj county and returned to Nyíregyháza, where he persisted, until the age of seventy-two, by the side of the cash-register ladies at the Betyár.

This had been the first case of ill luck for a long time among the fortunate Burgers.

But misfortune never comes unaccompanied.

The lands acquired and passed on by Jeremiás were still intact. The property did not increase in size for there was no opportunity, hemmed in as it was on one side by the lands of the Eger church, on another by the holdings of the Máramarossziget Calvinist college and the Dessewffy estates. The six- to eight-hundred-acre holdings of the Semsey, Mezőssy, Csengery, and Kanizsay families were too solid to break up. As for the ten- and twenty-acre lots held by the Tirpáks of Nyíregyháza, who ever heard of a Tirpák selling even a square foot of his land? They were the original Hungarian smallholders that we hear so much about nowadays. So the Burger estates stayed as they were, as if old Jeremiás had acquired all the land destined for his family. The men of the family mostly occupied themselves with cultivation of the land and managing their estates; they were not attracted by industrial enterprises or commercial activity but remained "peasants" instead, as they are proud to point out.

Well, there was one among these "peasant" Burgers, a young man, István by name, who only became famous after he died. He cultivated the two thousand acres in Szabolcs county that old Jeremiás had transferred to Mihály, from whom his son István inherited the property intact. He was a typical Szabolcs county landowner, who ran a model farm. He would come in to Nyíregyháza for an occasional spree with his friends Sándor Juhász, director of the savings bank, Ödön Lakner, and the present-day mayor of Nyíregyháza, Dr. Kálmán Bencs, who was a notary at the time. István was not pretentious, impulsive, or excessive in his enjoyment of the good life. He was a sober and decent young man of comfortable means who no doubt would have married, had he lived past the age of twenty-seven.

Fate intervened, however.

After the war the Romanian occupation of Nyíregyháza and Szabolcs county lasted nearly a year and a half. During this time it was advisable to hide hunting weapons and revolvers, and they lay unused, gathering rust. After the occupation was over, the estate steward appeared at István Burger's farmhouse and suggested that the night watchman at the tobacco shed ought to be armed, in order to frighten off the nocturnal tobacco thieves. István Burger took out a rusty revolver from a desk drawer and handed it to the steward. As the steward tried to clean the handgun it suddenly went off, sending a bullet into István Burger's abdomen. The wounded landowner was placed in a buggy—a well-padded hay wagon would have been more appropriate—and taken to the hospital in Nyíregyháza. After examining the wound the physicians concluded that the patient was beyond help.

István Burger managed to remain conscious and even cheerful all this time, providing a detailed description of the circumstances of the accident for the examining magistrate who was sent out to the hospital. He made a deposition, under oath, of his conviction that the steward was innocent of any wrongdoing.

"Why would he want to? He depended on me for his livelihood. I don't want him to be prosecuted."

The next man to enter after the examining magistrate was old Gyula Somogyi, by now chief notary of the city, who had once upon a time recorded Jeremiás Burger's last will and testament. Now he appeared with pen and paper by the deathbed of the grandson, to take part once more in the disposition of the Burger fortune. He knew, better than the owner, all the details of the estate the dying man had to dispose of.

"I leave my fine collection of gold cigarette cases in equal portions to my three friends Sándor Juhász, Kálmán Bencs, and Ödön Lakner, residing in Nyíregyháza."

These good friends were keeping the wake all night in the adjacent room. When the notary informed them about the testament of the dying man, all three responded as one man that they could not lay any claim to István Burger's bequest and protested that he should leave it to others...

"Fine," said the dying man, "let's write another will."

He lay in silence for a while, thinking things over, then touched the notary's hand.

"Tell me the truth Mr. Somogyi, is there any substance to the legend that my grandfather Jeremiás Burger really intended to leave his fortune for a charitable purpose?"

"Yes," was the notary's truthful reply.

"Well then, I'm going to realize my grandfather's wishes. I have no family, no children, so it's easier for me to do."

And in full possession of his faculties, in a calm voice, he stipulated that his two thousand acres, townhouse, and other valuables be placed in a charitable trust, one half of which was to go to the city of Nyíregyháza, and the other half to the local Jewish religious community and benevolent association.

With that, the dying man breathed his last. His will was dated 1920.

This was how the legendary Burger fortune gave rise to a charitable foundation.

As for the natives of Nyíregyháza—with good reason, as anyone can see—they have nothing to do with the wave of anti-Semitism that has been rampant in Hungary in recent years.

(6 July, 1924)

We, the Old-Time Hungarians

One hears this more and more frequently nowadays... Since kings are no longer handing out those dog-skin parchments conveying patents of nobility, people have been ennobling themselves by means of their past, their age, the length of their residence in these parts, their remembrances reaching back so many distant decades...

We, the old-time Hungarians—as we say—still remember Kálmán Tisza and his *fiacre*-driver, Schneider... We still recall Dezső Bánffy, and that day of incomparable glory when Dezső Szilágyi greeted Francis Joseph with such proud words on the occasion of the nation's millennial celebration, words of a self-esteem such as had not been uttered by a Hungarian perhaps since the days of Prince Ferenc Rákóczi... Yes, we still recall that gentleman from Szabolcs county, by the name of Andris Kállay, who, when asked by Archduke Albrecht, who had been passing through the land known as Nyírség [The Birches], "How long have you lived here?" replied quietly, "A thousand years, Your Majesty, when Your Majesty's ancestors were still on the way to becoming goatherds..." We recall the legends about Jókai, according to which Francis Joseph had bestowed the title of "Baron" on the poet, a title to which Jókai never laid claim. We recall those school-inspectors of proverbial dignity who, after serving the requisite number of years, were appointed royal councilors; we recall the various grades of the Order of Francis Joseph and those splendid frock-coats worn in Hungary by the majority of gentlemen over the age of forty, and the top hats that on Sundays were worn even in the provinces; we recall the old-time gentlemen, entitled to be addressed as "Respected Sir", quietly but profoundly looking down on one addressed merely as "Great Sir"; the fantastic Hungarianized names that were the laughing-stock of an entire generation; that pride rearing up in every Hungarian when referring to Széchenyi as the "greatest" and his king as the "foremost"; we recall the explosion of the Hentzi-monument, loud enough to be heard all the way to Vienna; and we recall the orations of those old-time opposition delegates, who reared back in the old Parliament building on Sándor Street as if Francis Joseph himself were in attendance in the galleries, listening to their speeches...

271

"We, the old-time Hungarians!"

...Never before has there been such a fashion for the old, the antique, the ancient, for things past, as now, when we are commemorating another sad anniversary, of *ten years ago*. Only a smidgen of time has passed since then, yet it seems that the rocks and dust of centuries now bury that former age. The dead soldiers of the former Austro-Hungarian Monarchy, wearing their blue recruit uniforms, or those of the "Red Devils", lie at attention under the surface of the fields. We can still hear those songs that accompanied the long military trains as they sped off toward Serbia. It seems only yesterday, that ecstasy on Erzsébet Boulevard on the day of the declaration of war; we still see the figures in the street on that unforgettable evening, the exultant and the swindlers, those ladies who burst into tears of joy and those waiters who started to dance and who have since lost their legs at the front. Yes, memory still roams crazed and topsy-turvy around the shades of that bygone day when the nation staked its thousand-year-old past on a throw of the dice... And now, after the passage of ten years, we are almost ashamed that our memory stretches back only that far. We want to reach back farther, deeper into the past, to a time when we were unaware that war existed in the world.

(27 July, 1924)

GLOSSARY

Compiled by László Kelecsényi

1. Persons

Ábrányi, Kornél, Jr.(1849–1913): author, journalist, editor of *Pesti Napló.*

Ady, Endre (1877–1919): the major Hungarian poet of the early twentieth century; also a prominent journalist. Associated with the *Nyugat* group of writers.

Ágai, Adolf (1836–1916): author, humorist, journalist. Founder and editor of the political humor periodical *Borsszem Jankó.* Wrote under pseudonyms Csicseri Bors, Mokány Berci, Sanyaró Vendel.

Ambrus, Zoltán (1861–1932): novelist, critic; director of the National Theater.

Andrássy, Count Gyula, Sr. (1823–1890): statesman; one of the chief authors of the Compromise of 1867; prime minister, then Austro-Hungarian minister of foreign affairs, 1871–79.

Apponyi, Count Albert (1846–1933): conservative politician, statesman, internationally active in the 1920s.

Arany, János (1817–1882): outstanding lyric poet, spent his last summers on Margit Island.

Bakonyi, Miksa (1861–19??): prominent journalist, editor of *Az Újság.*

Baltazzi, Aristide (18??–1915): Viennese man-about-town of Greek origin, active in horse racing; confidant of Crown Prince Rudolph.

Bánffy, Baron Dezső (1843–1911): Transylvanian aristocrat, Liberal politician, prime minister 1895–1899; joined the opposition in 1904.

Bánffy, Count Miklós (1873–1950): statesman, writer, artist. Member of Parliament, then foreign minister; intendant of the Opera House.

Bányai, Elemér (1875–1915): radical bourgeois writer (pseudonym: Zuboly), journalist, member of Ady's circle.

Bárczy, István (1866–1943): jurist, politician, mayor, then lord mayor of Budapest (1906–1919). Later minister of justice, then Liberal member of Parliament.

Baross, Gábor (1848–1892): minister of transportation, industry and commerce 1886–1892; reorganized railways.

Basch, Arpád (1873–1944): painter, art editor of *Magyar Géniusz.*

Báttaszéki, Lajos (1844–1921): Liberal lawyer, journalist, editor of Democratic periodical *Új Század.*

Batthyány, Count Lajos (1806–1849): statesman, first constitutional prime minister of Hungary 1848–49; sentenced to death by the Austrians in 1849, he committed suicide.

Batthyányi, Count Elemér (1847–1932): politician, horse breeder, chairman of the Horse Racing Association.

Bem, Josef (1795–1850): Polish soldier; 1848–49 revolutionary general.

Benczúr, Gyula (1844–1920): outstanding painter of historical scenes.

Berinkey, Dénes (1871–1848): lawyer, minister of justice then prime minister in the short-lived Károlyi government 1918/19.

Berzeviczy, Adám (18??–1924): Francis Joseph's general and mace-bearer; Queen Elisabeth's gentleman-in-waiting.

Bethlen, Count István (1874–1946): politician, statesman, prime minister during the political and economic consolidation after World War One.

Blaha, Lujza (1850–1926): actress, "the nation's nightingale", star of popular, folksy musical theater.

Blaskovich, Ernő (1834–1911): horse breeder, owner of Kincsem, the world-famous racehorse that never lost a race.

Blau, Diogénész: well-known character in turn-of-the-century Budapest nightlife.

Bottyán, János (1640–1709): officer in Rákóczy's war of liberation, blind in one eye.

Bródy, Lajos (1857–19??): journalist, editor in chief of German-language *Neues Pester Journal*; president of the Budapest Association of Journalists.

Bródy, Sándor (1863–1924): significant novelist, playwright; wrote with deep sympathy about poor people in Budapest.

Bulyovszky, Lilla (1833–1909): actress and author.

Buza, Barna (1873–1944): lawyer, politician, minister of agriculture from 31 October 1918 to 20 March 1919, prepared the agrarian reforms of the Károlyi government.

Carola Cecilia (Karola Szabó): nightclub diva of Gay Nineties, star of Somosy's Orfeum.

Charles IV of Habsburg (1887–1922): last king of Hungary (1916–1918), abdicated, then made two attempts to regain throne; died in exile on Island of Madeira.

Clair, Vilmos (1858–19??): journalist, author of Dueling Rule Book.

Csávolszky, Lajos (1841–1909): journalist, politician, founder and editor of *Egyetértés*, the Independence Party paper.

Deák, Ferenc (1803–1876): statesman, minister of justice in 1848/49, chief engineer of Compromise of 1867 between Austria and Hungary; known as the "sage of the homeland" thereafter.

Dreher, Anton (1810–1863): founder of the Schwechat brewery in Austria and the Kőbánya brewery in Hungary.

Elek, Colonel Gusztáv: nineteenth-century champion sharpshooter, colonel of the hussars, killed the journalist Szevér Reviczky in a duel.

Elizabeth, Empress of Austria, Queen of Hungary (1837–1898): born Princess Wittelsbach, married Francis Joseph in 1854; popular in Hungary, where she liked to sojourn; victim of assassination in Geneva.

Eötvös, Károly (1842–1916): lawyer, author, journalist, Independence Party politician. Successfully defended the Jews accused of ritual murder in the Tiszaeszlár trial in 1883, of which he wrote a two-volume account, *A nagy per* [The Great Trial].

Erdélyi, Gyula (1851–1912): journalist, known as "Sylvester" in Miklós Szemere's entourage.

Esterházy, Count Miklós (1839–1897): famous horse breeder, founder of the Vienna Jockey Club.

Farkas, Pál (1878–1921): writer, editor of *Magyar Figyelő*.

Fejérváry, Baron Géza (1833–1914): soldier, politician, Francis Joseph's trusted field-marshal, minister of defense 1884–1903; prime minister 1905–1906.

Ferenczi, Sándor (1873–1933): pioneering psychoanalyst, Freud's student.

Ferenczy, Ida (1846–1928): Queen Elizabeth's lady-in-waiting and traveling companion.

Festetich, Prince Tasziló (1850–1933): owner of stables, famous horse breeder.

Francis Joseph I (1830–1916): Emperor of Austria, King of Hungary from 1848 to 1916. Crowned king after Compromise of 1867.

Gályi, Lajos (185?–1916): gambler of international repute.

Gáspár, Imre (1854–1910): poet, journalist, editor of Liberal newspaper in Debrecen where he discovered the young Gyula Krúdy.

Gellért, Oszkár (1882–1967): poet, journalist, editor of N*yugat* after 1920.

Glücklich, Vilma (1872–1928): educator, feminist.

Goluchowski, Count Agenor (1849–1921): Austro-Hungarian minister of foreign affairs.

Göndör, Ferenc (1885–1954): left-wing journalist, emigrated to U.S. after 1919.

Görgey, Arthur (1818–1916): commander in chief of 1848–49 revolutionary armies; after surrender to Austrian and Russian forces he was for decades considered a "traitor" by public opinion.

Greiner, Jenő (?–1917): economist, member of Ady's circle.

Gulner, Gyula (1842–1909): politician, member of Parliament.

Hadik, Count János (1863–1934): the last prime minister appointed by a king (1918) before Károlyi's government took over.

Harsányi, Zsolt (1887–1943): author, dramatist, known for clever historical novels.

Hatvany (Deutsch), Baron Lajos (1880–1961): writer, critic, patron of writers (Ady, Krúdy, Attila József). One of the founders and active supporters of N*yugat.*

Haynau, Julius Jacob (1786–1853): Austrian general, notorious for brutal suppression in Hungary after Revolution of 1848/49.

Heltai, Jenő (1871–1957): writer, poet, journalist.

Herczeg, Ferenc (1863–1954): much-acclaimed author of popular novels.

Hirsch, Baron Maurice (1831–1896) banker and philanthropist.

Hock, János (1859–1936): Roman Catholic priest, outstanding orator, opponent of István Tisza's policies, president of National Council during 1918 democratic revolution.

Huba: one of the seven chieftains of the Magyar tribes at the time of the Conquest, to whom Miklós Szemere claimed to trace his genealogy.

Hunyadi, János (1407–1456): great military commander in the fight against the Turks, governor of Hungary, father of King Matthias Corvinus.

Hunyady, Count József: famous 19th century horse-breeder.

Imre, Saint (1007–1031): son of King St. Stephen.

Irányi, Dániel (1822–1892): lawyer, journalist, lived in exile after participation in 1848/49 Revolution; after his return home he was leader of the Independence Party.

Istóczy, Győző (1842–1915): member of Parliament; founder of Anti-Semitic Party in 1880s; notorious agitator at the time of the Tiszaeszlár trial.

Jankovich-Bésán, Count Gyula: horse breeder, stable owner.

Jókai, Mór (1825–1904): the major nineteenth-century Hungarian novelist; his romantic, historical narratives earned him the title of "the great storyteller".

Jósa, Dr. András (1834–1918): Szabolcs county physician, amateur archaeologist and ethnologist.

Joseph, Archduke (1833–1905): general, commander in chief of Hungarian Honv*éds.* Resided on Margit Island, wrote monograph on Romany language.

Jósika, Baron Miklós (1794–1865): novelist, author of romantic, historical novels.

Kállay, András (1875–19??): Szabolcs county lord lieutenant, conservative politician, member of ancient Kállay family.

Kaposi, József (1863–1922): literary historian, editor of M*agyar Szemle.*

Károlyi, Count István (1845–1907): member of Parliament.

Károlyi, Count Mihály (1875–1955): radical politician; a leader of the National Council in 1918, prime minister after the democratic revolution, president of the Republic, January–March 1919. Emigrated after declaration of Soviet Republic; Hungarian ambassador to France, 1947–49.

Kemény, Zsigmond (1814–1875): author of novels bridging the romantic and realist modes.

Kéri, Pál (1881–?): editor of *Pesti Napló*.

Kerim, Abdul (1811–1885): the "Lion of Sebastopol", Turkish pasha and general, hero of Crimean war against Russia; in 1877 pro-Turk, anti-Russian Hungarians presented him with a ceremonial sword.

Kisfaludy, Károly (1788–1830): Romantic poet and playwright; a literary society was named after him.

Klapka, György (1820–1892): general in the 1848–49 revolutionary war; successfully defended fortress of Komárom; emigrated to England.

Kóbor, Tamás (1867–1942): journalist, author of realistic novels about turn-of-the-century Budapest. Contributor to *Pesti Hírlap*.

Kohányi, Tihamér (1863–1913): journalist, editor of *Egyetértés*; emigrated to U.S. where he founded the Cleveland *Szabadság*.

Kossuth, Ferenc (1841–1914): son of Lajos Kossuth; after university studies in England he worked as a railway engineer in Italy before returning to Hungary when his father died. Independence Party politician, member of Parliament, and minister of commerce.

Kossuth, Lajos (1802–1894): lawyer, politician, statesman, leader of 1848–48 revolution; afterwards lived in exile in Turin.

Kun, Béla (1886–1939): leader of the 1919 Commune in Hungary. Afterwards emigrated to the Soviet Union.

"Kun" László: Hungarian king, reigned from 1272 to 1290 as László IV. Called "the Kun" because of his Cumanian mother.

Krúdy, Gyula, the Eldest (18?–1913): the author's grandfather, veteran of the 1848–49 revolutionary struggles; late in life was head of the 1848 veterans' National Home in Budapest.

Lotz, Károly (1833–1904): painter, known for his ceiling murals at the Opera House.

Lovászy, Márton (1864–1927): journalist, editor, politician. Member of the National Council and the Károlyi government.

Lovik, Károly (1874–1915): author, editor of *Vadász- és Versenylap* [Hunt and Turf Magazine].

Lukács, Dr. Pál: physician, friend of the poet Endre Ady.

Madarász, Lajos: left-wing Independence Party politician.

Malonyai, Dezső (1866–1916): publicist, art historian. Known for his five-volume survey of Hungarian folk art.

Maria Jozefa, Princess (1867–1944): mother of King Charles IV.

Maria Theresa, Empress of Austria, Queen of Hungary, (1717–1780)

Maria Valeria, Archduchess (1868–1924): youngest daughter of Francis Joseph and Elizabeth. Grew up in Hungary.

Márkus, József (1852–1915): jurist, lord mayor of Budapest in the 1890s.

Mayer, János (1871–19?): member of Parliament, under-secretary of state in the 1918 Berinkey government; later minister of agriculture.

Mednyánszky, Baron László (1853–1919): painter, outstanding landscape artist and portrayer of downtrodden figures.

Meszlényi, Adrienne (1870–1926): actress, protégée of Miklós Szemere.

Mezőssy, Béla (1870–19?): minister of agriculture.

Mezőssy, László (?–1893): owner of Hegyalja vineyard, veteran of 1848, friend of Krúdy's grandfather.

Mikszáth, Kálmán (1847–1910): outstanding author, whose gently ironic works depict country squires; his novel *St. Peter's Umbrella* was translated into English in 1901.

Mocsáry, Lajos (1826–1916): follower of Lajos Kossuth, leader of Independence Party.

Molnár, Ferenc (1878–1952): journalist, novelist and playwright.

Munczy, Lajos: Gypsy violinist, band leader.

Nagy, Iván (1824–1898): historian, author of genealogy of Hungarian nobility.

Nagy, Miklós (1840–1907): journalist; from 1867 on, editor of *Vasárnapi Újság*.

Ónody, Géza (1848–?): Parliamentary representative, one of the instigators of the Tiszaeszlár blood libel.

Osváth, Ernő (1876–1929): critic and editor, a founder of Nyugat, the foremost Hungarian literary periodical of the twentieth century.

Pálmay, Ilka (1859–1945): actress, star of operettas, later Countess Kinsky.

Petőfi, Sándor (1823–1849): the greatest Hungarian Romantic poet; a revolutionary, he perished on the battlefield.

Pilisy, Róza (1857–1931): started life as a flower girl, became the Madame of the most exclusive salon of demimondaines in Budapest.

Podmaniczky, Baron Frigyes (1824–1907): politician, author. From 1873 to 1905, as president of the Budapest Municipal Council of Public Works, he did much for the development of Budapest. For ten years he was the director of the Opera House and the National Theater. Leader of Liberal Party (1889–1905).

Polónyi, Géza (1848–1920): Independence Party politician, journalist, editor of Nemzeti Újság, minister of justice in 1906.

Purjesz, Lajos (1881–1925): journalist, editor in chief of Egyetértés, then of Világ.

Rácz, Károly: Gypsy violinist, band leader in Debrecen.

Rajna, Ferenc (1861–1933): journalist, playwright, author of the long-running Frauenbataillon at Somosy's Orfeum.

Rákosi, Jenő (1842–1929): author, journalist, nationalist politician; founder and editor of Budapesti Hírlap.

Reinitz, Béla (1878–1943): composer, music critic, friend of the poet Endre Ady, whose lyrics he put to music.

Révész, Béla (1876–1944): author, journalist, editor of Friss Újság, literary editor of Népszava. Close friend of Ady.

Rózsa, Sándor (1813–1878): outlaw, active in 1848–49 Revolution, hero of biographical novel by Krúdy.

Rudnyánszky, Gyula (1858–1913): poet and journalist in Debrecen, jailed for sedition. Emigrated to America in 1905; returned home blind and impoverished.

Rudolph, Crown Prince (1858–1889): heir to the throne; in 1881 he married Stephania, the Belgian princess; committed suicide at Mayerling along with seventeen-year old Maria Vetsera in 1888.

Schlauch, Lőrinc (1824–1902): cardinal, bishop of Nagyvárad.

Schratt, Katharine (1855–1928): actress, Francis Joseph's lady friend.

Sigray, Count Antal (1879–19?): Hungarian monarchist, active in horse racing.

Somosy, Károly: theatrical entrepreneur; in 1884 he opened the highly popular Orfeum cabaret on Nagymező Street.

Stephania, Princess (1864–1945): widow of Crown Prince Rudolph.

Széchenyi, Count István (1791–1860): called by Lajos Kosuth "the greatest Hungarian". Prominent figure of the Age of Reforms, he published numerous books and pamphlets on public affairs, economics, transport, and horse racing.

Szemere, Miklós (1856–1919): politician, author, prominent figure in horse racing.

Szilágyi, Dezső (1840–1901): prosecutor, Liberal politician, minister of justice and president of the House of Representatives in the 1890s.

Szücs, "Pátri" (1852–1910): lawyer, sergeant-at-arms in Chamber of Deputies; patriotic gadabout. Notorious trencherman.

Táncsics, Mihály (1799–1884): teacher, journalist, political radical.

Teleki, Count László (1811–1861): statesman, playwright, committed suicide.

Tisza, Count István (1861–1918): son of Kálmán Tisza. Prime minister 1903–1905, 1913–17. After instituting Parliamentary reforms, dissolved Liberal Party. Assassinated at the outbreak of the revolution in late October 1918.

Tisza, Count Kálmán (1830–1902): Liberal politician, prime minister 1875–1890; led economic consolidation.

Torkos, László (1839–1939): poet, editor.

Üchtritz, Baron Zsigmond (1846–1925): famous horse breeder and racing figure.

Vadnai, Károly (1832–1902): author, journalist, editor of *Fővárosi Lapok*.

Vaszary, Kolos (1832–1915): primate of Esztergom.

Vázsonyi, Vilmos (1868–1926): lawyer, founder of Democratic Circle (1894), member of Parliament, minister of justice.

Verhovay, Gyula (1848–1906): journalist, anti-Semitic politician.

Vértesi, Arnold (1834–1911): author of short stories and novels.

Vészi, József (1858–1940): journalist, editor in chief of *Budapesti Napló* and *Pester Lloyd*. Friend of Endre Ady.

Vetsera, Baroness Maria (1871–1889): paramour of Crown Prince Rudolph, committed suicide with him.

Wahrmann, Richard (18?–1914): well-known owner of racing stables.

Waldau, Jeanette: actress, star of the Kék Macska nightclub.

Wekerle, Sándor (1848–1921): statesman; minister of finance, prime minister 1892–95, 1906–1910.

Wesselényi, Count Miklós (1796–1850): early-nineteenth-century reform politician, famous for rescuing people in the flood of 1838.

Wlassics, Baron Gyula (1852–1937): jurist, politician; minister of culture and education (1895–1903).

Zarándy, A. Gáspár (1860–1911): founder of Anti-Semitic Party, genealogist

"Zemplén lawyer": see Kossuth, Lajos

Zichy-Ferraris, Count Viktor (1842–1880): lawyer, public official, killed in duel by Count István Károlyi.

Zichy, Count Nándor (1829–1911): politician, Knight of the Golden Fleece; led Conservative Catholic faction in the 1890s.

Zirzen, Janka (1824–1904): pioneer in women's education, director of teachers' college for women.

Zrínyi, Count Miklós (1620–1664): poet and prominent military figure in the fight against the Turks.

2. Places

Alföld: the vast lowland plains of eastern Hungary

Brassó (Braşov): city in southeast Transylvania.

Debrecen: the largest city of the Alföld. Krúdy started out as a young journalist there.

Érsekújvár (Nové Zámky, Slovakia): town in the Highlands.

Geszt: village in the eastern part of the Alföld; site of Count Tisza's estates.

Gödöllő: small town east of Budapest, site of Habsburg estates; Queen Elizabeth's favorite summering place.

Hajdúság: region embracing several counties in eastern Hungary.

Hegyalja: famous Tokaj wine region in northeastern Hungary.

Highlands (Felvidék): "Upper Hungary" in pre-Trianon times; the mountainous region north of the Danube that is Slovakia today.

Kál-Kápolna (Kápolna): village in central Hungary, site of extensive Károlyi estates, also of a battle in 1848/49.

Kassa (Košice, Slovakia): Highlands town rich in historical relics.

Késmárk (Kežmarok, Slovakia): small town in northern Carpathians.

Körmöcbánya (Kremnica, Slovakia): small town famous for its gold mines and mint.

Nagyvárad (Oradea, Romania): city in eastern Hungary with a lively cultural life.

Nyíregyháza: Krúdy's birthplace in eastern Hungary, Szabolcs-Szatmár-Bereg county seat.

Nyírség: "The Birches", Krúdy's native region in Szabolcs county in eastern Hungary.

Pozsony (Bratislava, Slovakia): city in western Hungary, site of the Diet until 1848.

Püspökladány: important railway junction in the middle of the Alföld.

Sáros: formerly a county in Upper Hungary, now part of Slovakia.

Somogy: county in southwestern Hungary.

Szentes: small town in the southern Alföld.

Szepesbéla (Spišská Belá, Slovakia): small town in northern Carpathians.

Tisza: second largest river in Hungary, flows into the Danube from the east.

Tiszaeszlár: small village in northeast Hungary.

3. Publications, Periodicals

Alkotmány [Constitution]: conservative Catholic newspaper (1896–1919) founded by Count Nándor Zichy.

Athenaeum: largest Hungarian publisher (1868–1948) of books and daily papers (Az Est, Magyarország, Pesti Napló).

A Nap [The Sun]: sensation-hungry political daily (1904–1922).

A Polgár [The Citizen]: Democratic daily (1905–1913), chief forum of the opposition politician Vilmos Vázsonyi.

Az Újság [News]: daily newspaper (1903–1944) along the lines of Western bourgeois ideals; contributors included Kálmán Mikszáth, Ferenc Herczeg, Tamás Kóbor, Sándor Márai.

Borsszem Jankó: political humor periodical edited by A. Ágai in late 19th century.

Egyetértés [Concord]: opposition political daily (1874–1913); pro-Kossuth and anti-Habsburg.

Fővárosi Lapok [Pages from the Capital]: literary daily (1864–1903).

Képes Budapest [Budapest Pictorial]: a short-lived periodical in the early 1900s.

Magyar Állam [Hungarian State]: Catholic daily (1868–1908).

Magyar Figyelő [Hungarian Observer]: conservative literary periodical (1911–1918).

Magyar Szemle [Hungarian Review]: Catholic literary monthly (1888–1906).

Nemzet [The Nation]: pro-government daily newspaper (1882–1899), edited by Mór Jókai.

Nyugat [West]: the major Hungarian literary monthly (1908–1941); Krúdy was one of its contributors.

Pester Lloyd: German-language daily (1854–1945).

Pesti Hírlap [Pest Journal]: independent political daily newspaper (1878–1944).

Pesti Napló [Pest Diary]: one of the oldest Hungarian newspapers (1850–1939).

The Crimson Coach (1913), Krúdy's first real best-selling novel.

Új Század [New Century]: democratic periodical (1900–1905), edited by Lajos Báttaszéki.

4. Institutions, Establishments, Concepts, etc.

Alispán: subprefect or deputy Lord Lieutenant, the most powerful country official.

Catholic Circle [Katolikus Kör]: a literary organization founded in 1892 by József Kaposi to introduce young writers to Conservative Inner City audiences, presided over by Miklós Móric Esterházy.

Conquest: The "conquest of the homeland", referring to the occupation of the Carpathian Basin by the alliance of tribes led by the Magyars in the late ninth century.

Csángó: Hungarian ethnic minority in Moldavia.

Díszmagyar: traditional ornate ceremonial Hungarian outfit consisting of a short, jewel-bedecked and gold-chained fur dolman or cape, draped around one shoulder, worn over a sumptuous silk or velvet doublet edged with fur, topped by a fur cap with jeweled aigrette; tight-fitting, embroidered breeches and Hessian boots with gilt spurs, and a scimitar in a jeweled scabbard.

English Misses [Angolkisasszonyok] : famous Catholic school for girls, founded by English Catholic women who fled to Europe in the seventeenth century.

Egyke: the practice of having only one child in a family.

Forint: monetary unit consisting of 100 fillér.

"Gentry Casino" [Országos Kaszinó] : the club for the lesser nobility, founded in 1883, also located on Kossuth Lajos Street.

Gyurkovics-girls: characters in a series of popular novels (1893) by Ferenc Herczeg.

Hajdúk [Haiduk]: foot-soldiers in the seventeenth-century wars of liberation.

Honvéd: (literally "defender of the fatherland"); name coined for soldiers in the 1848/49 War of Independence.

Independence Party: the major opposition party in Hungary (1868–1905).

Korona: Austro–Hungarian monetary unit.

Kossuth-song: anti-Austrian 1848/49 revolutionary recruiting song; prohibited during subsequent years of oppression.

Kufstein: fortified prison where Hungarian revolutionaries of 1848–49 were jailed by the Austrians.

K.u.K. [*Kaiserlich und Königlich*]: Imperial and Royal (pertaining to the Dual Monarchy).

Kuruc: fighter in Prince Rákóczi's war of liberation.

Liberal Party: the ruling government political party in Hungary (1875–1906); its leader was Kálmán Tisza.

M.Á.V.: Hungarian State Railways.

Millennial Exhibition of 1896: organized to celebrate the 1000th anniversary of the Conquest, a series of cultural, commercial and entertaining exhibitions in the Budapest Municipal Park.

National Casino [Nemzeti Kaszinó]: exclusive club for aristocrats, founded in 1827 by Count István Széchenyi. It was located on Kossuth Lajos Street, with summer quarters at the Park Club on Stefánia Road.

Otthon Circle: journalists' club, 1891–1948.

Palóc: inhabitant of northeast Hungary, with a characteristic accent.

Park Club: summer quarters of the aristocracy's National Casino.

Pázmány Association: short-lived literary association named after Péter Pázmány (1570–1637), counter-reformation prelate of Esztergom.

Saint Stephen Association: Catholic publishing house (1848–1948).

St. Stephen's Day: 20 August, feast-day of St. Stephen, the first king of Hungary (1000–1038).

Turul: mythical eagle or falcon-like totem bird of the ancient Magyars.

5. Budapest Sights

Abbázia: coffeehouse on Oktogon, seat of sixth-district Democrats, frequented by Károly Eötvös and Vilmos Vásonyi.

Andrássy Avenue: built in 1870s, about 2 kms long, reaches from Inner City to Municipal Park.

Basilica: the main Catholic church in the fifth district of Pest.

Beliczay: coffeehouse on Andrássy Avenue.

Emke: coffeehouse on corner of Rákóczi Road and Great Ring Boulevard.

Erzsébetváros: the Seventh District of Pest.

Griff: Hotel in Józsefváros, on Rákóczi Avenue; burned down in 1865. The Hotel Pannónia was built in its place.

Hentzi Memorial: statue erected on Buda Castle Hill to honor the Austrian commander during the 1848 revolution; offensive to Hungarian national sentiments.

Inner City: the oldest part of Pest, the Fifth District.

Józsefváros: the Eigth District in Pest.

Király Street: a busy, narrow thoroughfare separating the Sixth and Seventh districts

Korona [Magyar Korona]: restaurant and coffeehouse in the Inner City, frequented by prominent politicos.

Margit Island: a 2.5 km long island in the Danube between Buda and Pest.

Matthias Church: medieval church, restored in the 19th century, on Trinity Place, Buda, Castle Hill.

New York: the most prominent literary coffeehouse, on Erzsébet Boulevard.

Orfeum: Somosy's popular nightclub on Nagymező Street.

Pannónia: hotel on Rákóczi Avenue; Miklós Szemere lived there.

Pekáry House: ornate mid-nineteenth-century apartment building on Király Street; Krúdy and his first wife lived there.

Terézváros: the Sixth District in Pest.

Three Ravens [Három Holló]: tavern on Andrássy Avenue near the Opera house; Endre Ady's favorite nightspot.

BIBLIOGRAPHY

Irói arcképek (Literary Portraits), I–II. Selected and with an Afterword and Notes by Sándor Kozocsa. Budapest: Magvető, 1957.

Pesti levelek (Letters from Pest: Journalistic articles). Selected, edited and with an Afterword and bibliography by Lajos Tóth and Dénes Udvarhelyi. Budapest: Magvető, 1963.

Álmoskönyv (Book of Dreams). Seventh, enlarged edition, edited and with an Afterword by András Barta. Budapest: Magvető, 1966.

Régi pesti historiák (Stories of Old-Time Pest: Feature articles). Selected and edited by András Barta. With an Afterword by István Kristó-Nagy. Budapest: Magvető, 1967.

Komédia. Selected and edited by András Barta. Magvető, 1968.

Budapest võlegénye (Budapest's Bridegroom). Selected and edited by Zsuzsa Krúdy with an Introduction by Ede Szabó. Budapest: Szépirodalmi, 1973.

A szobrok megmozdulnak (The Statues Stir). Selected, edited, and with an Afterword and Notes by Sándor Kozocsa. Budapest: Gondolat, 1974.

Kossuth fia (Kossuth's son). Edited, with Notes and an Afterword by Anna Fábri. Budapest: Magvető, 1976.

Szent Terézia utcái (Streets of Saint Theresa). With a facsimile of the manuscript and an essay by András Barta. Budapest: Magyar Helikon, 1978.

Magyar Tükör (Hungarian Mirror). Selected and edited by András Barta. Budapest: Szépirodalmi, 1984.

Pesti Album (Budapest Album). Selected, edited, and with a Note by András Barta. Budapest: Szépirodalmi, 1985.

A XIX. század vizitkártyái [Visiting Cards from the 19th Century]. Selected and edited by András Barta. Budapest: Szépirodalmi, 1986.

Egy krónikás könyvéből (From a Chronicler's Book). Selected and edited by András Barta. Budapest: Szépirodalmi, 1987.

A Magyar Köztársaság Almanachja (Almanac of the Hungarian Republic). Edited by Lajos V. Mohai, with an Afterword by Anna Fábri. Budapest: Zrinyi Kiadó, 1988.

Ady Endre éjszakái (Endre Ady's Nights). Arranged for publication and with an Afterword by Anna Fábri. Budapest: Helikon Kiadó, 1989.

Irodalmi kalendárium (Literary Almanac). Selected and edited by András Barta. Budapest: Szépirodalmi, 1989.

Öreg szó az ifjakhoz (Old Words for the Young) I–II. Selected, edited, and with an Afterword by László Kelecsényi. Budapest: Aqua Kiadó, 1995.

Erzsébet királyné (Queen Elizabeth). Selected, edited, and with an Afterword by László Kelecsényi. Budapest: Palatinus kiadó, 1998.

INDEX

286